Go Systems Progra

Master Linux and Unix system level programming with Go

Mihalis Tsoukalos

BIRMINGHAM - MUMBAI

Go Systems Programming

First published: September 2017

Production reference: 1210917

Published by Packt Publishing Ltd.
Livery Place
35 Livery Street
Birmingham
B3 2PB, UK.
ISBN 978-1-78712-564-3

www.packtpub.com

Credits

Author
Mihalis Tsoukalos

Reviewer
Chris "mac" McEniry

Acquisition Editor
Frank Pohlmann

Project Editor
Radhika Atitkar

Content Development Editor
Monika Sangwan

Technical Editor
Anupam Tiwari

Copy Editor
Tom Jacob

Proofreader
Safis Editing

Indexer
Tejal Daruwale Soni

Graphics
Kirk D'Penha

Production Coordinator
Arvindkumar Gupta

About the Author

Mihalis Tsoukalos is a Unix administrator, programmer, DBA, and mathematician, who enjoys writing technical books and articles and learning new things. He has written more than 250 technical articles for many magazines including *Sys Admin*, *MacTech*, *Linux User and Developer*, *USENIX ;login:*, *Linux Format*, and *Linux Journal*. His research interests include databases, operating systems, Statistics, and machine learning.

You can reach him at http://www.mtsoukalos.eu/ and @mactsouk.

Mihalis is also a photographer (http://www.highiso.net/).

He is also the technical editor for *MongoDB in Action, Second Edition*, published by *Manning*.

I would like to thank all the magazines that I have written articles for because they gave me the opportunity to improve my technical writing skills and finally write my first book! I would also like to thank Agisilaos Ziotopoulos for telling me during a Skype call that after writing so many magazine articles, I should write a book! Lastly, I would like to thank the people at Packt Publishing for helping me write this book, including Frank Pohlmann, my technical reviewer; Chris McEniry, for his really good comments; and especially my editor, Radhika Atitkar for answering all my questions and encouraging me during the whole process. For all potential writers everywhere: if you wish to become a writer, start writing!

About the Reviewer

Chris "mac" McEniry has been a practicing systems administrator and engineer for over twenty years. He regularly presents, writes tools, and works on improving how we maintain systems.

www.PacktPub.com

For support files and downloads related to your book, please visit `www.PacktPub.com`. Did you know that Packt offers eBook versions of every book published, with PDF and ePub files available? You can upgrade to the eBook version at `www.PacktPub.com`and as a print book customer, you are entitled to a discount on the eBook copy.

Get in touch with us at `service@packtpub.com` for more details. At `www.PacktPub.com`, you can also read a collection of free technical articles, sign up for a range of free newsletters and receive exclusive discounts and offers on Packt books and eBooks.

`https://www.packtpub.com/mapt`

Get the most in-demand software skills with Mapt. Mapt gives you full access to all Packt books and video courses, as well as industry-leading tools to help you plan your personal development and advance your career.

Why subscribe?

- Fully searchable across every book published by Packt
- Copy and paste, print, and bookmark content
- On demand and accessible via a web browser

Customer Feedback

Thanks for purchasing this Packt book. At Packt, quality is at the heart of our editorial process. To help us improve, please leave us an honest review on this book's Amazon page at https://www.amazon.com/dp/1787125645.

If you'd like to join our team of regular reviewers, you can email us at customerreviews@packtpub.com. We award our regular reviewers with free eBooks and videos in exchange for their valuable feedback. Help us be relentless in improving our products!

Table of Contents

Preface

Go Systems Programming is a book that will help you develop systems software using Go, which is a systems programming language that started as an internal Google project before becoming popular. What makes Go really popular is that it keeps the developer happy by being easy to write, easy to read, easy to understand, and by having a compiler that is there to help you. This book does not cover every possible aspect and feature of the Go programming language—only the ones that are related to systems programming. Should you wish to learn more about the Go programming language, you should wait from my next book, *Mastering Go*, which will be ready in 2018!

The book you are about to read is an honest book in the sense that it will present working Go code without overlooking its potential faults, its restrictions, and its logical gaffes, which will allow you to improve it on your own and create a better version of it in the future. What you will not be able to improve is the fundamental information that will be presented, which is the basis of the way Unix systems work. I will consider the book to be successful if it helps you understand what systems programming is about, why it is important, and how you can start developing systems software in Go. I will be equally happy if Go becomes your favorite programming language!

What this book covers

Chapter 1, *Getting started with Go and Unix Systems Programming*, starts by defining what systems programming is before talking about the advantages and the disadvantages of Go, the features of Go version 1.8, two handy Go tools named `gofmt` and `godoc`, as well as the various states of Unix processes.

Chapter 2, *Writing Programs in Go*, helps you learn how to compile Go code and how to use the environment variables that Go supports, and understand how Go reads the command line arguments of a program. Then, we will talk about getting user input and output, which are fundamental tasks, show you how to define functions in Go, where the `defer` keyword is mentioned for the first time in this book and continue by discussing the data structures that Go offers using handy code examples. In the remaining sections of the chapter, we will discuss Go interfaces and random number generation. I am sure that you are going to enjoy this chapter!

Chapter 3, *Advanced Go Features*, goes deeper and starts talking about some advanced Go features, including error handling, which is critical when developing systems software and error logging. Then it introduces you to pattern matching and regular expressions, Go Reflection, and talks about unsafe code. After that, it compares Go to other programming languages and presents two utilities, named dtrace(1) and strace(1), that allow you to see what happens behind the scenes when you execute a program. Lastly, it talks about how you can use the go tool to detect unreachable code and how to avoid some common Go mistakes.

Chapter 4, *Go Packages, Algorithms, and Data Structures*, talks about algorithms and sorting in Go and about the sort.Slice() function, which requires Go version 1.8 or newer. Then it shows Go implementations of a linked list, a binary tree and a hash table. After that, it discusses Go packages and teaches you how to create and use your own Go packages. The last part of the chapter discusses Garbage collection in Go.

Chapter 5, *Files and Directories*, is the first chapter of this book that deals with a systems programming topic, which is the handling of files, symbolic links, and directories. In this chapter, you will find Go implementations of the core functionality of Unix tools such as which(1), pwd(1), and find(1), but first you will learn how to use the flag package in order to parse the command-line arguments and options of a Go program. Additionally, you will learn how to delete, rename, and move files as well as how to traverse directory structures the Go way. The last part of this chapter implements a utility that creates a copy of all the directories of a directory structure!

Chapter 6, *File Input and Output*, shows you how to read the contents of a file, how to change them, and how to write your own data to files! In this chapter, you will learn about the io package, the io.Writer and io.Reader interfaces, and the bufio package that is used for buffered input and output. You will also create Go versions of the cp(1), wc(1), and dd(1) utilities. Lastly, you will learn about sparse files, how to create sparse files in Go, how to read and write records from files, and how to lock files in Go.

Chapter 7, *Working with System Files*, teaches you how to deal with Unix system files, which includes writing data to Unix log files, appending data to existing files, and altering the data of text files. In this chapter, you will also learn about the log and log/syslog standard Go packages, about Unix file permissions, and take your pattern matching and regular expressions knowledge even further using practical examples. You will also learn about finding the user ID of a user as well as the Unix groups a user belongs to. Lastly, you will discover how to work with dates and times in Go using the time package and how to create and rotate log files on your own.

Chapter 8, *Processes and Signals*, begins by discussing the handling of Unix signals in Go with the help of the os/signal package by presenting three Go programs. Then it shows a Go program that can rotate its log files using signals and signal handling and another Go program that uses signals to present the progress of a file copy operation. This chapter will also teach you how to plot data in Go and how to implement Unix pipes in Go. Then it will implement the cat(1) utility in Go before briefly presenting the Go code of a Unix socket client. The last section of the chapter quickly discusses how you can program a Unix shell in Go.

Chapter 9, *Goroutines – Basic Features*, discusses a very important Go topic, which is goroutines, by talking about how you can create goroutines and how you can synchronize them and wait for them to finish before ending a program. Then it talks about channels and pipelines, which help goroutines communicate and exchange data in a safe way. The last part of the chapter presents a version of the wc(1) utility that is implemented using goroutines. However, as goroutines is a big subject, the next chapter will continue talking about them.

Chapter 10, *Goroutines – Advanced Features*, talks about more advanced topics related to goroutines and channels, including buffered channels, signal channels, nil channels, channels of channels, timeouts, and the select keyword. Then it discusses issues related to shared memory and mutexes before presenting two more Go versions of the wc(1) utility that use channels and shared memory. Lastly, this chapter will talk about race conditions and the GOMAXPROCS environment variable.

Chapter 11, *Writing Web Applications in Go*, talks about developing web applications and web servers and clients in Go. Additionally, it talks about communicating with MongoDB and MySQL databases using Go code. Then, it illustrates how to use the html/template package, which is part of the Go standard library and allows you to generate HTML output using Go HTML template files. Lastly, it talks about reading and writing JSON data before presenting a utility that reads a number of web pages and returns the number of times a given keyword was found in those web pages.

Chapter 12, *Network Programming*, discusses topics related to TCP/IP and its protocols using the net Go standard package. It shows you how to create TCP and UDP clients and servers, how to perform various types of DNS lookups, and how to use Wireshark to inspect network traffic. Additionally, it talks about developing RPC clients and servers in Go as well as developing a Unix socket server and a Unix socket client.

As you will see, at the end of each chapter there are some exercises for you to do in order to gain more information about important Go packages and write your own Go programs. Please, try to do all the exercises of this book.

What you need for this book

This book requires a computer running a Unix variant with a relatively recent Go version, which includes any machine running Mac OS X, macOS, or Linux.

Apple used to call its operating system as Mac OS X followed by the version number; however, after Mac OS X 10.11 (El Capitan), Apple changed that, and Mac OS X 10.12 is now called macOS 10.12 (Sierra) – in this book, the terms Mac OS X and macOS are used interchangeably. Additionally, there is a big chance that by the time you read this book, the latest version of macOS will be macOS 10.13 (High Sierra). You can learn more about the various versions of macOS by visiting https://en.wikipedia.org/wiki/MacOS.

All of the Go code in this book has been tested with Go 1.8.x running on a iMac using macOS 10.12 Sierra and with Go version 1.3.3 running on a Debian Linux machine. Most of the code can run on both Go versions without any code changes. However, when newer Go features are used, the code will fail to compile with Go 1.3.3—the book states the Go programs that will not compile with Go version 1.3.3 or require Go version 1.8 or newer.

Please note that at the time of writing this text, the latest Go version is 1.9. Given the way Go works, you will be able to compile all the Go code of this book in newer Go versions without any changes.

Who this book is for

This book is for Unix users, power Unix users, Unix system administrators, and Unix system developers that use Go on one or more Unix variants and want to start developing systems software using the Go programming language.

Although this book might not be the best choice for people that do not feel comfortable with the Unix operating system or for people who have no previous programming experience, amateur programmers will find lots of practical information about Unix that might inspire them to start developing their own system utilities.

Conventions

In this book, you will find a number of text styles that distinguish between different kinds of information. Here are some examples of these styles and an explanation of their meaning. Code words in text, database table names, folder names, filenames, file extensions, pathnames, dummy URLs, user input, and Twitter handles are shown as follows: "This is because the `main()` function is where the program execution begins."

A block of code is set as follows:

```
package main

import "fmt"
import "os"

func main() {
   arguments := os.Args
   for i := 0; i < len(arguments); i++ {
         fmt.Println(arguments[i])
   }
}
```

When we wish to draw your attention to a particular part of a code block, the relevant lines or items are set in bold:

```
package main

import "fmt"
import "os"

func main() {
   arguments := os.Args
   for i := 0; i < len(arguments); i++ {
         fmt.Println(arguments[i])
   }
}
```

Any command-line input or output is written as follows:

```
$ go run hw.go
Hello World!
```

New terms and **important words** are shown in bold.

Warnings or important notes appear like this.

Tips and tricks appear like this.

Reader feedback

Feedback from our readers is always welcome. Let us know what you think about this book-what you liked or disliked. Reader feedback is important for us as it helps us develop titles that you will really get the most out of. To send us general feedback, simply email feedback@packtpub.com, and mention the book's title in the subject of your message. If there is a topic that you have expertise in and you are interested in either writing or contributing to a book, see our author guide at www.packtpub.com/authors.

Customer support

Now that you are the proud owner of a Packt book, we have a number of things to help you to get the most from your purchase.

Downloading the example code

You can download the example code files for this book from your account at http://www.packtpub.com. If you purchased this book elsewhere, you can visit http://www.packtpub.com/support and register to have the files emailed directly to you. You can download the code files by following these steps:

1. Log in or register to our website using your email address and password.
2. Hover the mouse pointer on the **SUPPORT** tab at the top.
3. Click on **Code Downloads & Errata**.
4. Enter the name of the book in the **Search** box.
5. Select the book for which you're looking to download the code files.
6. Choose from the drop-down menu where you purchased this book from.
7. Click on **Code Download**.

Once the file is downloaded, please make sure that you unzip or extract the folder using the latest version of:

* WinRAR / 7-Zip for Windows
* Zipeg / iZip / UnRarX for Mac
* 7-Zip / PeaZip for Linux

The code bundle for the book is also hosted on GitHub at
`https://github.com/PacktPublishing/Go-Systems-Programming`. We also have other code
bundles from our rich catalog of books and videos available at
`https://github.com/PacktPublishing/`. Check them out!

Downloading the color images of this book

We also provide you with a PDF file that has color images of the screenshots/diagrams used
in this book. The color images will help you better understand the changes in the output.
You can download this file from
`https://www.packtpub.com/sites/default/files/downloads/GoSystemsProgramming_Col`
`orImages.pdf`.

Errata

Although we have taken every care to ensure the accuracy of our content, mistakes do
happen. If you find a mistake in one of our books-maybe a mistake in the text or the code-
we would be grateful if you could report this to us. By doing so, you can save other readers
from frustration and help us improve subsequent versions of this book. If you find any
errata, please report them by visiting `http://www.packtpub.com/submit-errata`, selecting
your book, clicking on the **Errata Submission Form** link, and entering the details of your
errata. Once your errata are verified, your submission will be accepted and the errata will
be uploaded to our website or added to any list of existing errata under the Errata section of
that title. To view the previously submitted errata, go to
`https://www.packtpub.com/books/content/support` and enter the name of the book in the
search field. The required information will appear under the **Errata** section.

Piracy

Piracy of copyrighted material on the internet is an ongoing problem across all media. At
Packt, we take the protection of our copyright and licenses very seriously. If you come
across any illegal copies of our works in any form on the internet, please provide us with
the location address or website name immediately so that we can pursue a remedy. Please
contact us at `copyright@packtpub.com` with a link to the suspected pirated material. We
appreciate your help in protecting our authors and our ability to bring you valuable
content.

Questions

If you have a problem with any aspect of this book, you can contact us at questions@packtpub.com, and we will do our best to address the problem.

1
Getting Started with Go and Unix Systems Programming

An operating system is the kind of software that allows you to communicate with the hardware, which means that you cannot use your hardware without an operating system. Unix is an operating system with many variants that have many things in common including their programming interface.

The Unix operating system was mainly programmed in C and not entirely in the assembly language, which makes it portable to other computer architectures without having to rewrite everything from scratch. It is important to understand that even if you are developing a Go program on a Unix machine, at the end of the day, your code will be translated to C functions and system calls because this is the only way to directly communicate with the Unix kernel. The main benefits you get from writing Go code instead of C code are smaller programs with less silly bugs. You will learn more about this in Chapter 3, *Advanced Go Features.*

As this book will use Go, you will need to have a version of Go installed on your Unix machine. The good news is that there is a port of the Go programming language for almost all modern Unix systems including macOS, Linux, and FreeBSD. There is also a Windows port of Go, but this book will not deal with Microsoft Windows.

Although there is a good chance that your Unix variant has a package for Go, you can also get Go from `https://golang.org/dl/`.

In this chapter, you will learn the following topics:

- Systems programming
- The advantages and disadvantages of Go
- The states of a Unix process
- Two Go tools –`gofmt` and `godoc`
- The features of the latest Go version (1.8)

The structure of the book

This book has three parts. The first part, which includes this chapter, is about Go and the Go features that can be handy when developing systems software—this does not mean that you should use all of them when developing your programs. The second part is all about programming with files, directories, and processes, which is the most common type of systems software. The third part explores goroutines, web applications, and network programming in Go, which is the most advanced type of systems software. The good thing is that you do not need to read the third part of the book right away.

What is systems programming?

Systems programming is a special area of programming on Unix machines. Note that systems programming is not limited to Unix machines—it is just that this book deals with the Unix operating system only. Most commands that have to do with system administration tasks, such as disk formatting, network interface configuration, module loading, and kernel performance tracking, are implemented using the techniques of systems programming. Additionally, the /etc directory, which can be found on all Unix systems, contains plain text files that deal with the configuration of a Unix machine and its services and are also manipulated using systems software.

You can group the various areas of systems software and related system calls in the following sets:

- **File I/O**: This area deals with file reading and writing operations, which is the most important task of an operating system. File input and output must be fast and efficient, and above all, reliable.
- **Advanced file I/O**: Apart from the basic input and output system calls, there are also more advanced ways to read or write to a file including asynchronous I/O and non-blocking I/O.

- **System files and configuration**: This group of system software includes functions that allow you to handle system files, such as /etc/passwd, and get system specific information, such as system time and DNS configuration.
- **Files and directories**: This cluster includes functions and system calls that allow the programmer to create and delete directories and get information such as the owner and the permissions of a file or a directory.
- **Process control**: This group of software allows you to create and interact with Unix processes.
- **Threads**: When a process has multiple threads, it can perform multiple tasks. However, threads must be created, terminated, and synchronized, which is the purpose of this collection of functions and system calls.
- **Server processes**: This set includes techniques that allow you to develop server processes, which are processes that get executed in the background without the need for an active terminal. Go is not that good at writing server processes in the traditional Unix way—but let me explain this a little more. Unix servers such as Apache use fork(2) to create one or more child processes (this process is called **forking** and refers to cloning the parent process into a child process) and continue executing the same executable from the same point, and most importantly, sharing memory. Although Go does not offer an equivalent to the fork(2) function, this is not an issue because you can use goroutines to cover most of the uses of fork(2).
- **Interprocess communication**: This set of functions allows processes that run on the same Unix machine to communicate with each other using features such as pipes, FIFOs, message queues, semaphores, and shared memory.
- **Signal processing**: Signals offer processes a way of handling asynchronous events, which can be very handy. Almost all server processes have extra code that allows them to handle Unix signals using the system calls of this group.
- **Network programming**: This is the art of developing applications that work over computer networks with the help of TCP/IP and is not systems programming per se. However, most TCP/IP servers and clients are dealing with system resources, users, files, and directories. So, most of the time, you cannot create network applications without doing some kind of systems programming.

The challenging thing with systems programming is that you cannot afford to have an incomplete program; you can either have a fully working, secure program that can be used on a production system or nothing at all. This mainly happens because you cannot trust end users and hackers. The key difficulty in systems programming is the fact that an erroneous system call can make your Unix machine misbehave or, even worse, crash!

Most security issues on Unix systems usually come from wrongly implemented systems software because bugs in systems software can compromise the security of an entire system. The worst part is that this can happen many years after using a certain piece of software.

 When writing systems software, you should take good care of both error messages and warnings because they are the friends that help you understand what is going on and why your program did not behave as expected. Putting it simply, there is a big difference between the*File not found* and *Not enough permissions to read file* error messages.

Back when Unix was first introduced, the only way to write systems software was using C; nowadays, you can program systems software using programming languages including Go, which will be the subject of this book.

You should understand that the two main benefits you get from using a programming language other than C for developing systems software are as follows:

- Using a modern programming language along with its tools
- Simplicity, as you usually have to write, debug, and maintain less code

Apart from Go, other good candidates for developing system tools are Python, Perl, Rust, and Ruby.

Learning systems programming

The only way you can learn systems programming is by developing your own utilities using this book as a reference and a tutorial. At first, you will make a large amount of ridiculous mistakes, but as you get better, you will make a smaller amount of much more clever and hard to debug mistakes! However, it is fine to try new things when learning. In fact, it is necessary to try new things and fail because this means that you are really learning something new. Just make sure that you do not use a production web server for learning systems programming.

If you have difficulties finding out what to develop, you can start by creating your own versions of some of the existing Unix command line utilities such as`ls(1)`,`mkdir(1)`, `ln(1)`,`wc(1)`, and`which(1)`. You do not have to create a fully featured version of each one of them with support for all command-line options; what is important is to develop a stable and secure version that implements the main functionality and works without problems.

The best book that can teach you Unix systems programming in C is *Advanced Unix Programming in the Unix Environment* by *W. Richard Stevens*. Its third edition is available now, but all its editions are useful and contain a plethora of valuable details.

About Go

Go is a modern generic purpose open source programming language that was officially announced at the end of 2009. It began as an internal Google project and has been inspired by many other programming languages including C, Pascal, Alef, and Oberon. Its spiritual fathers are *Robert Griesemer, Ken Thomson,* and *Rob Pike*, who designed Go as a language for professional programmers who want to build reliable and robust software. Apart from its syntax and standard functions, Go comes with a pretty rich standard library.

At the time of writing this book, the latest stable Go version is 1.8, which includes some handy new features including the following—feel free to skip this if you have not used Go before:

- New conversion rules exist that allow you to easily convert between types that are almost equal provided that some criteria are met. You can fix the import paths of the `golang.org/x/net/name` form to just the name of the Go source file using the `go tool` command without having to open the source files yourselves.
- The operation of the tool is stricter in some cases and looser in cases that used to generate false positives.
- There is now a default value for **GOPATH Environment Variables** when **GOPATH** is undefined. For Unix systems, the default value is **$HOME/go**.
- There are various improvements to the Go runtime that speed up Go.
- There is a `sort.slice()` function that allows you to sort a slice by providing a comparator callback instead of implementing `sort.Interface`.
- There is now a `Shutdown` method to `http.Server`.
- There exist various small changes to the `database/sql` package that give the developer more control over queries.
- You can create bugs using the `go bug` command.

Getting ready for Go

You can easily find your version of Go using this command:

```
$ go version
go version go1.7.5 darwin/amd64
```

The previous output is from a macOS machine hence the `darwin` string. A Linux machine would give the following kind of output:

```
$ go version
go version go1.3.3 linux/amd64
```

You will learn more about `go tool`, which you will use all the time, in the next chapters.

As I can imagine, you must be impatient to see some Go code; so here is the Go version of the famous Hello World program:

```
package main

import "fmt"

// This is a demonstrative comment!
func main() {
    fmt.Println("Hello World!")
}
```

If you are familiar with C or C++, you will find Go code pretty easy to understand. Each file that contains Go code begins with a package declaration followed by the needed import declarations. The package declaration shows the package that this file belongs to. Note that semicolons are not required for successfully terminating a Go statement unless you want to put two or more Go statements in the same line.

In Chapter 2, *Writing Programs in Go,* you will find out how to compile and execute Go code. For now, it is enough to remember that Go source files are stored using the `.go` file extension—your task is to choose a descriptive filename.

When searching for Go-related information, use `Golang` or `golang` as the keyword for the Go programming language because the word Go can be found almost everywhere in the English language and it will not help your search!

Two useful Go tools

The Go distribution comes with a plethora of tools that can make your life as a programmer easier. The two most useful of them are gofmt and godoc.

Note that go tool itself can also invoke various tools—you can see a list of them by executing go tool.

The gofmt utility formats Go programs in a given way, which is really important when different people are going to work with the same code for a big project. You can find more information about gofmt at https://golang.org/cmd/gofmt/.

The following is a poorly formatted version of the hw.go program that is hard to read and understand:

```
$ cat unglyHW.go
package main
import
    "fmt"
// This is a demonstrative comment!
        func main() {
  fmt.Println("Hello World!")
}
```

Processing the previous code, which is saved as unglyHW.go with gofmt, generates the following easy to read and comprehend output:

```
$ gofmt unglyHW.go
package main
import "fmt"
// This is a demonstrative comment!
func main() {
        fmt.Println("Hello World!")
}
```

Remembering that the gofmt utility does not automatically save the generated output is important, which means that you should either use the -w option followed by a valid filename or redirect the output of gofmt to a new file.

The godoc utility allows you to see the documentation of existing Go packages and functions. You can find more information about godoc at http://godoc.org/golang.org/x/tools/cmd/godoc.

You are going to use `godoc` a lot as it is a great tool for learning the details of Go functions.

The following screenshot shows the output of the `godoc` command generated on a Terminal when asked for information about the `Println()` function of the `fmt` package:

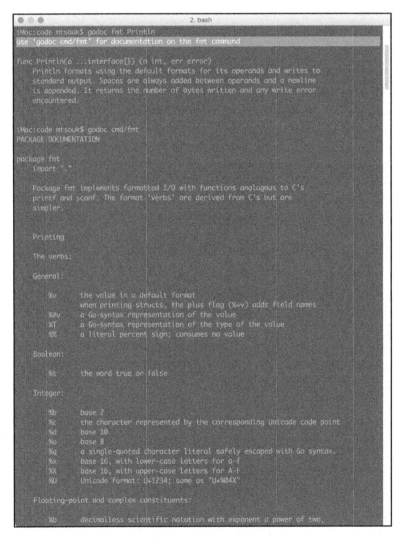

The output of the godoc command

Another handy feature of `godoc` is that it can start its own web server and allow you to see its documentation using a web browser:

```
$ godoc -http=:8080
```

The following screenshot shows the kind of output you get on a web browser after visiting `http://localhost:8080/pkg/` while the previous command is running. You can use any port number you want, provided that it is not already in use:

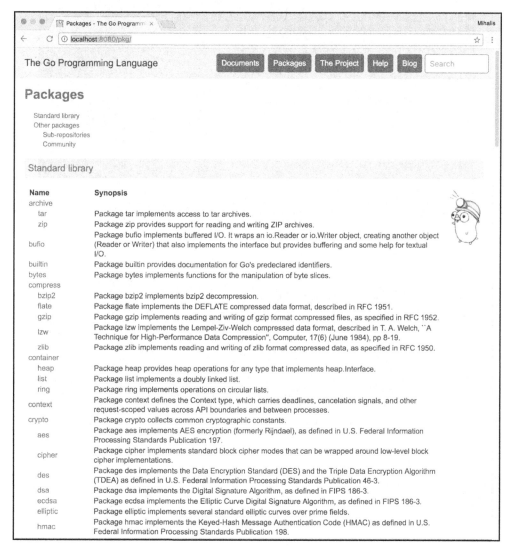

Using the godoc utility from your web browser

The most important tool for a programmer is the editor they use for writing the source code. When I am on a Mac, I typically use the TextMate editor, but when I am on a different Unix machine, I prefer vi. Choosing an editor is not an easy task because you are going to spend a lot of time with it. However, any text editor will do the job as long as it does not put any control characters inside the source code files. The following screenshot shows the TextMate editor in action:

```go
package main

import (
    "fmt"
    "io/ioutil"
    "os"
)

func main() {
    if len(os.Args) != 3 {
        fmt.Println("Please use two command line arguments!")
        os.Exit(-1)
    }

    in := os.Args[1]
    out := os.Args[2]

    input, err := ioutil.ReadFile(in)
    if err != nil {
        fmt.Println("Error reading the input!")
    }

    err = ioutil.WriteFile(out, input, 0644)
    if err != nil {
        fmt.Println("Error creating the destination file!")
    }

}
```

The TextMate editor showing the look of a some Go code

Advantages and disadvantages of Go

Go is not perfect but it has some very interesting features. The list of the Go strong features includes the following:

- Go code is easy to read and easy to understand.
- Go wants happy developers because a happy developer writes better code!
- The Go compiler prints practical warning and error messages that help you solve the actual problem. Putting it simply, the Go compiler is there to help you, not to make your life difficult!
- Go code is portable.
- Go is a modern programming language.
- Go has support for procedural, concurrent, and distributed programming.
- Go supports **Garbage Collection** (**GC**) so you do not have to deal with memory allocation and deallocation. However, GC might slow down your programs a little.
- Go does not have a preprocessor and does high-speed compilation. Consequently, Go can be used as a scripting language.
- Go can build web applications. Building a web application in C is simply not very efficient unless you use a nonstandard external library. Additionally, Go provides programmers with a simple web server for testing purposes.
- The standard Go library offers many packages that simplify the work of the programmer. Additionally, the methods found in the standard Go library are tested and debugged in advance, which means that most of the time they contain no bugs.
- Go uses static linking by default, which means that the produced binary files can be easily transferred to other machines with the same OS. Consequently, the developer does not need to worry about libraries, dependencies, and different library versions.
- You will not need a GUI for developing, debugging, and testing Go applications as Go can be used from the command line.
- Go supports Unicode. This means that you do not need any extra code to print characters from multiple human languages.
- Go keeps concepts orthogonal because a few orthogonal features work better than many overlapping ones.

The list of Go disadvantages includes the following:

- Well, Go is not C, which means that you or your team should learn a new programming language to develop systems software.
- Go does not have direct support for object-oriented programming, which can be a problem for programmers that are used to writing code in an object-oriented manner. Nevertheless, you can use composition in Go to mimic inheritance.
- Back when Unix was first introduced, C was the only programming language for writing systems software. Nowadays, you can also use Rust, C++, and Swift for writing systems software, which means that not everybody will be using Go.
- C is still faster than any other programming language for systems programming mainly because Unix is written in C.

Despite the advantages or the disadvantages of a programming language, you have the final word on whether you like it or not. The important thing is that you choose a programming language that you like and can do the job you want! Personally, I do not like C++ despite the fact that it is a very capable programming language and I have written an FTP client in C++! Additionally, I never liked Java. There is no right or wrong thing in personal tastes so do not feel guilty about your choices.

The various states of a Unix process

Strictly speaking, a process is an execution environment that contains instructions, user-data and system-data parts, and other kinds of resources that are obtained during runtime. A program is a file that contains instructions and data, which are used for initializing the instruction and user-data parts of a process.

Back when the Unix operating system was first introduced, computers had single CPUs without multiple cores and a small amount of RAM. However, Unix was a multiuser and multitasking operating system. In order to actually be a multiuser and do multitasking, it had to be able to run each individual process sporadically, which means that a process should have multiple states. The following figure shows the possible states of a process as well as the right path to go from one state to another:

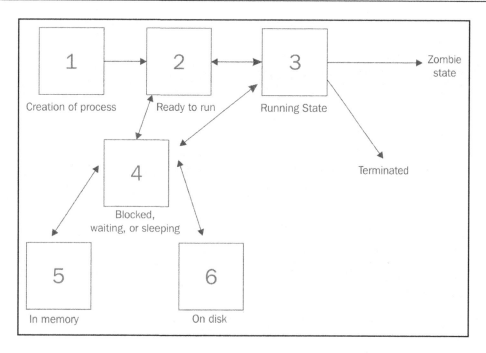

The states of a Unix process

There are three categories of processes: user processes, Kernel processes, and Daemon processes:

- User processes run in user space and usually have no special access rights
- Kernel processes are being executed in kernel space only and can fully access all kernel data structures
- Daemon processes are programs that can be found in the user space and run in the background without the need for a Terminal

Realizing that you cannot control the state of a process is really important, as this is the job of the **scheduler** of the operating system that runs in the kernel. Putting it simply, you cannot tell when the state of a process is going to change or when the process is going to go into the running state, so your code cannot count on any such assumptions!

 The C way for creating new processes involves the calling of the `fork()` system call. The return value of `fork()` allows the programmer to differentiate between the parent and child processes. However, Go does not support a similar functionality.

Exercises

1. Visit the Go website: `https://golang.org/`.
2. Install Go on your system and find out its version.
3. Type the code of the Hello World program on your own and save it to a file.
4. If you are on a Mac, download TextMate from `http://macromates.com/`.
5. If you are on a Mac, download the TextWrangler editor from `http://www.barebones.com/products/TextWrangler/` and try it.
6. Try to learn vi or Emacs on your own if you are not already familiar with another Unix text editor.
7. Look at any Go code you can find and try to make small changes to it.

Summary

In this chapter, you learned how to get Go on your computer, the features of the latest Go version, the advantages and disadvantages of Go, and the `gofmt` and `godoc` Go tools, as well as some important things about the Unix operating system.

The next chapter will not only tell you how to compile your Go code but it will also discuss other important Go topics such as reading and using command-line arguments, environment variables, writing functions, data structures, interfaces, getting user input, and printing output.

2

Writing Programs in Go

This chapter will talk about many essential, interesting, and handy Go topics that will help you be more productive. I think it would be a good idea to start this chapter by compiling and running the Go code of the hw.go program from the previous chapter. Then, you will learn how to deal with the environment variables that can be used by Go, how to process the command-line arguments of a Go program, and how to print the output on the screen and get input from the user. Finally, you will see how to define functions in Go, learn about the extremely important defer keyword, look at the data structures that come with Go, and learn what Go interfaces are before checking out code that generates random numbers.

Therefore, in this chapter, you will become familiar with many Go concepts, including the following:

- Compiling your Go programs
- Go environment variables
- Using the command-line arguments given to a Go program
- Getting user input and printing the output on your screen
- Go functions and the defer keyword
- Go data structures and interfaces
- Creating random numbers

Compiling Go code

Go does not care about the name of the source file of an autonomous program as long as the package name is main and there is a main() function in it. This is because the main() function is where the program execution begins. This also means that you cannot have multiple main() functions in the files of a single project.

There exist two ways to run a Go program:

- The first one, go run, just executes the Go code without generating any new files, only some temporary ones that are deleted afterward
- The second way, go build, compiles the code, generates an executable file, and waits for you to run the executable file

This book is written on an Apple Mac OS Sierra system using the Homebrew (https://brew.sh/) version of Go. However, you should have no difficulties compiling and running the presented Go code on most Linux and FreeBSD systems, provided that you have a relatively recent version of Go.

So, the first way is as follows:

```
$ go run hw.go
Hello World!
```

The aforementioned way allows Go to be used as a scripting language. The following is the second way:

```
$ go build hw.go
$ file hw
hw: Mach-O 64-bit executable x86_64
```

The generated executable file is named after the name of the Go source file, which is much better than a.out, which is the default filename of the executable files generated by the C compiler.

If there is an error in your code, such as a misspelled Go package name when calling a Go function, you will get the following kind of error message:

```
$ go run hw.go
# command-line-arguments
./hw.go:3: imported and not used: "fmt"
./hw.go:7: undefined: mt in mt.Println
```

If you accidentally misspell the main() function, you will get the following error message because the execution of an autonomous Go program begins from the main() function:

```
$ go run hw.go
# command-line-arguments
runtime.main_main f: relocation target main.main not defined
runtime.main_main f: undefined: "main.main"
```

Lastly, I want to show you an error message that will give you a good idea about a formatting rule of Go:

```
$ cat hw.gocat
package main
import "fmt"
func main()
{
        fmt.Println("Hello World!")
}
$ go run hw.go
# command-line-arguments
./hw.go:6: syntax error: unexpected semicolon or newline before {
```

The previous error message shows us that Go prefers putting curly braces in a certain way, which is not the case with most programming languages such as Perl, C, and C++. This might look frustrating at first, but it saves you from one extra line of code and makes your programs more readable. Note that the preceding code uses the *Allman formatting style*, which Go does not accept.

The official explanation for this error is that Go requires the use of semicolons as statement terminators in many contexts, and the compiler automatically inserts the required semicolons when it thinks they are necessary, which in this case is at the end of a non-blank line. Therefore, putting the opening brace ({) on its own line will make the Go compiler to put a semicolon at the end of the previous line, which produces the error message.

If you think that the gofmt tool can save you from similar errors, you will be disappointed:

```
$ gofmt hw.go
hw.go:6:1: expected declaration, found '{'
```

The Go compiler has another rule, as you can see in the following output:

```
$ go run afile.go
# command-line-arguments
./afile.go:4: imported and not used: "net"
```

This means that you should not import packages without actually using them in your programs. Although this could have been a harmless warning message, your Go program will not get compiled. Bear in mind that similar warnings and error messages are a good indication that you are missing something, and you should try to correct them. You will create a higher quality of code if you treat warnings and errors the same.

Checking the size of the executable file

So, after successfully compiling `hw.go`, you might want to check the size of the generated executable file:

```
$ ls -l hw
-rwxr-xr-x  1 mtsouk  staff  1628192 Feb  9 22:29 hw
$ file hw
hw: Mach-O 64-bit executable x86_64
```

Compiling the same Go program on a Linux machine will create the following file:

```
$ go versiongo
go version go1.3.3 linux/amd64
$ go build hw.go
$ ls -l hw
-rwxr-xr-x 1 mtsouk mtsouk 1823712 Feb 18 17:35 hw
$ file hw
hw: ELF 64-bit LSB executable, x86-64, version 1 (SYSV), statically linked,
not stripped
```

> To get a better sense of how big the Go executable is, consider that the executable for the same program written in C is about 8432 bytes!

So, you might ask why such a huge executable file for such a small program? The main reason is that Go executable files are statically build, which means that they require no external libraries to run. The use of the `strip(1)` command can make the generated executable files a little smaller, but do not expect miracles:

```
$ strip hw
$ ls -l hw
-rwxr-xr-x  1 mtsouk  staff  1540096 Feb 18 17:41 hw
```

The previous process has nothing to do with Go itself because `strip(1)` is a Unix command that removes or modifies the symbol table of files and therefore reduces their size. Go can perform the work of the `strip(1)` command on its own and create smaller executable files, but this method does not always work:

```
$ ls -l hw
-rwxr-xr-x 1 mtsouk mtsouk 1823712 Feb 18 17:35 hw
$ CGO_ENABLED=0 go build -ldflags "-s" -a hw.go
$ ls -l hw
-rwxr-xr-x 1 mtsouk mtsouk 1328032 Feb 18 17:44 hw
$ file hw
hw: ELF 64-bit LSB executable, x86-64, version 1 (SYSV), statically linked,
stripped
```

The preceding output is from a Linux machine; when the same compilation command is used on a macOS machine, it will make no difference to the size of the executable file.

Go environment variables

The `go tool` can use many Unix shell environment variables dedicated to Go, including GOROOT, GOHOME, GOBIN, and GOPATH. The most important Go environment variable is GOPATH, which specifies the location of your workspace. Usually, this is the only environment variable that you will need to define when developing Go code; it is to do with the way the files of a project will be organized. This means that each project will be organized into three main directories, named `src`, `pkg`, and `bin`. However, many people, including me, prefer not to use GOPATH and manually organize their project files.

So, if you are a big fan of shell variables, you can put all these kinds of definitions in either `.bashrc` or `.profile`, which means that these environment variables will be active every time you log in to your Unix machine. If you are not using the Bash shell, which is the default Linux and macOS shell, then you might need to use another start up file. Check out the documentation of your favorite Unix shell to find out which file to use.

The upcoming screenshot shows part of the output of the following command, which displays all the environment variables used by Go:

```
$ go help environment
```

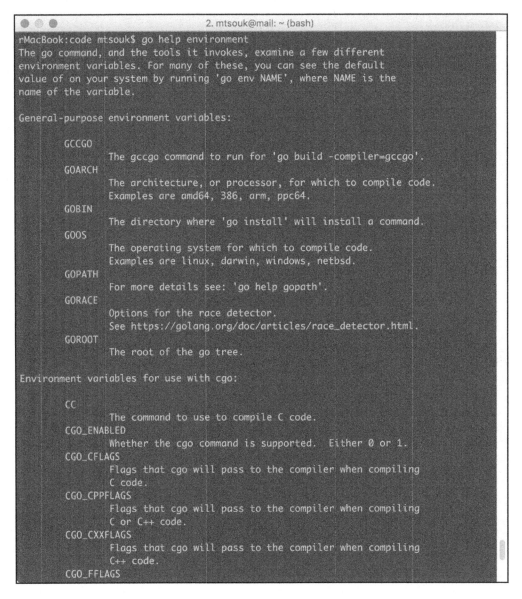

The output of the "go help environment" command

You can find additional information about a particular environment variable by executing the next command and replacing NAME with the environment variable that interests you:

```
$ go env NAME
```

All these environment variables have nothing to do with the actual Go code or the execution of the program, but they might affect the development environment; therefore, if you happen to see any strange behavior while trying to compile a Go program, check the environment variables you are using.

Using command-line arguments

Command-line arguments allow your programs to get input, such as the names of the files you want to process, without having to write a different version of the program. Hence, you cannot create any useful systems software if you're unable to process the command-line arguments passed to it.

So here is a naïve Go program, named cla.go, that prints all its command-line arguments, including the name of the executable file:

```
package main

import "fmt"
import "os"

func main() {
    arguments := os.Args
    for i := 0; i < len(arguments); i++ {
            fmt.Println(arguments[i])
    }
}
```

As you can see, Go needs an extra package named os in order to read the command-line arguments of a program that are stored in the os.Args array. In case you do not like having multiple import statements, you can rewrite the two import statements as follows, which I find much easier to read:

```
import (
    "fmt"
    "os"
)
```

The `gofmt` utility puts package names in alphabetical order when you are importing all your packages using a single import block.

The Go code of `cla.go` is simple as it stores all the command-line arguments in an array and uses a `for` loop for printing them. As you will see in forthcoming chapters, the `os` package can do many more things. If you are familiar with C, you should know that in C, command-line arguments are automatically passed to programs, and you do not need to include any extra header files in order to read them. Go uses a different approach that gives you more control but requires slightly more code.

Executing `cla.go` after building it first will create the following kind of output:

```
$ ./cla 1 2 three
./cla
1
2
three
```

Finding the sum of the command-line arguments

Now, let us try something different and tricky: you are going to try to find the summary of the command-line arguments given to your Go program. Therefore, you are going to consider the command-line arguments as numbers. Although the main idea remains the same, the implementation is totally different because you will have to convert your command-line arguments into numbers. The name of the Go program will be `addCLA.go`, and it can be split into two parts.

The first part is the preamble of the program:

```
package main

import (
    "fmt"
    "os"
    "strconv"
)
```

You need the `fmt` package for printing your output and the `os` package for reading the command-line arguments. As command-line arguments are stored as strings, you will also need the `srtconv` package for converting them into integers.

The second part is the implementation of the `main()` function:

```go
func main() {
    arguments := os.Args
    sum := 0
    for i := 1; i < len(arguments); i++ {
        temp, _ := strconv.Atoi(arguments[i])
        sum = sum + temp
    }
    fmt.Println("Sum:", sum)
}
```

The `strconv.Atoi()` function returns two values: the first one is an integer number, provided that the conversion was successful, and the second one is an error variable.

Note that most Go functions return an error variable, which should always be examined, especially on production software.

If you do not use the `strconv.Atoi()` function, then you will have two problems:

- The first one is that the program will try to perform additions, which are mathematical operations, using strings
- The second one is that you will not be able to tell whether a command-line argument is a valid integer number or not, which can be done by examining the return value of `strconv.Atoi()`

So, `strconv.Atoi()` not only does the desired job, but it also tells us whether a given argument is a valid integer or not, which is equally important because it allows us to process inappropriate arguments differently.

The other crucial Go code found in `addCLA.go` is the one that ignores the value of the error variable from the `strconv.Atoi()` function using pattern matching. The `_` character means "match everything" in Go pattern matching terms, but do not save it in any variable.

Go has support for four different sizes of signed and unsigned integers, named int8, int16, int32, int64, uint8, uint16, uint32, and uint64, respectively. However, Go also has `int` and `uint`, which are the most efficient signed and unsigned integers for your current platform. Therefore, when in doubt, use either `int` or `uint`.

Executing `addCLA.go` with the right kind of command-line arguments creates the following output:

```
$ go run addCLA.go 1 2 -1 -3
Sum: -1
$ go run addCLA.go
Sum: 0
```

The good thing is that `addCLA.go` does not crash if it gets no arguments, without you taking care of it. Nevertheless, it would be more interesting to see how the program handles erroneous input because you can never assume that you are going to get the right type of input:

```
$ go run addCLA.go !
Sum: 0
$ go run addCLA.go ! -@
Sum: 0
$ go run addCLA.go ! -@ 1 2
Sum: 3
```

As you can see, if the program gets the wrong type of input, it does not crash and does not include the erroneous input in its calculations. What is a major issue here is that `addCLA.go` does not print any warning message to let the user know that some of their input was ignored. This kind of dangerous code creates unstable executables that might generate security issues when given the wrong kind of input. So, the general advice here is that you should never expect or rely on the Go compiler, or any other compiler or program, to take care of such things because this is your job.

`Chapter 3`, *Advanced Go Features*, will talk about error handling in Go in more detail and will present a better and safer version of the previous program. For now, we should all be happy that we can prove that our program does not crash with any kind of input.

> Although this is not a perfect situation, it is not that bad if you know that your program does not work as expected for some given kinds of input. The bad thing is when the developer has no idea that there exist certain kinds of input that can make a program fail, because you cannot correct what you do not believe or recognize is wrong.

Although processing command-line arguments looks easy, it might get pretty complex if your command-line utility supports a large number of options and parameters. `Chapter 5`, *Files and Directories*, will talk more about processing command-line options, arguments, and parameters using the `flag` standard Go package.

User input and output

According to the Unix philosophy, when a program finishes its job successfully, it generates no output. However, for a number of reasons, not all programs finish successfully and they need to inform the user about their issues by printing appropriate messages. Additionally, some system tools need to get input from the user in order to decide how to handle a situation that might come up.

The hero of Go user input and output is the fmt package, and this section is going to show you how to perform these two tasks by starting with the simplest one.

 The best place to learn more about the fmt package is its documentation page, which can be found at https://golang.org/pkg/fmt/.

Getting user input

Apart from using command-line arguments to get user input, which is the preferred approach in systems programming, there exist ways to ask the user for input.

Two such examples are the rm(1) and mv(1) commands when used with the -i option:

```
$ touch aFile
$ rm -i aFile
remove aFile? y
$ touch aFile
$ touch ../aFile
$ mv -i ../aFile .
overwrite ./aFile? (y/n [n]) y
```

So, this section will show you how to mimic the previous behavior in your Go code by making your program understand the -i parameter without actually implementing the functionality of either rm(1) or mv(1).

The simplest function for getting user input is called fmt.Scanln() and reads an entire line. Other functions for getting user input include fmt.Scan(), fmt.Scanf(), fmt.Sscanf(), fmt.Sscanln(), and fmt.Sscan().

However, there exists a more advanced way to get input from the user in Go; it involves the use of the bufio package. Nevertheless, using the bufio package to get a simple response from a user is a bit of an overkill.

The Go code of `parameter.go` is as follows:

```
package main

import (
    "fmt"
    "os"
    "strings"
)

func main() {
    arguments := os.Args
    minusI := false
    for i := 0; i < len(arguments); i++ {
            if strings.Compare(arguments[i], "-i") == 0 {
                    minusI = true
                    break
            }
    }

    if minusI {
            fmt.Println("Got the -i parameter!")
            fmt.Print("y/n: ")
            var answer string
            fmt.Scanln(&answer)
            fmt.Println("You entered:", answer)
    } else {
            fmt.Println("The -i parameter is not set")
    }
}
```

The presented code is not particularly clever. It just visits all command-line arguments using a `for` loop and checks whether the current argument is equal to the `-i` string. Once it finds a match with the help of the `strings.Compare()` function, it changes the value of the `minusI` variable from false to true. Then, as it does not need to look any further, it exits the `for` loop using a `break` statement. In case the `-i` parameter is given, the block with the `if` statement asks the user to enter `y` or `n` using the `fmt.Scanln()` function.

Note that the `fmt.Scanln()` function uses a pointer to the `answer` variable. Since Go passes its variables by value, we have to use a pointer reference here in order to save the user input to the `answer` variable. Generally speaking, functions that read data from the user tend to work this way.

Executing `parameter.go` creates the following kind of output:

```
$ go run parameter.go
The -i parameter is not set
$ go run parameter.go -i
Got the -i parameter!
y/n: y
You entered: y
```

Printing output

The simplest way to print something in Go is using the `fmt.Println()` and `fmt.Printf()` functions. The `fmt.Printf()` function has many similarities with the C `printf(3)` function. You can also use the `fmt.Print()` function instead of `fmt.Println()`.

The main difference between `fmt.Print()` and `fmt.Println()` is that the latter automatically prints a newline character each time you call it. The biggest difference between `fmt.Println()` and `fmt.Printf()` is that the latter requires a format specifier for everything it will print, just like the C `printf(3)` function. This means that you have better control over what you are doing, but you have to write more code. Go calls these specifiers **verbs**, and you can find out more about supported verbs at `https://golang.org/pkg/fmt/`.

Go functions

Functions are an important element of every programming language because they allow you to break big programs into smaller and more manageable parts, but they must be as independent of each other as possible and must do one job and only one job. So, if you find yourself writing functions that do multiple things, you may want to consider writing multiple functions instead. However, Go will not refuse to compile functions that are long, complicated, or do multiple things.

A safe indication that you need to create a new function is when you find yourself using the same Go code multiple times in your program. Similarly, a safe indication that you need to put some of your functions in a module is when you find yourself using the same functions all the time in most of your programs.

The single most popular Go function is `main()`, which can be found in every autonomous Go program. If you look at the definition of the `main()` function, you'll soon realize that function declarations in Go start with the `func` keyword.

 As a rule of thumb, you must try to write functions that are less than 20-30 lines of Go code. A good side effect of having smaller functions is that they can be optimized more easily because you can clearly find out where the bottleneck is.

Naming the return values of a Go function

Unlike C, Go allows you to name the return values of a Go function. Additionally, when such a function has a return statement without any arguments, the function automatically returns the current value of each named return value. Note that such functions return their values in the order they were declared in the definition of the function.

 Naming return values is a very handy Go feature that can save you from various types of bugs, so use it.

My personal advice is this: name the return values of your functions unless there is a very good reason not to do so.

Anonymous functions

Anonymous functions can be defined in line, without the need for a name, and they are usually used for implementing things that require a small amount of code. In Go, a function can return an anonymous function or take an anonymous function as one of its arguments. Additionally, anonymous functions can be attached to Go variables.

 It is considered a good practice for anonymous functions to have a small implementation and local usage. If an anonymous function does not have local utilization, then you might need to consider making it a regular function.

When an anonymous function is suitable for a job, then it is extremely convenient and makes your life easier; just do not use too many anonymous functions in your programs without a good reason.

Illustrating Go functions

This subsection will present examples of the previous types of functions using the Go code of the functions.go program. The first part of the program contains the expected preamble and the implementation of the unnamedMinMax() function:

```
package main

import (
    "fmt"
)

func unnamedMinMax(x, y int) (int, int) {
    if x > y {
        min := y
        max := x
        return min, max
    } else {
        min := x
        max := y
        return min, max
    }
}
```

The unnamedMinMax() function is a regular function that gets two integer numbers as input, named x and y, respectively. It returns two integer numbers as output using a return statement.

The next part of functions.go defines another function but this time with named returned values, which are called min and max:

```
func minMax(x, y int) (min, max int) {
    if x > y {
        min = y
        max = x
    } else {
        min = x
        max = y
    }
    return min, max
}
```

The next function is an improved version of `minMax()` because you do not have to explicitly define the return variables of the return statement:

```go
func namedMinMax(x, y int) (min, max int) {
    if x > y {
            min = y
            max = x
    } else {
            min = x
            max = y
    }
    return
}
```

However, you can easily discover which values will be returned by looking at the definition of the `namedMinMax()` function. The `namedMinMax()` function will return the current values of `min` and `max`, in that order.

The next function shows how to sort two integers without having to use a temporary variable:

```go
func sort(x, y int) (int, int) {
    if x > y {
            return x, y
    } else {
            return y, x
    }
}
```

The previous code also shows how handy it is that Go functions can return more than one value. The last part of `functions.go` contains the `main()` function; this could be explained in two parts.

The first part is to do with anonymous functions:

```go
func main() {
    y := 4
    square := func(s int) int {
            return s * s
    }
    fmt.Println("The square of", y, "is", square(y))

    square = func(s int) int {
            return s + s
    }
    fmt.Println("The square of", y, "is", square(y))
```

Here, you define two anonymous functions: the first one calculates the square of the given integer whereas the second doubles the given integer number. What is important here is that both of them are assigned to the same variable, which is a totally wrong and is a dangerous practice. Therefore, improper use of anonymous functions can create nasty bugs, so take extra care and do not assign the same variable to different anonymous functions.

Note that even if a function is assigned to a variable, it is still considered an anonymous function.

The second part of `main()` uses some of the defined functions:

```
fmt.Println(minMax(15, 6))
fmt.Println(namedMinMax(15, 6))
min, max := namedMinMax(12, -1)
fmt.Println(min, max)
}
```

What is interesting here is that you can get the two returned values of the `namedMinMax()` function using two variables, all in one statement.

Executing `functions.go` generates the following output:

```
$ go run functions.go
The square of 4 is 16
The square of 4 is 8
6 15
6 15
-1 12
```

The next section shows more examples of anonymous functions combined with the `defer` keyword.

The defer keyword

The `defer` keyword defers the execution of a function until the surrounding function returns, and is widely used in file I/O operations. This is because it saves you from having to remember when to close an open file.

The file with the Go code that illustrates the use of `defer` is called `defer.go` and has four main parts.

The first part is the expected preamble as well as the definition of the `a1()` function:

```
package main

import (
    "fmt"
)

func a1() {
    for i := 0; i < 3; i++ {
        defer fmt.Print(i, " ")
    }
}
```

In the previous example, the `defer` keyword is used with a simple `fmt.Print()` statement.

The second part is the definition of the `a2()` function:

```
func a2() {
    for i := 0; i < 3; i++ {
        defer func() { fmt.Print(i, " ") }()
    }
}
```

After the `defer` keyword, there is an anonymous function that is not attached to a variable, which means that after the termination of the `for` loop, the anonymous function will automatically disappear. The presented anonymous function takes no arguments but uses the `i` local variable in the `fmt.Print()` statement.

The next part defines the `a3()` function and has the following Go code:

```
func a3() {
    for i := 0; i < 3; i++ {
        defer func(n int) { fmt.Print(n, " ") }(i)
    }
}
```

This time, the anonymous function requires an integer parameter that is named `n` and takes its value from the `i` variable.

The last part of defer.go is the implementation of the main() function:

```
func main() {
    a1()
    fmt.Println()
    a2()
    fmt.Println()
    a3()
    fmt.Println()
}
```

Executing defer.go will print the following, which might surprise you at first:

```
$ go run defer.go
2 1 0
3 3 3
2 1 0
```

So, now it is time to explain the output of defer.go by examining the way a1(), a2(), and a3() execute their code. The first line of output verifies that deferred functions are executed in **Last In First Out (LIFO)** order after the return of the surrounding function. The for loop in a1() defers a single function call that uses the current value of the i variable. As a result, all numbers are printed in reverse order because the last used value of i is 2. The a2() function is a tricky one because due to defer, the function body is evaluated after the for loop ends while it is still referencing the local i variable, which at that time was equal to 3 for all evaluations of the body. As a result, a2() prints the number 3 three times. Put simply, you have three function calls that use the last value of a variable because this is what is passed to the function. However, this is not the case with the a3() function because the current value of i is passed as an argument to the deferred function, due to the (i) code at the end of the a3() function definition. So, each time the deferred function is executed, it has a different i value to process.

 As using defer can be complicated, you should write your own examples and try to guess their output before executing the actual Go code to make sure that your program behaves as expected. Try to be able to tell when the function arguments are evaluated and when the function body is actually executed.

You will see the defer keyword in action again in Chapter 6, *File Input and Output*.

Using pointer variables in functions

Pointers are memory addresses that offer improved speed in exchange for difficult-to-debug code and nasty bugs. C programmers know more about this. The use of pointer variables in Go functions is illustrated inside the `pointers.go` file, which can be divided into two main parts. The first part contains the definition of two functions and one new structure named `complex`:

```go
func withPointer(x *int) {
    *x = *x * *x
}

type complex struct {
    x, y int
}

func newComplex(x, y int) *complex {
    return &complex{x, y}
}
```

The second part illustrates the use of the previous definitions in the `main()` function:

```go
func main() {
    x := -2
    withPointer(&x)
    fmt.Println(x)

    w := newComplex(4, -5)
    fmt.Println(*w)
    fmt.Println(w)
}
```

As the `withPointer()` function uses a pointer variable, you do not need to return any values because any changes to the variable you pass to the function are automatically stored in the passed variable. Note that you need to put `&` in front of the variable name to pass it as a pointer instead of as a value. The `complex` structure has two members, named `x` and `y`, which are both integer variables.

On the other hand, the `newComplex()` function returns a pointer to a `complex` structure, previously defined in `pointers.go`, which needs to be stored in a variable. In order to print the contents of a complex variable returned by the `newComplex()` function, you will need to put a `*` character in front of it.

Executing `pointers.go` generates the following output:

```
$ go run pointers.go
4
{4 -5}
&{4 -5}
```

 I do not recommend the use of pointers to amateur programmers outside of what is required by the libraries you use because they might cause problems. However, as you get more experienced, you might want to experiment with pointers and decide whether you want to use them or not depending on the problem you are trying to solve.

Go data structures

Go comes with many handy **data structures** that can help you store your own data, including arrays, slices, and maps. The most important task that you should be able to perform on any data structure is accessing all of its elements in some way. The second important task is having direct access to a specific element once you know its index or key. The last two equally important tasks are inserting elements and deleting elements from data structures. Once you know how to perform these four tasks, you will have complete control over the data structure.

Arrays

Arrays are the most popular data structure due to their speed and are supported by almost all programming languages. You can declare an array in Go as follows:

```
myArray := [4]int{1, 2, 4, -4}
```

Should you wish to declare an array with two or three dimensions, you can use the following notation:

```
twoD := [3][3]int{{1, 2, 3}, {4, 5, 6}, {7, 8, 9}}
threeD := [2][2][2]int{{{1, 2}, {3, 4}}, {{5, 6}, {7, 8}}}
```

The index of the first element of each dimension of an array is 0, the index of the second element of each dimension is 1, and so on. Accessing, assigning, or printing a single element from one of the previous three arrays can also be done easily:

```
myArray[0]
twoD[1][2] = 15
threeD[0][1][1] = -1
```

The most common way to access all the elements of an array is by finding its size using the `len()` function and then using a `for` loop. However, there exist cooler ways to visit all the elements of an array that involve the use of the `range` keyword inside a `for` loop and allow you to bypass the use of the `len()` function, which is pretty handy when you have to deal with arrays with two or more dimensions.

All of the code in this subsection is saved as `arrays.go`, and you should watch it on your own. Running `arrays.go` creates the following output:

```
$ go run arrays.go
1 2 4 -4
0 2 -2 6 7 8
1 2 3 4 5 15 7 8 9
[[1 2] [3 -1]] [[5 6] [7 8]]
```

Now let's try to break things by trying to access some strange array elements, such as an element with an index number that does not exist or an element with a negative index number, using the following Go program that is named `breakMe.go`:

```go
package main

import "fmt"

func main() {
    myArray := [4]int{1, 2, 4, -4}
    threeD := [2][2][2]int{{{1, 2}, {3, 4}}, {{5, 6}, {7, 8}}}
    fmt.Println("myArray[-1]:", myArray[-1])
    fmt.Println("myArray[10]:", myArray[10])
    fmt.Println("threeD[-1][20][0]:", threeD[-1][20][0])
}
```

Executing `breakMe.go` will generate the following output:

```
$ go run breakMe.go
# command-line-arguments
./breakMe.go:8: invalid array index -1 (index must be non-negative)
./breakMe.go:9: invalid array index 10 (out of bounds for 4-element array)
./breakMe.go:10: invalid array index -1 (index must be non-negative)
./breakMe.go:10: invalid array index 20 (out of bounds for 2-element array)
```

Go considers compiler issues that can be detected as compiler errors because this helps the development workflow, which is the reason for printing all the out of bounds array access errors of `breakMe.go`.

Trying to break things is an extremely educational process that you should attempt all the time. Put simply, knowing when something does not work is equally useful to knowing when it works.

Despite their simplicity, Go arrays have many and severe shortcomings:

- First, once you define an array, you cannot change its size, which means that Go arrays are not dynamic. Put simply, if you want to include an additional element to an existing array that has no space, you will need to create a bigger array and copy all the elements from the old array to the new one.
- Second, when you pass an array to a function, you actually pass a copy of the array, which means that any changes you make to an array inside a function will be lost after the function finishes.
- Last, passing a large array to a function can be pretty slow, mostly because Go has to create a second copy of the array. The solution to all these problems is to use slices instead.

Slices

You'll not find the concept of **slice** in many programming languages, despite the fact that it is both smart and handy. A slice has many similarities with an array, and it allows you to overcome the shortcomings of an array.

Slices have a capacity and length property, which are not always the same. The length of a slice is the same as the length of an array with the same number of elements and can be found using the `len()` function. The capacity of a slice is the current room that has been allocated for this particular slice and can be found with the `cap()` function. As slices are dynamic in size, if a slice runs out of room, Go automatically doubles its current length to make room for more elements.

As slices are passed by reference to functions, any modifications you make to a slice inside a function will not be lost after the function ends. Additionally, passing a big slice to a function is significantly faster than passing the same array because Go will not have to make a copy of the slice; it will just pass the memory address of the slice variable.

The code of this subsection is saved in `slices.go`, and it can be separated into three main parts.

The first part is the preamble as well as the definition of two functions that get `slice` as input:

```
package main

import (
    "fmt"
)

func change(x []int) {
    x[3] = -2
}

func printSlice(x []int) {
    for _, number := range x {


            fmt.Printf("%d ", number)
    }
    fmt.Println()
}
```

Note that when you use `range` over a slice, you get a pair of values in its iteration. The first one is the index number and the second one is the value of the element. When you are only interested in the stored element, you can ignore the index number as it happens with the `printSlice()` function.

The `change()` function just changes the fourth element of the input slice, whereas `printSlice()` is a utility function that prints the contents of its slice input variable. Here, you can also see the use of the `fmt.Printf()` function for printing an integer number.

The second part creates a new slice named `aSlice`and makes a change to it with the help of the `change()` function you saw in the first part:

```
func main() {
    aSlice := []int{-1, 4, 5, 0, 7, 9}
    fmt.Printf("Before change: ")
    printSlice(aSlice)
    change(aSlice)
    fmt.Printf("After change: ")
    printSlice(aSlice)
```

Although the way you define a populated slice has some similarities with the way you define an array, the biggest difference is that you do not have to declare the number of elements your slice will have.

The last part illustrates the capacity property of a Go slice as well as the `make()` function:

```
    fmt.Printf("Before. Cap: %d, length: %d\n", cap(aSlice), len(aSlice))
    aSlice = append(aSlice, -100)
    fmt.Printf("After. Cap: %d, length: %d\n", cap(aSlice), len(aSlice))
    printSlice(aSlice)
    anotherSlice := make([]int, 4)
    fmt.Printf("A new slice with 4 elements: ")
    printSlice(anotherSlice)
}
```

The `make()` function automatically initializes the elements of a slice to the zero value for that type, which can be verified by the output of the `printSlice(anotherSlice)` statement. Note that you need to specify the number of elements of a slice when you create it with the `make()` function.

Executing `slices.go` generates the following output:

```
$ go run slices.go
Before change: -1 4 5 0 7 9
After change: -1 4 5 -2 7 9
Before. Cap: 6, length: 6
After. Cap: 12, length: 7
-1 4 5 -2 7 9 -100
A new slice with 4 elements: 0 0 0 0
```

As you can see from the third line of the output, the capacity and the length of a slice were the same at the time of its definition. However, after adding a new element to the slice using `append()`, its length goes from 6 to 7 but its capacity doubles and goes from 6 to 12. The main advantage you get from doubling the capacity of a slice is better performance because Go will not have to allocate memory space all the time.

You can create a slice from the elements of an existing array, and you can copy an existing slice to another one using the `copy()` function. Both operations have some tricky points, and you should experiment with them.

Chapter 6,*File Input and Output*, will talk about a special type of slice, named byte slice, that can be used in file I/O operations.

Maps

The Map data type in Go is equivalent to the well-known hash table found in other programming languages. The main advantage of maps is that they can use almost any data type as their index, which in this case is called a **key**. For a data type to be used as a key, it must be comparable.

So, let's take a look at an example Go program, named `maps.go`, which we will use for illustrative purposes. The first part of `maps.go` contains the preamble Go code you would expect:

```go
package main

import (
    "fmt"
)

func main() {
```

Then, you can define a new empty map that has strings as its keys and integer numbers as values, as follows:

```go
aMap := make(map[string]int)
```

Post this, you can add new key and value pairs to the `aMap` map, as follows:

```go
aMap["Mon"] = 0
aMap["Tue"] = 1
aMap["Wed"] = 2
aMap["Thu"] = 3
aMap["Fri"] = 4
aMap["Sat"] = 5
aMap["Sun"] = 6
```

Then, you can get the value of an existing key:

```
fmt.Printf("Sunday is the %dth day of the week.\n", aMap["Sun"])
```

However, the single most important operation you can perform on an existing map is illustrated in the following Go code:

```
_, ok := aMap["Tuesday"]
if ok {
        fmt.Printf("The Tuesday key exists!\n")
} else {
        fmt.Printf("The Tuesday key does not exist!\n")
}
```

What the aforementioned Go code does is use the error-handling capabilities of Go in order to verify that a key of a map already exists before you try to get its value. This is the proper and safe way of trying to get the value of a map key because asking for a value for which there is no key will result in returning zero. This gives you no way of determining whether the result was zero because the key you requested was not there or because the element with the corresponding key actually had the zero value.

The following Go code shows how you can iterate over all the keys of an existing map:

```
count := 0
for key, _ := range aMap {
        count++
        fmt.Printf("%s ", key)
}
fmt.Printf("\n")
fmt.Printf("The aMap has %d elements\n", count)
```

If you have no interest in visiting the keys and the values of a map and you just want to count its pairs, then you can use the next, much simpler variation of the previous for loop:

```
count = 0
delete(aMap, "Fri")
for _, _ = range aMap {
        count++
}
fmt.Printf("The aMap has now %d elements\n", count)
```

The last part of the `main()` function contains the following Go code that illustrates an alternative way of defining and initializing a map at the same time:

```
anotherMap := map[string]int{
        "One":   1,
        "Two":   2,
        "Three": 3,
        "Four":  4,
}
anotherMap["Five"] = 5
count = 0
for _, _ = range anotherMap {
        count++
}
fmt.Printf("anotherMap has %d elements\n", count)
}
```

However, apart from the different initialization, all the other `map` operations work exactly the same. Executing `maps.go` generates the following output:

```
$ go run maps.go
Sunday is the 6th day of the week.
The Tuesday key does not exist!
Wed Thu Fri Sat Sun Mon Tue
The aMap has 7 elements
The aMap has now 6 elements
anotherMap has 5 elements
```

Maps are a very handy data structure, and there is a big chance that you are going to need them when developing systems software.

Converting an array into a map

This subsection will perform a practical operation, which is converting an array into a map without knowing the size of `array` in advance. The Go code of `array2map.go` can be divided into three main parts. The first part is the standard Go code that includes the required packages and the beginning of the `main()` function:

```
package main

import (
    "fmt"
    "strconv"
)

func main() {
```

The second part, which implements the core functionality, is as follows:

```
anArray := [4]int{1, -2, 14, 0}
aMap := make(map[string]int)

length := len(anArray)
for i := 0; i < length; i++ {
    fmt.Printf("%s ", strconv.Itoa(i))
    aMap[strconv.Itoa(i)] = anArray[i]
}
```

You first define the `array` variable and the `map` variable you will use. The `for` loop is used for visiting all the array elements and adding them to `map`. The `strconv.Itoa()` function converts the index number of `array` into a string.

 Bear in mind that if you know that all the keys of a map will be consecutive positive integer numbers, you might consider using an array or a slice instead of a map. In fact, even if the keys are not consecutive, arrays and slices are cheaper data structures than maps, so you might end up with a sparse matrix.

The last part, which is just for printing the contents of the generated map, uses the expected range form of the `for` loop:

```
for key, value := range aMap {
    fmt.Printf("%s: %d\n", key, value)
    }
}
```

As you can easily guess, developing the inverse operation is not always possible because `map` is a richer data structure than `array`. However, the price you pay for a more powerful data structure is time because array operations are usually faster.

Structures

Although arrays, slices, and maps are all very useful, they cannot hold multiple values in the same place. When you need to group various types of variables and create a new handy type, you can use a structure--the various elements of a structure are called fields.

The code of this subsection is saved as `dataStructures.go` and can be divided into three parts. The first part contains the preamble and the definition of a new structure named `message`:

```
package main

import (
    "fmt"
    "reflect"
)

func main() {

    type message struct {
            X       int
            Y       int
            Label string
    }
```

The message structure has three fields, named X, Y, and Label. Note that structures are usually defined at the beginning of a program and outside the `main()` function.

The second part uses the message structure to define two new message variables, named p1 and p2. Then, it uses reflection to get information about the p1 and p2 variables of the message structure:

```
    p1 := message{23, 12, "A Message"}
    p2 := message{}
    p2.Label = "Message 2"

    s1 := reflect.ValueOf(&p1).Elem()
    s2 := reflect.ValueOf(&p2).Elem()
    fmt.Println("S2= ", s2)
```

The last part shows how to print all the fields of a structure without knowing their names using a `for` loop and the `Type()` function:

```
    typeOfT := s1.Type()
    fmt.Println("P1=", p1)
    fmt.Println("P2=", p2)

    for i := 0; i < s1.NumField(); i++ {
            f := s1.Field(i)

            fmt.Printf("%d: %s ", i, typeOfT.Field(i).Name)
            fmt.Printf("%s = %v\n", f.Type(), f.Interface())
    }
```

```
}
```

Running `dataStructures.go` will generate the following kind of output:

```
$ go run dataStructures.go
S2=  {0 0 Message 2}
P1= {23 12 A Message}
P2= {0 0 Message 2}
0: X int = 23
1: Y int = 12
2: Label string = A Message
```

If the name of a field of a `struct` definition begins with a lowercase letter (x instead of X), the previous program will fail with the following error message:

```
panic: reflect.Value.Interface: cannot return value obtained from
unexported field or method
```

This happens because lowercase fields do not get exported; therefore, they cannot be used by the `reflect.Value.Interface()` method. You will learn more about `reflection` in the next chapter.

Interfaces

Interfaces are an advanced Go feature, which means that you might not want to use them in your programs if you are not feeling very comfortable with Go. However, interfaces can be very practical when developing big Go programs, which is the main reason for talking about interfaces in this book.

But first, I will talk about methods, which are functions with a special receiver argument. You declare methods as ordinary functions with an additional parameter that appears just before the function name. This particular parameter connects the function to the type of that extra parameter. As a result, that parameter is called the receiver of the method. You will see such functions in a while.

Put simply, interfaces are abstract types that define a set of functions that need to be implemented so that a type can be considered an instance of the interface. When this happens, we say that the type satisfies this interface. So, an interface is two things--a set of methods and a type--and it is used for defining the behavior of a type.

Let's describe the main advantage of interfaces with an example. Imagine that you have a type named ATYPE and an interface for the ATYPE type. Any function that accepts an ATYPE variable can accept any other variable that implements the interface of ATYPE.

The Go code of `interfaces.go` can be divided into three parts. The first part is as follows:

```
package main

import (
    "fmt"
)

type coordinates interface {
    xaxis() int
    yaxis() int
}

type point2D struct {
    X int
    Y int
}
```

In this part, you define an interface called coordinates and a new structure called `point2D`. The interface has two functions, named `xaxis()` and `yaxis()`. The definition of the coordinates interface says that if you want to convert to the coordinates interface, you will have to implement these two functions.

It is important to notice that the interface does not state any other specific types apart from the interface itself. On the other hand, the two functions of the interface should state the types of their return values.

The second part has the following Go code:

```
func (s point2D) xaxis() int {
    return s.X
}

func (s point2D) yaxis() int {
    return s.Y
```

```
}

func findCoordinates(a coordinates) {
    fmt.Println("X:", a.xaxis(), "Y:", a.yaxis())
}

type coordinate int

func (s coordinate) xaxis() int {
    return int(s)
}

func (s coordinate) yaxis() int {
    return 0
}
```

In the second part, you first implement the two functions of the coordinates interface for the
point2D type. Then you develop a function named findCoordinates() that accepts a
variable that implements the coordinates interface. The findCoordinates() function just
prints the two coordinates of a point using a simple fmt.Println() function call. Then,
you define a new type named coordinate that is used for points that belong to the *x*-axis.
Last, you implement the coordinates interface for the coordinate type.

At the time of writing the code for interfaces.go, I believed that the coordinates and
coordinate names were fine. After writing the previous paragraph, I realized that the
coordinate type could have been renamed to xpoint for better readability. I left the
names coordinates and coordinate to point out that everybody makes mistakes and
that the variable and type names you are using must be chosen wisely.

The last part has the following Go code:

```
func main() {

    x := point2D{X: -1, Y: 12}
    fmt.Println(x)
    findCoordinates(x)

    y := coordinate(10)
    findCoordinates(y)
}
```

In this part, you first create a `point2D` variable and print its coordinates using the `findCoordinates()` function, then you create a coordinate variable named `y` that holds a single coordinate value. Lastly, you print the `y` variable using the same `findCoordinates()` function used for printing a `point2D` variable.

Although Go is not an object-oriented programming language, I will use some object-oriented terminology here. So, in object-oriented terminology, this means that both `point2D` and `coordinate` types are coordinate objects. However, none of them are *only* a `coordinate` object.

Executing `interfaces.go` creates the following output:

```
$ go run interfaces.go
{-1 12}
X: -1 Y: 12
X: 10 Y: 0
```

I believe that Go interfaces are not necessary when developing systems software, but they are a handy Go feature that can make the development of a systems application more readable and simpler, so do not hesitate to use them.

Creating random numbers

As a practical programming example, this section will talk about creating random numbers in Go. Random numbers have many uses, including the generation of good passwords as well as the creation of files with random data that can be used for testing other applications. However, bear in mind that usually programming languages generate pseudorandom numbers that approximate the properties of a true random number generator.

Go uses the `math/rand` package for generating random numbers and needs a seed to start producing random numbers. The seed is used for initializing the entire process and is extremely important because if you always start with the same seed, you will always get the same sequence of random numbers.

The `random.go` program has three main parts. The first part is the preamble of the program:

```
package main

import (
    "fmt"
    "math/rand"
    "os"
```

```
    "strconv"
    "time"
)
```

The second part is the definition of the `random()` function that returns a random number each time it is called, using the `rand.Intn()` Go function:

```
func random(min, max int) int {
    return rand.Intn(max-min) + min
}
```

The two parameters of the `random()` function define the lower and upper limits of the generated random number. The last part of `random.go` is the implementation of the `main()` function that is mainly used for calling the `random()` function:

```
func main() {
    MIN := 0
    MAX := 0
    TOTAL := 0
    if len(os.Args) > 3 {
        MIN, _ = strconv.Atoi(os.Args[1])
        MAX, _ = strconv.Atoi(os.Args[2])
        TOTAL, _ = strconv.Atoi(os.Args[3])
    } else {
        fmt.Println("Usage:", os.Args[0], "MIX MAX TOTAL")
        os.Exit(-1)
    }

    rand.Seed(time.Now().Unix())
    for i := 0; i < TOTAL; i++ {
        myrand := random(MIN, MAX)
        fmt.Print(myrand)
        fmt.Print(" ")
    }
    fmt.Println()
}
```

A big part of the `main()` function involves dealing with the reading of command-line arguments as integer numbers and printing a descriptive error message in case you did not get the correct number of command-line arguments. This is the standard practice that we will follow in this book. The `random.go` program uses the Unix epoch time as the seed for the random number generator by calling the `time.Now().Unix()` function. The important thing to remember is that you do not have to call `rand.Seed()` multiple times. Lastly, `random.go` does not examine the error variable returned by `strconv.Atoi()` to save book space, not because it is not necessary.

Executing `random.go` generates the following kind of output:

```
$ go run random.go 12 32 20
29 27 20 23 22 28 13 16 22 26 12 29 22 30 15 19 26 24 20 29
```

Should you wish to generate more secure random numbers in Go, you should use the `crypto/rand` package, which implements a cryptographically secure pseudorandom number generator. You can find more information about the `crypto/rand` package by visiting its documentation page at `https://golang.org/pkg/crypto/rand/`.

If you are really into random numbers, then the definitive reference to the theory of random numbers is the second volume of *The Art of Computer Programming* by Donald Knuth.

Exercises

1. Browse the Go documentation site:`https://golang.org/doc/`.
2. Write a Go program that keeps reading integers until you give the number 0 as input, then it prints the minimum and maximum integer in the input.
3. Write the same Go program as before, but this time, you will get your input using command-line arguments. Which version do you think is better? Why?
4. Write a Go program that supports two command-line options (`-i` and `-k`) in random order using if statements. Now change your program to support three command-line arguments. As you will see, the complexity of the latter program is just too much to handle using if statements.
5. If the indices of a map were natural numbers, are there any cases that it would be wise and efficient to use a map instead of an array?
6. Try to put the functionality of `array2map.go` into a separate function.
7. Try to develop your own random number generator in Go that will still use the current time as a seed but not the `math/rand` package.
8. Learn how to create a slice from an existing array. What happens when you make changes to the slice?
9. Use the `copy()` function to make a copy of an existing slice. What happens when the destination slice is smaller than the source slice? What happens when the destination slice is bigger than the source slice?
10. Try to write an interface for supporting points in 3D space. Then, use this interface to support points that reside on the x-axis.

Summary

You learned many things in this chapter, including getting user input and processing command-line arguments. You familiarized yourself with the basic Go structures and you created a Go program that generates random numbers. Try to do the offered exercises and do not get discouraged if you fail in some of them.

The next chapter will talk about many advanced Go features, including error handling, pattern matching, regular expressions, reflection, unsafe code, calling C code from Go, and the `strace(1)` command-line utility. I will compare Go with other programming languages and give you practical advice in order to avoid some common Go pitfalls.

3
Advanced Go Features

In the previous chapter, you learned how to compile Go code, how to get input from the user and print the output on the screen, how to create your own Go functions, the data structures that Go supports, and how to process command-line arguments.

This chapter will discuss many fascinating things, so you better prepare yourselves for lots of interesting and practical Go code that will help you perform many different yet really important tasks, starting with error handling and ending with how to avoid some common Go mistakes. If you are familiar with Go, you can skip what you already know, but please do not skip the proposed exercises.

So, this chapter will talk about some advanced Go features, including:

- Error handling
- Error logging
- Pattern matching and regular expressions
- Reflection
- How to use the `strace(1)` and `dtrace(1)` tools to watch the system calls of Go executable files
- How to detect unreachable Go code
- How to avoid various common Go mistakes

Error handling in Go

Errors happen all the time, so it is our job to both catch and handle them, especially when writing code that deals with sensitive system information and files. The good news is that Go has a special data type called `error` that helps signify erroneous states; if an `error` variable has a `nil` value, then there is no error situation.

As you saw in the `addCLA.go` program that was developed in the previous chapter, you can ignore the `error` variable that is returned by most Go functions using the _ character:

```
temp, _ := strconv.Atoi(arguments[i])
```

However, this is not considered good practice and should be avoided, especially on systems software and other kinds of critical software, such as server processes.

As you will see in `Chapter` 6, *File Input and Output*, even **End of File (EOF)** is a type of error that is returned when there is nothing left to read from a file. As `EOF` is defined in the `io` package, you can handle it as follows:

```
if err == io.EOF {


    // Do something
}
```

However, the most important task to learn is how to develop functions that return `error` variables and how to handle them, which is explained next.

Functions can return error variables

Go functions can return `error` variables, which means that an error condition can be handled inside a function, outside of a function, or both inside and outside the function; the latter situation does not happen very often. So, this subsection will develop a function that returns error messages. The relevant Go code can be found in `funErr.go` and will be presented in three parts.

The first part contains the following Go code:

```
package main

import (
    "errors"
    "fmt"
    "log"
)

func division(x, y int) (int, error, error) {
    if y == 0 {
        return 0, nil, errors.New("Cannot divide by zero!")
    }
    if x%y != 0 {
        remainder := errors.New("There is a remainder!")
```

```
            return x / y, remainder, nil
    } else {
            return x / y, nil, nil
    }

}
```

Apart from the expected preamble, the preceding code defines a new function named division(), which returns an integer and two error variables. If you remember from your Math classes, when you divide two integer numbers, the division operation is not always perfect, which means that you might get a remainder that is not zero. The errors.New() function from the errors Go package that you see in funErr.go creates a new error variable, using the provided string as the error message.

The second part of funErr.go has the following Go code:

```
func main() {
    result, rem, err := division(2, 2)
    if err != nil {
            log.Fatal(err)
    } else {
            fmt.Println("The result is", result)
    }

    if rem != nil {
            fmt.Println(rem)
    }
```

It is a very common Go practice to compare an error variable with nil to quickly find out whether there is an error condition or not.

The last part of funErr.go is as follows:

```
    result, rem, err = division(12, 5)
    if err != nil {
            log.Fatal(err)
    } else {
            fmt.Println("The result is", result)
    }

    if rem != nil {
            fmt.Println(rem)
    }

    result, rem, err = division(2, 0)
    if err != nil {
            log.Fatal(err)
```

```
    } else {
        fmt.Println("The result is", result)
    }

    if rem != nil {
        fmt.Println(rem)
    }
}
```

This part showcases two erroneous conditions. The first one is an integer division that has a remainder, whereas the second one is an invalid division because you cannot divide a number by zero. As the name `log.Fatal()` implies, this logging function should be used for critical errors only because when called, it automatically terminates your program. However, as you will see in the next subsection, there exist other, more gentle, ways to log your error messages.

Executing `funErr.go` generates the next output:

```
$ go run funErr.go
The result is 1
The result is 2
There is a remainder!
2017/03/07 07:39:19 Cannot divide by zero!
exit status 1
```

The last line is automatically generated by the `log.Fatal()` function, just before terminating the program. It is important to understand that any Go code after the call to `log.Fatal()` will not be executed.

About error logging

Go offers functions that can help you log your error messages in various ways. You already saw `log.Fatal()` in `funErr.go`, which is a somewhat cruel way to deal with simple errors. Put simply, you should have a very good reason to use `log.Fatal()` in your code. Generally speaking, `log.Fatal()` should be used instead of the `os.Exit()` function because it allows you to print an error message and exit your program using just one function call.

Go offers additional error logging functions in the `log` standard package that behave more gently depending on the situation, which includes `log.Printf()`, `log.Print()`, `log.Println()`, `log.Fatalf()`, `log.Fatalln()`, `log.Panic()`, `log.Panicln()`, and `log.Panicf()`. Please note that logging functions can be handy for debugging purposes so do not underestimate their power.

The `logging.go` program illustrates two of the mentioned logging functions using the following Go code:

```
package main

import (
    "log"
)

func main() {
    x := 1
    log.Printf("log.Print() function: %d", x)
    x = x + 1
    log.Printf("log.Print() function: %d", x)
    x = x + 1
    log.Panicf("log.Panicf() function: %d", x)
    x = x + 1
    log.Printf("log.Print() function: %d", x)
}
```

As you can see, `logging.go` does not need the `fmt` package because it has its own functions for printing the output. Executing `logging.go` will produce the following output:

```
$ go run logging.go
2017/03/10 16:51:56 log.Print() function: 1
2017/03/10 16:51:56 log.Print() function: 2
2017/03/10 16:51:56 log.Panicf() function: 3
panic: log.Panicf() function: 3
goroutine 1 [running]:
log.Panicf(0x10b78d0, 0x19, 0xc42003df48, 0x1, 0x1)
        /usr/local/Cellar/go/1.8/libexec/src/log/log.go:329 +0xda
main.main()
        /Users/mtsouk/ch3/code/logging.go:14 +0x1af
exit status 2
```

Although the `log.Printf()` function works in the same way as `fmt.Printf()`, it automatically prints the date and time the log message was printed, just like the `log.Fatal()` function did in `funErr.go`. Additionally, the `log.Panicf()` function works in a similar way to `log.Fatal()`--they both terminate the current program. However, `log.Panicf()` prints some additional information, useful for debugging purposes.

Go also offers the `log/syslog` package that is a simple interface to the system log service running on your Unix machine. Chapter 7,*Working with System Files*, will talk more about the `log/syslog` package.

The addCLA.go program revisited

This subsection will present an improved version of the addCLA.go program we developed in the previous chapter, to make it able to handle any kind of user input. The new program will be called addCLAImproved.go, but instead of presenting its full Go code, you will only see the differences between addCLAImproved.go and addCLA.go using the diff(1) command-line utility:

```
$ diff addCLAImproved.go addCLA.go
13,18c13,14
<           temp, err := strconv.Atoi(arguments[i])
<           if err == nil {
<                 sum = sum + temp
<           } else {
<                 fmt.Println("Ignoring", arguments[i])
<           }
---
>           temp, _ := strconv.Atoi(arguments[i])
>           sum = sum + temp
```

What this output basically tells us is that the last two lines of code, which can be found in addCLA.go and begin with the > character, were replaced by the lines of code that begin with the < character in addCLAImproved.go. The remaining code of both files is exactly the same.

The diff(1) utility compares text files line by line and is a handy way of spotting code differences between different versions of the same file.

Executing addCLAImproved.go will generate the following kind of output:

```
$ go run addCLAImproved.go
Sum: 0
$ go run addCLAImproved.go 1 2 -3
Sum: 0
$ go run addCLAImproved.go 1 a 2 b 3.2 @
Ignoring a
Ignoring b
Ignoring 3.2
Ignoring @
Sum: 3
```

So, the new and improved version works as expected, behaves reliably, and allows us to differentiate between valid and invalid input.

Pattern matching and regular expressions

Pattern matching, which plays a key role in Go, is a technique for searching a string for a set of characters based on a specific search pattern that is based on **regular expressions**. If pattern matching is successful, it allows you to extract the desired data from the string or replace or delete it. **Grammar** is a set of production rules for strings in a formal language. The production rules describe how to create strings from the alphabet of the language that are valid according to the syntax of the language. Grammar does not describe the meaning of a string or what can be done with it in whatever context, only its form. What is important is to realize that grammar is at the heart of regular expressions because without it, you cannot define or use a regular expression.

Regular expressions and pattern matching are not a panacea, so you should not try to solve every problem using regular expressions since they are not suitable for every kind of problem you may come up against. Furthermore, they might introduce unnecessary complexity to your software.

The Go package responsible for the pattern matching capabilities of Go is called `regexp`, which you can see in action in `regExp.go`. The code of `regExp.go` will be presented in four parts.

The first part is the expected preamble:

```
package main

import (
    "fmt"
    "regexp"
)
```

The second part is as follows:

```
func main() {
match, _ := regexp.MatchString("Mihalis", "Mihalis Tsoukalos")
    fmt.Println(match)
    match, _ = regexp.MatchString("Tsoukalos", "Mihalis tsoukalos")
    fmt.Println(match)
```

Both calls to `regexp.MatchString()` try to find a static string, which is the first parameter, in a given string, which is the second parameter.

The third part contains a single, yet crucial, line of Go code:

```
parse, err := regexp.Compile("[Mm]ihalis")
```

The `regexp.Compile()` function reads the provided regular expression and tries to parse it. If the parsing of the regular expressing is successful, then `regexp.Compile()` returns a value of the `regexp.Regexp` variable typethat you can use afterward. The `[Mm]` expression in the `regexp.Compile()` function means that what you are looking for can begin with an uppercase M or a lowercase m. Both [and] are special characters that are not part of the regular expression. So, the provided grammar is naive and only matches the words `Mihalis` and `mihalis`.

The last part uses the previous regular expression that is stored in the `parse` variable:

```
if err != nil {
        fmt.Printf("Error compiling RE: %s\n", err)
} else {
        fmt.Println(parse.MatchString("Mihalis Tsoukalos"))
        fmt.Println(parse.MatchString("mihalis Tsoukalos"))
        fmt.Println(parse.MatchString("M ihalis Tsoukalos"))
        fmt.Println(parse.ReplaceAllString("mihalis Mihalis", "MIHALIS"))
}
}
```

Running `regExp.go` generates the next output:

```
$ go run regExp.go
true
false
true
true
false
MIHALIS MIHALIS
```

So, the first call to `regexp.MatchString()` was a match, but the second was not because pattern matching is case-sensitive and `Tsoukalos` does not match `tsoukalos`. The `parse.ReplaceAllString()` function at the end searches the string that is given as an input (`"mihalis Mihalis"`) and replaces each match with the string that is given as its second parameter (`"MIHALIS"`).

The rest of this section will present various examples using static text because you do not know how to read text files yet. However, as the static text will be stored in an array and processed line by line, the presented code can be easily modified to support getting your input from external text files.

Printing all the values from a given column of a line

This is a very common scenario, as you often will need to get all the data from a given column of a structured text file in order to analyze it afterward. The code of readColumn.go, which prints values in the third column, will be presented in two parts.

The first part is as follows:

```
package main

import (
    "fmt"
    "strings"
)

func main() {
    var s [3]string
    s[0] = "1 2 3"
    s[1] = "11 12 13 14 15 16"
    s[2] = "-1 2 -3 -4 -5 6"
```

Here, you import the required Go packages and define a string with three lines using an array with three elements.

The second part contains the following Go code:

```
    column := 2

    for i := 0; i < len(s); i++ {
        data := strings.Fields(s[i])
        if len(data) >= column {
            fmt.Println((data[column-1]))
        }
    }
}
```

First, you define the column that interests you. Then, you start iterating over the strings stored in the array. This is similar to reading a text file line by line. The Go code inside the `for` loop splits the fields of the input line, stores them in the `data` array, verifies that the value from the desired column is present, and prints it on your screen. All of the hard work is done by the handy `strings.Fields()` function that splits a string based on whitespace characters, as defined in `unicode.IsSpace()`, and returns a slice of strings. Although `readColumn.go` does not use the `regexp.Compile()` function, the logic behind its implementation with the use of `strings.Fields()` is still based on the principles of regular expressions.

An important thing to remember is that you should never trust your data. Put simply, always verify that the data you expect to grab is there.

Executing `readColumn.go` will generate the following kind of output:

```
$ go run readColumn.go
2
12
2
```

`Chapter 6`,*File Input and Output*, will show an improved version of `readColumn.go` that you can use as a starting point in case you want to modify the rest of the examples shown.

Creating summaries

In this section, we will develop a program that adds all the values of a given column of text with multiple lines. To make things even more interesting, the column number will be given as a parameter in the program. The main difference between the program of this subsection and `readColumn.go` from the previous subsection is that you will need to convert each value into an integer number.

The name of the program that will be developed is `summary.go` and can be divided into three parts.

The first part is this:

```
package main

import (
    "fmt"
    "os"
    "strconv"
    "strings"
)

func main() {
    var s [3]string
    s[0] = "1 b 3"
    s[1] = "11 a 1 14 1 1"
    s[2] = "-1 2 -3 -4 -5"
```

The second part has the following Go code:

```
arguments := os.Args
column, err := strconv.Atoi(arguments[1])
if err != nil {
        fmt.Println("Error reading argument")
        os.Exit(-1)
}
if column == 0 {
        fmt.Println("Invalid column")
        os.Exit(1)
}
```

The previous code reads the index of the column that interests you. If you want to make summary.go even better, you can check for negative values in the column variable and print the appropriate error message.

The last part of summary.go is as follows:

```
sum := 0
for i := 0; i < len(s); i++ {
        data := strings.Fields(s[i])
        if len(data) >= column {
                temp, err := strconv.Atoi(data[column-1])
                if err == nil {
                        sum = sum + temp
                } else {
                        fmt.Printf("Invalid argument: %s\n", data[column-1])
                }
        } else {
                fmt.Println("Invalid column!")
```

```
        }
    }
    fmt.Printf("Sum: %d\n", sum)
}
```

As you can see, most of the Go code in `summary.go` is about dealing with exceptions and potential errors. The core functionality of `summary.go` is implemented in a few lines of Go code.

Executing `summary.go` will give you the following output:

```
$ go run summary.go 0
Invalid column
exit status 1
$ go run summary.go 2
Invalid argument: b
Invalid argument: a
Sum: 2
$ go run summary.go 1
Sum: 11
```

Finding the number of occurrences

A very common programming problem is finding out the number of times an IP address appears in a log file. So, the example in this subsection will show you how to do this using a handy map structure. The `occurrences.go` program will be presented in three parts.

The first part is as follows:

```
package main

import (
    "fmt"
    "strings"
)

func main() {

    var s [3]string
    s[0] = "1 b 3 1 a a b"
    s[1] = "11 a 1 1 1 1 a a"
    s[2] = "-1 b 1 -4 a 1"
```

The second part is as follows:

```
counts := make(map[string]int)

for i := 0; i < len(s); i++ {
        data := strings.Fields(s[i])
        for _, word := range data {
                _, ok := counts[word]
                if ok {
                        counts[word] = counts[word] + 1
                } else {
                        counts[word] = 1
                }
        }
}
```

Here, we use the knowledge from the previous chapter to create a map named counts and populate it with the desired data using two for loops.

The last part is pretty small as it just prints the contents of the counts map:

```
for key, _ := range counts {


        fmt.Printf("%s -> %d \n", key, counts[key])
}
}
```

Executing occurrences.go and using the sort(1) command-line utility to sort the output of occurrences.go will generate the following kind of output:

```
$ go run occurrences.go | sort -n -r -t\  -k3,3
1 -> 8
a -> 6
b -> 3
3 -> 1
11 -> 1
-4 -> 1
-1 -> 1
```

As you can see, traditional Unix tools are still useful.

Find and replace

The example in this subsection will search the provided text for two variations of a given string and replace it with another string. The program will be named `findReplace.go` and will actually use Go regular expressions. The main reason for using the `regexp.Compile()` function, in this case, is that it greatly simplifies things and allows you to access your text only once.

The first part of the `findReplace.go` program is as follows:

```
package main

import (
    "fmt"
    "os"
    "regexp"
)
```

The next part is as follows:

```
func main() {

    var s [3]string
    s[0] = "1 b 3"
    s[1] = "11 a B 14 1 1"
    s[2] = "b 2 -3 B -5"

    parse, err := regexp.Compile("[bB]")


    if err != nil {
            fmt.Printf("Error compiling RE: %s\n", err)
            os.Exit(-1)
    }
```

The previous Go code will find every occurrence of an uppercase B or a lowercase b (`[bB]`). Note that there is also `regexp.MustCompile()` that works like `regexp.Compile()`. However, `regexp.MustCompile()` does not return an `error` variable; it just panics if the given expression is erroneous and cannot be parsed. As a result, `regexp.Compile()` is a better choice.

The last part is as follows:

```
for i := 0; i < len(s); i++ {
        temp := parse.ReplaceAllString(s[i], "C")
        fmt.Println(temp)
    }
}
```

Here you replace each match with an uppercase C using `parse.ReplaceAllString()`.

Executing `findReplace.go` generates the expected output:

```
$ go run findReplace.go
1 C 3
11 a C 14 1 1
C 2 -3 C -5
```

> The `awk(1)` and `sed(1)` command-line tools can do most of the previous
> tasks more easily, but `sed(1)` and `awk(1)` are not general-purpose
> programming languages.

Reflection

Reflection is an advanced Go feature that allows you to dynamically learn the type of an arbitrary object as well as information about its structure. You should recall that the `dataStructures.go` program from Chapter 2, *Writing Programs in Go*, used reflection to find out the fields of a data structure as well as the type of each fields. All of this happened with the help of the `reflect` Go package and the `reflect.TypeOf()` function that returns a `Type` variable.

Reflection is illustrated in the `reflection.go` Go program that will be presented in four parts.

The first one is the preamble of the Go program and has the following code:

```
package main

import (
    "fmt"
    "reflect"
)
```

The second part is as follows:

```
func main() {

    type t1 int
    type t2 int

    x1 := t1(1)
    x2 := t2(1)
    x3 := 1
```

Here, you create two new types, named t1 and t2, that are both int and three variables, named x1, x2, and x3.

The third part has the following Go code:

```
st1 :- reflect.ValueOf(&x1).Elem()
st2 := reflect.ValueOf(&x2).Elem()
st3 := reflect.ValueOf(&x3).Elem()

typeOfX1 := st1.Type()
typeOfX2 := st2.Type()
typeOfX3 := st3.Type()

fmt.Printf("X1 Type: %s\n", typeOfX1)
fmt.Printf("X2 Type: %s\n", typeOfX2)
fmt.Printf("X3 Type: %s\n", typeOfX3)
```

Here, you find the type of the x1, x2, and x3 variables using reflect.ValueOf() and Type().

The last part of reflection.go deals with a struct variable:

```
type aStructure struct {
        X     uint
        Y     float64
        Text string
}

x4 := aStructure{123, 3.14, "A Structure"}
st4 := reflect.ValueOf(&x4).Elem()
typeOfX4 := st4.Type()

fmt.Printf("X4 Type: %s\n", typeOfX4)
fmt.Printf("The fields of %s are:\n", typeOfX4)

for i := 0; i < st4.NumField(); i++ {
        fmt.Printf("%d: Field name: %s ", i, typeOfX4.Field(i).Name)
```

```
fmt.Printf("Type: %s ", st4.Field(i).Type())
fmt.Printf("and Value: %v\n", st4.Field(i).Interface())
    }
}
```

 There exist some laws that govern reflection in Go, but talking about them is beyond the scope of this book. What you should remember is that your programs can examine their own structure using reflection, which is a very powerful capability.

Executing `reflection.go` prints the following output:

```
$ go run reflection.go
X1 Type: main.t1
X2 Type: main.t2
X3 Type: int
X4 Type: main.aStructure
The fields of main.aStructure are:
0: Field name: X Type: uint and Value: 123
1: Field name: Y Type: float64 and Value: 3.14
2: Field name: Text Type: string and Value: A Structure
```

The first two lines of the output show that Go does not consider the types `t1` and `t2` as equal, even though both `t1` and `t2` are aliases of the `int` type.

Old habits die hard!

Despite the fact that Go tries to be a safe programming language, sometimes it is forced to forget about safety and allows the programmer to do whatever he/she wants.

Calling C code from Go

Go allows you to call C code because there are times when the only way to perform some tasks, such as communicating with a hardware device or a database server, is by using C. Nevertheless, if you find yourself using this capability many times in the same project, you might need to reconsider your approach and your choice of programming language.

Talking more about this capability in Go is beyond the scope of this book. What you should remember is that most likely, you will never need to call C code from your Go program. Nevertheless, should you wish to explore this Go feature, you can start by visiting the documentation of the `cgo` tool at `https://golang.org/cmd/cgo/` as well as by looking at the code found at `https://github.com/golang/go/blob/master/misc/cgo/gmp/gmp.go`.

Unsafe code

Unsafe code is Go code that bypasses the type safety and memory security of Go and requires the use of the unsafe package. You will most likely never need to use unsafe code in your Go programs but if for some strange reason you ever need to, it will probably have to do with pointers.

Using unsafe code can be dangerous for your programs, so only use it when it is absolutely necessary. If you are not completely sure that you need it, then do not use it.

The example code in this subsection is saved as unsafe.go and will be presented in two parts.

The first part is as follows:

```
package main

import (
    "fmt"
    "unsafe"
)

func main() {
    var value int64 = 5


    var p1 = &value
    var p2 = (*int32)(unsafe.Pointer(p1))
```

You first create a new int64 variable that is named value. Then, you create a pointer to it named p1. Next, you create another pointer that points to p1. However, the p2 pointer that points to p1 is a pointer to an int32 integer, despite the fact that p1 points to an int64 variable. Although this is not permitted by Go rules, the unsafe.Pointer() function makes this possible.

The second part is as follows:

```
fmt.Println("*p1: ", *p1)
fmt.Println("*p2: ", *p2)
*p1 = 312121321321213212
fmt.Println(value)
fmt.Println("*p2: ", *p2)
*p1 = 31212132
fmt.Println(value)
```

```
    fmt.Println("*p2: ", *p2)
}
```

Executing `unsafe.go` will create the following output:

```
$ go run unsafe.go
*p1:  5
*p2:  5
312121321321213212
*p2:  606940444
31212132
*p2:  31212132
```

The output shows how dangerous an unsafe pointer can be. When the value of the `value` variable fits into an `int32` memory space (`5` and `31212132`), then `p2` works fine and shows the correct result. However, when the `value` variable holds a value (`312121321321213212`) that does not fit into an `int32` memory space, then `p2` shows an erroneous result (`606940444`), without giving you a warning or an error message.

Comparing Go to other programming languages

Go is not perfect, but neither are the rest of the programming languages. This section will briefly discuss other programming languages and compare them to Go in order to give you a better understanding of the choices you have. So, the list of programming languages that can be compared to Go includes:

- C: C is the most popular programming language for developing systems software because the portable part of each Unix operating system is written in C. However, it has some critical drawbacks, including the fact that C pointers, which are great and fast, can lead to difficult-to-detect bugs and memory leaks. Additionally, C does not offer garbage collection; back when C was created, garbage collection was a luxury that had the ability slow down computers. However, nowadays computers are pretty fast and garbage collection does not slow things down anymore. Moreover, C programs require more code for developing a given task than other systems programming languages. Lastly, C is an old programming language that does not support modern programming paradigms, such as object-oriented and functional programming.

- **C++**: As previously mention, I do not like C++ anymore. If you think that you should use C++, then you may want to consider using C instead. However, the main advantage of C++ over Go is that if needed, C++ can be used as if it were C. However, neither C nor C++ have good support for concurrent programming.
- **Rust**: Rust is a new systems programming language that tries to avoid unpleasant bugs caused by unsafe code. Currently, the syntax of Rust is changing too fast, but this will end in the near feature. If for some reason you do not like Go, you should try Rust.
- **Swift**: In its current status, Swift is more suitable for developing systems software for macOS systems. However, I am sure that in the near feature, Swift will be more popular on Linux machines, so you should keep an eye on it.
- **Python**: Python is a scripting language, which is its main disadvantage. This is because usually, you do not want to make the source of your systems software available to everyone.
- **Perl**: What was said about Python can be also said about Perl. However, both programming languages have a plethora of modules that will make your life a lot easier and your code a lot smaller.

If you ask my opinion, I think that Go is a modern, portable, mature, and safe programming language for writing systems software. You should try Go before looking for any alternatives. However, if you are a Go programmer and want to try something else, I suggest that you pick Rust or Swift. Yet, if you need to write reliable concurrent programs, Go should be your first choice.

If you cannot choose between Go and Rust, then just try C. Learning the basics of systems programming is more important than the programming language you select.

Despite their disadvantages, bear in mind that all scripting programming languages are perfect for writing prototypes and have the advantage that they allow you to create graphical interfaces for your software. Still, delivering systems software in a scripting language is rarely accepted, unless there is a really good reason to do so.

Analysing software

There are times that a program fails for some unknown reason or does not perform well, and you want to find out why without having to rewrite your code and add a plethora of debugging statements. So, this section will talk about strace(1) and dtrace(1), which allow you to see what is going on behind the scenes when you execute a program on a Unix machine. Although both tools can work with the go run command, you will get less unrelated output if you first create an executable file using go build and use this file. This mainly occurs because go run makes temporary files before actually running your Go code, and you want to debug the actual program, not the compiler used to build the program.

Remember that although dtrace(1) is more powerful than strace(1) and has its own programming language, strace(1) is more versatile for watching the system calls a program makes.

Using the strace(1) command-line utility

The strace(1) command-line utility allows you to trace system calls and signals. As strace(1) is not available on Mac machines, this section will use a Linux machine to showcase strace(1). However, as you will see in a later, macOS machines have the dtrace(1) command-line utility that can do many more things.

The number after the name of a program refers to the section of the manual its page belongs to. Although most of the names can be found only once, which means that putting the section number is not necessary, there are names that can be located in multiple sections because they have multiple meanings, such ascrontab(1) and crontab(5). Therefore, if you try to retrieve such a page without specifically stating the section number, you will get the entry in the section of the manual that has the smallest section number.

To get a good sense of the output generated by strace(1), look at the following figure where strace(1) is used to examine the executable of addCLAImproved.go:

```
●  ●  ●                    2. mtsouk@mail: ~/Desktop/goBook/ch/ch3/code (ssh)
code$ strace ./addCLAImproved 1 2
execve("./addCLAImproved", ["./addCLAImproved", "1", "2"], [/* 22 vars */]) = 0
arch_prctl(ARCH_SET_FS, 0x544990)        = 0
sched_getaffinity(0, 128, {1})           = 8
mmap(0xc000000000, 65536, PROT_NONE, MAP_PRIVATE|MAP_ANONYMOUS, -1, 0) = 0xc000000000
munmap(0xc000000000, 65536)              = 0
mmap(NULL, 262144, PROT_READ|PROT_WRITE, MAP_PRIVATE|MAP_ANONYMOUS, -1, 0) = 0x7f09f6cf6000
mmap(0xc208000000, 1048576, PROT_READ|PROT_WRITE, MAP_PRIVATE|MAP_ANONYMOUS, -1, 0) = 0xc20
8000000
mmap(0xc207ff0000, 65536, PROT_READ|PROT_WRITE, MAP_PRIVATE|MAP_ANONYMOUS, -1, 0) = 0xc207f
f0000
mmap(0xc000000000, 4096, PROT_READ|PROT_WRITE, MAP_PRIVATE|MAP_ANONYMOUS, -1, 0) = 0xc00000
0000
mmap(NULL, 65536, PROT_READ|PROT_WRITE, MAP_PRIVATE|MAP_ANONYMOUS, -1, 0) = 0x7f09f6ce6000
mmap(NULL, 1439992, PROT_READ|PROT_WRITE, MAP_PRIVATE|MAP_ANONYMOUS, -1, 0) = 0x7f09f6b8600
0
mmap(NULL, 131072, PROT_READ|PROT_WRITE, MAP_PRIVATE|MAP_ANONYMOUS, -1, 0) = 0x7f09f6b66000
sigaltstack({ss_sp=0xc208006000, ss_flags=0, ss_size=32768}, NULL) = 0
rt_sigprocmask(SIG_SETMASK, [], NULL, 8) = 0
rt_sigaction(SIGHUP, NULL, {SIG_DFL, [], 0}, 8) = 0
rt_sigaction(SIGHUP, {0x428480, ~[], SA_RESTORER|SA_STACK|SA_RESTART|SA_SIGINFO, 0x4284f0},
NULL, 8) = 0
rt_sigaction(SIGINT, NULL, {SIG_DFL, [], 0}, 8) = 0
rt_sigaction(SIGINT, {0x428480, ~[], SA_RESTORER|SA_STACK|SA_RESTART|SA_SIGINFO, 0x4284f0},
NULL, 8) = 0
rt_sigaction(SIGQUIT, {0x428480, ~[], SA_RESTORER|SA_STACK|SA_RESTART|SA_SIGINFO, 0x4284f0}
, NULL, 8) = 0
rt_sigaction(SIGILL, {0x428480, ~[], SA_RESTORER|SA_STACK|SA_RESTART|SA_SIGINFO, 0x4284f0},
NULL, 8) = 0
rt_sigaction(SIGTRAP, {0x428480, ~[], SA_RESTORER|SA_STACK|SA_RESTART|SA_SIGINFO, 0x4284f0}
, NULL, 8) = 0
rt_sigaction(SIGABRT, {0x428480, ~[], SA_RESTORER|SA_STACK|SA_RESTART|SA_SIGINFO, 0x4284f0}
, NULL, 8) = 0
rt_sigaction(SIGBUS, {0x428480, ~[], SA_RESTORER|SA_STACK|SA_RESTART|SA_SIGINFO, 0x4284f0},
NULL, 8) = 0
rt_sigaction(SIGFPE, {0x428480, ~[], SA_RESTORER|SA_STACK|SA_RESTART|SA_SIGINFO, 0x4284f0},
NULL, 8) = 0
rt_sigaction(SIGUSR1, {0x428480, ~[], SA_RESTORER|SA_STACK|SA_RESTART|SA_SIGINFO, 0x4284f0}
, NULL, 8) = 0
rt_sigaction(SIGSEGV, {0x428480, ~[], SA_RESTORER|SA_STACK|SA_RESTART|SA_SIGINFO, 0x4284f0}
, NULL, 8) = 0
rt_sigaction(SIGUSR2, {0x428480, ~[], SA_RESTORER|SA_STACK|SA_RESTART|SA_SIGINFO, 0x4284f0}
, NULL, 8) = 0
rt_sigaction(SIGPIPE, {0x428480, ~[], SA_RESTORER|SA_STACK|SA_RESTART|SA_SIGINFO, 0x4284f0}
, NULL, 8) = 0
rt_sigaction(SIGALRM, {0x428480, ~[], SA_RESTORER|SA_STACK|SA_RESTART|SA_SIGINFO, 0x4284f0}
, NULL, 8) = 0
rt_sigaction(SIGTERM, {0x428480, ~[], SA_RESTORER|SA_STACK|SA_RESTART|SA_SIGINFO, 0x4284f0}
, NULL, 8) = 0
rt_sigaction(SIGSTKFLT, {0x428480, ~[], SA_RESTORER|SA_STACK|SA_RESTART|SA_SIGINFO, 0x4284f
0}, NULL, 8) = 0
```

Using the strace(1) command on a Linux machine

The really interesting part of the `strace(1)` output is the following line, which cannot be seen in the preceding figure:

```
$ strace ./addCLAImproved 1 2 2>&1 | grep write
write(1, "Sum: 3\n", 7Sum: 3
```

We used the `grep(1)` command-line utility to extract the lines that contain the C system call that interests us, which in this case is `write(2)`. This is because we already know that `write(2)` is used for printing output. So, you learned that in this case, a single `write(2)` C system call is used for printing all of the output on the screen; its first parameter is the file descriptor, and its second parameter is the text you want to print.

Note that you might want to use `strace(1)` with the `-f` option in order to also trace any child processes that might get created during the execution of a program.

Bear in mind that there existtwo more variations of `write(2)`, named `pwrite(2)` and `writev(2)`, which offer the same core functionality as `write(2)` but in a slightly different way.

The following variation of the previous command requires more calls to `write(2)` because it generates more output:

```
$ strace ./addCLAImproved 1 a b 2>&1 | grep write
write(1, "Ignoring a\n", 11Ignoring a
write(1, "Ignoring b\n", 11Ignoring b
write(1, "Sum: 1\n", 7Sum: 1
```

Unix uses file descriptors, which are positive integer values, as an internal representation for accessing all its files. By default, all Unix systems support three special and standard filenames: `/dev/stdin`, `/dev/stdout`, and `/dev/stderr`. They can also be accessed using file descriptors 0, 1, and 2, respectively. These three file descriptors are also called standard input, standard output, and standard error, respectively. Additionally, the file descriptor 0 can be accessed as `/dev/fd/0` on a Mac machine and as `/dev/pts/0` on a Debian Linux machine because everything in Unix is a file.

So, the reason for needing to put `2>&1` at the end of the command is to redirect all of the output, from standard error (file descriptor 2) to standard output (file descriptor 1), in order to be able to search it using the `grep(1)` command, which searches standard output only. Note that there exist many variations of `grep(1)`, including `zegrep(1)`, `fgrep(1)`, and `fgrep(1)`, that might work faster when they have to deal with large or huge text files.

What you can see here is that even if you are writing in Go, the generated executable uses C system calls and functions because apart from using machine language, C is the only way to communicate with the Unix kernel.

The DTrace utility

Although debugging utilities, such as `strace(1)` and `truss(1)`, which work on FreeBSD, can trace system calls produced by a process, they can be slow and therefore not appropriate for solving performance problems on busy Unix systems. Another tool named `dtrace(1)`, which uses the **DTrace** facility, allows you to see what happens behind the scenes on a system-wide basis without the need to modify or recompile anything. It also allows you to work on production systems and watch running programs or server processes dynamically without introducing a big overhead.

This subsection will use the `dtruss(1)` command-line utility, which is just a `dtrace(1)` script, that shows the system calls of a process. The output that `dtruss(1)` generates when examining the `addCLAImproved.go` executable on a macOS machine looks similar to the one that you can see in the following screenshot:

```
rMacBook:code mtsouk$ sudo dtruss ./addCLAImproved 1
SYSCALL(args)               = return
fatal error: runtime: bsdthread_register error

runtime stack:
runtime.throw(0x10b6e6d, 0x21)
        /usr/local/Cellar/go/1.8/libexec/src/runtime/panic.go:596 +0x95 fp=0x7fff5fbff
b20 sp=0x7fff5fbffb00
runtime.goenvs()
        /usr/local/Cellar/go/1.8/libexec/src/runtime/os_darwin.go:108 +0xa0 fp=0x7fff5
fbffb50 sp=0x7fff5fbffb20
runtime.schedinit()
        /usr/local/Cellar/go/1.8/libexec/src/runtime/proc.go:486 +0xa1 fp=0x7fff5fbffb
90 sp=0x7fff5fbffb50
runtime.rt0_go(0x7fff5fbffbc0, 0x2, 0x7fff5fbffbc0, 0x0, 0x2, 0x7fff5fbffce0, 0x7fff5f
bffcf1, 0x0, 0x7fff5fbffcf3, 0x7fff5fbffd01, ...)
        /usr/local/Cellar/go/1.8/libexec/src/runtime/asm_amd64.s:158 +0x183 fp=0x7fff5
fbffb98 sp=0x7fff5fbffb90
stat64("/usr/lib/libc++.1.dylib\0", 0x7FFF5FBFDD48, 0x1)                  = 0 0
stat64("/usr/lib/libSystem.B.dylib\0", 0x7FFF5FBFDD48, 0x1)               = 0 0
stat64("/usr/lib/libc++abi.dylib\0", 0x7FFF5FBFDC58, 0x1)                 = 0 0
stat64("/usr/lib/system/libcache.dylib\0", 0x7FFF5FBFD788, 0x1)           = 0 0
stat64("/usr/lib/system/libcommonCrypto.dylib\0", 0x7FFF5FBFD788, 0x1)        = 0 0
stat64("/usr/lib/system/libcompiler_rt.dylib\0", 0x7FFF5FBFD788, 0x1)         = 0 0
stat64("/usr/lib/system/libcopyfile.dylib\0", 0x7FFF5FBFD788, 0x1)            = 0 0
stat64("/usr/lib/system/libcorecrypto.dylib\0", 0x7FFF5FBFD788, 0x1)          = 0 0
stat64("/usr/lib/system/libdispatch.dylib\0", 0x7FFF5FBFD788, 0x1)            = 0 0
stat64("/usr/lib/system/libdyld.dylib\0", 0x7FFF5FBFD788, 0x1)            = 0 0
stat64("/usr/lib/system/libkeymgr.dylib\0", 0x7FFF5FBFD788, 0x1)              = 0 0
stat64("/usr/lib/system/liblaunch.dylib\0", 0x7FFF5FBFD788, 0x1)              = 0 0
stat64("/usr/lib/system/libmacho.dylib\0", 0x7FFF5FBFD788, 0x1)           = 0 0
stat64("/usr/lib/system/libquarantine.dylib\0", 0x7FFF5FBFD788, 0x1)          = 0 0
stat64("/usr/lib/system/libremovefile.dylib\0", 0x7FFF5FBFD788, 0x1)          = 0 0
stat64("/usr/lib/system/libsystem_asl.dylib\0", 0x7FFF5FBFD788, 0x1)          = 0 0
stat64("/usr/lib/system/libsystem_blocks.dylib\0", 0x7FFF5FBFD788, 0x1)       = 0 0
stat64("/usr/lib/system/libsystem_c.dylib\0", 0x7FFF5FBFD788, 0x1)        = 0 0
stat64("/usr/lib/system/libsystem_configuration.dylib\0", 0x7FFF5FBFD788, 0x1)    =
0 0
stat64("/usr/lib/system/libsystem_coreservices.dylib\0", 0x7FFF5FBFD788, 0x1)     =
0 0
stat64("/usr/lib/system/libsystem_coretls.dylib\0", 0x7FFF5FBFD788, 0x1)      =
0 0
```

Using the dtruss(1) command on a macOS machine

Once again, the following part of the output verifies that at the end of the day, everything on Unix machines is translated into C system calls and functions because this is the only way to communicate with the Unix kernel. You can display all the calls to the `write(2)` system call as follows:

```
$ sudo dtruss -c ./addCLAImproved 2000 2>&1 | grep write
```

However, this time you are going to get lots of output because the macOS executable uses `write(2)` multiple times instead of just once to print the same output.

> Starting to realize that not all Unix systems work the same way, despite their numerous similarities, is marvelous. But this also means that you should not make any assumptions about the way a Unix system works behind the scenes.

What is really interesting is the last part of the output of the following command:

```
$ sudo dtruss -c ./addCLAImproved 2000
CALL                                COUNT
__pthread_sigmask                     1
exit                                  1
getpid                                1
ioctl                                 1
issetugid                             1
read                                  1
thread_selfid                         1
ulock_wake                            1
bsdthread_register                    2
close                                 2
csops                                 2
open                                  2
select                                2
sysctl                                3
mmap                                  7
mprotect                              8
stat64                               41
write                                83
```

The reason you get this output is the `-c` option that tells `dtruss(1)` to count all system calls and print a summary of them, which in this case shows that `write(2)` has been called 83 times and `stat64(2)` 41 times.

The `dtrace(1)` utility is much more powerful than `strace(1)` and has its own programming language but is more difficult to learn. Additionally, even though there is a Linux version of `dtrace(1)`, `strace(1)` is more mature on Linux systems and does the job of tracing system calls in a simpler way.

You can learn more about the `dtrace(1)` utility by reading *DTrace: Dynamic Tracing in Oracle Solaris, Mac OS X, and FreeBSD* by Brendan Gregg and Jim Mauro and by visiting `http://dtrace.org/`.

Disabling System Integrity Protection on macOS

There is a big chance that you will have trouble running `dtrace(1)` and `dtruss(1)` on your Mac OS X machine the first time you try them and get the following error message:

```
$ sudo dtruss ./addCLAImproved 1 2 2>&1 | grep -i write
dtrace: error on enabled probe ID 2132 (ID 156: syscall::write:return):
invalid kernel access in action #12 at DIF offset 92
```

In this case you might need to disable the DTrace restrictions but still keep System Integrity Protection active for everything else. You can learn more about System Integrity Protection by visiting `https://support.apple.com/en-us/HT204899`.

Unreachable code

Unreachable code is code that can never be executed and is a logical kind of error. As the Go compiler itself cannot catch such logical errors, you will need to use the `go tool vet` command to help.

You should not confuse unreachable code with code that never gets executed intentionally, such as the code of a function that is not needed and is therefore not called in a program.

The example code in this section is saved as `cannotReach.go` and can be divided into two parts.

The first part has the following Go code:

```
package main

import (
    "fmt"
)


func x() int {


    return -1
    fmt.Println("Exiting x()")
    return -1
}

func y() int {
    return -1
    fmt.Println("Exiting y()")
    return -1
}
```

The second part is as follows:

```
func main() {
    fmt.Println(x())
    fmt.Println("Exiting program...")
}
```

As you can see, the unreachable code is in the first part. Both x() and y() functions have unreachable code because their return statements were put at the wrong place. However, we are not done yet because we will have to let the go tool vet tool discover the unreachable code. The process is simple and includes the execution of the following command:

```
$ go tool vet cannotReach.go
cannotReach.go:9: unreachable code
cannotReach.go:14: unreachable code
```

Additionally, you can see that go tool vet detects unreachable code even if the surrounding function is not going to be executed at all, as happens with y().

Avoiding common Go mistakes

This section will briefly talk about some common Go mistakes so that you can avoid them in your programs:

- If you have an error in a Go function, either log it or return it; do not do both unless you have a really good reason to do so.
- Go interfaces define behaviors, not data and data structures.
- Use the `io.Reader` and `io.Writer` interfaces because they make your code more extensible.
- Make sure that you pass a pointer to a variable to a function only when needed. The rest of the time, just pass the value of the variable.
- Error variables are not strings; they are `error` values.
- If you are afraid of making mistakes, you will most likely end up doing nothing useful. So experiment as much as you can.

The following are general pieces of advice that can be applied in every programming language:

- Test your Go code and functions in small and autonomous Go programs to make sure that they behave the way you think they should
- If you do not really know a Go feature, test it before using it for the first time, especially if you are developing a systems utility
- Do not test systems software on production machines
- When you deploy your systems software on a production machine, do it when the production machine is not busy and make sure that you have a backup plan

Exercises

1. Find and visit the documentation page of the `log` package
2. Use `strace(1)` to examine `hw.go` from the previous chapter
3. If you are on a Mac, try to examine the `hw.go` executable using `dtruss(1)`
4. Write a program that gets input from the user and examine its executable file using either `strace(1)` or `dtruss(1)`

5. Visit the website of Rust at `https://www.rust-lang.org/`

6. Visit the website of Swift at `https://swift.org/`

7. Visit the documentation page of the `io` package at `https://golang.org/pkg/io/`

8. Use the `diff(1)` command-line utility on your own in order to learn how to interpret its output better

9. Visit and read the main page of `write(2)`

10. Visit the main page of `grep(1)`

11. Play with reflection on your own by examining your own structures

12. Write an improved version of `occurrences.go` that will only display frequencies that are above a known numeric threshold, which will be given as a command-line argument

Summary

This chapter taught you some advanced Go features, including error handling, pattern matching and regular expressions, reflection, and unsafe code. Also, it talked about the `strace(1)` and `dtrace(1)` tools.

The next chapter will cover many interesting things, including the use of the new `sort.slice()` Go function, which is available in the latest Go version (1.8), as well as the big O notation, sorting algorithms, Go packages, and garbage collection.

4
Go Packages, Algorithms, and Data Structures

The main topics of this chapter will be Go packages, algorithms, and data structures. If you combine all of these, you will end up with a complete program because Go programs come in packages that contain algorithms that deal with data structures. These packages include both the ones that come with Go and the ones that you create on your own in order to manipulate your data.

Hence, in this chapter, you will learn about the following:

- The Big O notation
- Two sorting algorithms
- The `sort.Slice()` function
- Linked lists
- Trees
- Creating your own hash table data structure in Go
- Go packages
- **Garbage collection (GC)** in Go

About algorithms

Knowing about algorithms and the way they work will definitely help you when you have to manipulate lots of data. Additionally, if you choose to use the wrong algorithm for a given job, you might slow down the entire process and make your software unusable.

Traditional Unix command-line utilities such as `awk(1)`, `sed(1)`, `vi(1)`, `tar(1)`, and `cp(1)` are great examples of how good algorithms can help, and these utilities can work with files that are much bigger than the memory of a machine. This was extremely important in the early Unix days because the total amount of RAM on a Unix machine then was about 64K or even less!

The Big O notation

The **Big O notation** is used for describing the complexity of an algorithm, which is directly related to its performance. The efficiency of an algorithm is judged by its computation complexity, which mainly has to do with the number of times the algorithm needs to access its input data to do its job. Usually, you would want to know about the worst-case scenario and the average situation.

So, an $O(n)$ algorithm, where n is the size of the input, is considered better than an $O(n^2)$ algorithm, which is better than an $O(n^3)$ algorithm. However, the worst algorithms are the ones with an $O(n!)$ running time because this makes them almost unusable for inputs with more than 300 elements. Note that the Big O notation is more about estimating and not about giving an exact value. Therefore, it is largely used as a comparative value and not an absolute value.

Also, most Go lookup operations in built-in types, such as finding the value of a map key or accessing an array element, have a constant time, which is represented by $O(1)$. This means that built-in types are generally faster than custom types and that you should usually prefer them unless you want full control over what is going on behind the scenes. Additionally, not all data structures are created equal. Generally speaking, array operations are faster than map operations, whereas maps are more versatile than arrays!

Sorting algorithms

The most common category of algorithm has to deal with sorting data, that is, placing it in a given order. The two most famous sorting algorithms are the following:

- **Quicksort**: This is considered one of the fastest sorting algorithms. The average time thatquicksort takes to sort its data is O (n log n), but this can grow up to $O(n^2)$ in the worst-case scenario, which mainly has to do with the way the data is presented for processing.
- **Bubble sort**: This algorithm is pretty easy to implement with an $O(n^2)$ average complexity. If you want to start learning about sorting, start with bubble sort before looking into the more difficult to develop algorithms.

Although every algorithm has its disadvantages, if you do not have lots of data, the algorithm is not really important as long as it does the job.

What you should remember is, the way Go implements sorting internally cannot be controlled by the developer and it can change in the future; so, if you want to have full control over sorting, you should write your own implementation.

The sort.Slice() function

This section will illustrate the use of the sort.Slice() function that first came with Go version 1.8. The use of the function will be illustrated in sortSlice.go, which will be presented in three parts.

The first part is the expected preamble of the program and the definition of a new structure type, given as follows:

```
package main

import (
    "fmt"
    "sort"
)

type aStructure struct {
    person string
    height int
    weight int
}
```

As you might expect, you have to import the `sort` package to be able to use its `Slice()` function.

The second part contains the definition of a slice, which has four elements:

```
func main() {

    mySlice := make([]aStructure, 0)
    a := aStructure{"Mihalis", 180, 90}

    mySlice = append(mySlice, a)
    a = aStructure{"Dimitris", 180, 95}
    mySlice = append(mySlice, a)
    a = aStructure{"Marietta", 155, 45}
    mySlice = append(mySlice, a)
    a = aStructure{"Bill", 134, 40}
    mySlice = append(mySlice, a)
```

Therefore, in the first part, you declared a slice of structure that will be sorted in two ways in the rest of the program, which contains the following code:

```
    fmt.Println("0:", mySlice)
    sort.Slice(mySlice, func(i, j int) bool {
        return mySlice[i].weight <mySlice[j].weight
    })
    fmt.Println("<:", mySlice)
    sort.Slice(mySlice, func(i, j int) bool {
        return mySlice[i].weight >mySlice[j].weight
    })
    fmt.Println(">:", mySlice)
}
```

This code contains all the magic—you only have to define the way you want to `sort` your `slice` and the rest is done by Go. The `sort.Slice()` function takes the anonymous sorting function as one of its arguments; the other argument is the name of the `slice` variable you want to `sort`. Note that the sorted slice is saved in the `slice` variable.

Executing `sortSlice.go` will generate the following output:

```
$ go run sortSlice.go
0: [{Mihalis 180 90} {Dimitris 180 95} {Marietta 155 45} {Bill 134 40}]
<: [{Bill 134 40} {Marietta 155 45} {Mihalis 180 90} {Dimitris 180 95}]
>: [{Dimitris 180 95} {Mihalis 180 90} {Marietta 155 45} {Bill 134 40}]
```

As you can see, you can easily `sort` in ascending or descending order by just changing a single character in the Go code!

Also, if your Go version does not support `sort.Slice()`, you will get an error message similar to the following:

```
$ go version
go version go1.3.3 linux/amd64
$ go run sortSlice.go
# command-line-arguments
./sortSlice.go:27: undefined: sort.Slice
./sortSlice.go:31: undefined: sort.Slice
```

Linked lists in Go

A **linked list** is a structure with a finite set of elements where each element uses at least two memory locations—one for storing the data and the other for a pointer that links the current element to the next one in the sequence of elements that make the linked list. The biggest advantages of linked lists are that they are easy to understand and implement, and generic enough to be used in many different situations and model many different kinds of data.

The first element of a linked list is called the **head**, whereas the last element of a list is often called the **tail**. The first thing you should do when defining a linked list is to keep the head of the list in a separate variable because the head is the only thing that you need to access the entire linked list.

Note that if you lose the pointer to the first node of a single linked list, there is no possible way to find it again.

The following figure shows the graphical representation of a linked list and a doubly linked list. Doubly linked lists are more flexible, but require more housekeeping:

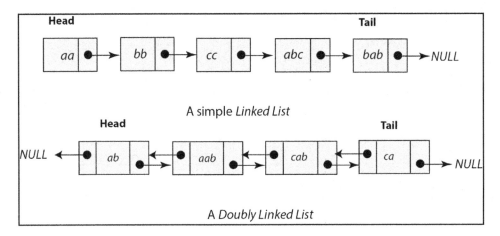

The graphical representation of a linked list and a doubly linked list

So, in this section, we will present a simple implementation of a linked list in Go saved in `linkedList.go`.

 When creating your own data structures, the single most important element is the definition of the node, which is usually implemented using a structure.

The code of `linkedList.go` will be presented in four parts.

The first part is as follows:

```
package main

import (
    "fmt"
)
```

The second part contains the following Go code:

```
type Node struct {
    Value int
    Next  *Node
}

func addNode(t *Node, v int) int {
```

```
    if root == nil {
            t = &Node{v, nil}
            root = t
            return 0
    }

    if v == t.Value {
            fmt.Println("Node already exists:", v)
            return -1
    }

    if t.Next == nil {
            t.Next = &Node{v, nil}
            return -2
    }

    return addNode(t.Next, v)



}
```

Here, you define the structure that will hold each element of the list and a function that allows you to add a new node to the list. In order to avoid duplicate entries, you should check whether a value already exists in the list or not. Note that addNode() is a recursive function because it calls itself and that this approach might be a little slower and require more memory than iterating.

The third part of the code is the traverse() function:

```
func traverse(t *Node) {
    if t == nil {
            fmt.Println("-> Empty list!")
            return
    }

    for t != nil {

            fmt.Printf("%d -> ", t.Value)
            t = t.Next
    }
    fmt.Println()
}
```

The for loop implements the iterative approach for visiting all the nodes in a linked list.

The last part is as follows:

```
var root = new(Node)
func main() {
    fmt.Println(root)
    root = nil
    traverse(root)
    addNode(root, 1)
    addNode(root, 1)
    traverse(root)
    addNode(root, 10)
    addNode(root, 5)
    addNode(root, 0)
    addNode(root, 0)
    traverse(root)
    addNode(root, 100)
    traverse(root)
}
```

For the first time in this book, you see the use of a global variable that is not a constant. Global variables can be accessed and changed from anywhere in a program, which makes their use both practical and dangerous for that reason. The reason for using a global variable, which is named root, to hold the root of the linked list is to show whether the linked list is empty or not. This happens because integer values in Go are initialized as 0; so new(Node) is in fact {0 <nil>}, which makes it impossible to tell whether the head of the list is nil or not without passing an extra variable to each function that manipulates the linked list.

Executing linkedList.go will generate the following output:

```
$ go run linkedList.go
&{0 <nil>}
-> Empty list!
Node already exists: 1
1 ->
Node already exists: 0
1 -> 10 -> 5 -> 0 ->
1 -> 10 -> 5 -> 0 -> 100 ->
```

Trees in Go

A **graph** is a finite and nonempty set of vertices and edges. A **directed graph** is a graph whose edges have a direction associated with them. A **directed acyclic graph** is a directed graph with no cycles in it. A **tree** is a directed acyclic graph that satisfies three more principles: firstly, it has a root node—the entry point to the tree; secondly, every vertex, except the root, has one and only one entry point; and thirdly, there is a path that connects the root with each vertex and belongs to the tree.

As a result, the root is the first node of the tree. Each node can be connected to one or more nodes depending on the tree type. If each node leads to one and only one other node, then the tree is a linked list!

The most commonly used type of tree is called a binary tree because each node can have up to two children. The following figure shows a graphical representation of a binary tree's data structure:

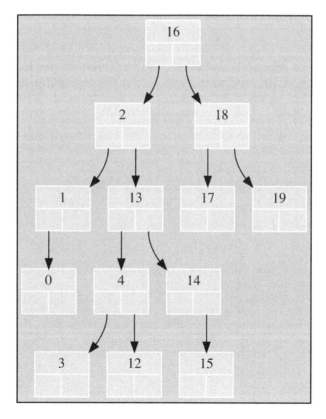

A binary tree

The presented code will only show you how to create a binary tree and how to traverse it in order to print all of its elements as proof that Go can be used for creating a tree data structure. Therefore, it will not implement the full functionality of a binary tree, which also includes deleting a tree node and balancing a tree.

The code of `tree.go` will be presented in three parts.

The first part is the expected preamble as well as the definition of the node, as given here:

```
package main

import (
    "fmt"
    "math/rand"
    "time"
)
type Tree struct {
    Left   *Tree
    Value int
    Right *Tree
}
```

The second part contains functions that allow you to traverse a tree in order to print all of its elements, create a tree with randomly generated numbers, and insert a node into it:

```
func traverse(t *Tree) {
    if t == nil {
        return
    }
    traverse(t.Left)
    fmt.Print(t.Value, " ")
    traverse(t.Right)
}

func create(n int) *Tree {
    var t *Tree
    rand.Seed(time.Now().Unix())
    for i := 0; i< 2*n; i++ {
        temp := rand.Intn(n)
        t = insert(t, temp)
    }
    return t
}

func insert(t *Tree, v int) *Tree {
    if t == nil {
        return&Tree{nil, v, nil}
```

```
    }
    if v == t.Value {
        return t
    }
    if v <t.Value {
        t.Left = insert(t.Left, v)
        return t
    }
    t.Right = insert(t.Right, v)
    return t
}
```

The second `if` statement of `insert()` checks whether a value already exists in the tree, in order to not add it again. The third `if` statement identifies whether the new element will be on the left or right-hand side of the current node.

The last part is the implementation of the `main()` function:

```
func main() {
    tree := create(30)
    traverse(tree)
    fmt.Println()
    fmt.Println("The value of the root of the tree is", tree.Value)
}
```

Executing `tree.go` will generate the following output:

```
$ go run tree.go
0 3 4 5 6 7 8 9 10 11 12 13 14 15 16 17 18 19 21 22 23 24 25 26 27 28 29
The value of the root of the tree is 16
```

Please note that as the values of the nodes of the tree are generated randomly, the output of the program will be different each time you run it. If you want to get the same elements all the time, then use a constant for the seed value in the `create()` function.

Developing a hash table in Go

Strictly speaking, a **hash table** is a data structure that stores one or more key and value pairs and uses the `hashFunction` of the key to compute an index into an array of buckets or slots, from which the correct value can be retrieved. Ideally, the `hashFunction` should assign each key to a unique bucket, provided that you have the required number of buckets.

A good `hashFunction` must be able to produce a uniform distribution of hash values because it is inefficient to have unused buckets or big differences in the cardinalities of the buckets. Additionally, the `hashFunction` should work consistently and output the same hash value for identical keys because otherwise it would be impossible to find the information you want! If you think that hash tables are not that useful, handy, or clever, you should consider the following: when a hash table has n keys and k buckets, its search speed goes from O (n) for a linear search to O (n/k)! Although the improvement might look small, you should realize that for a hash array with only 20 slots, the search time would be reduced by 20 times! This makes hash tables good for applications such as dictionaries or any other analogous application where you have to search lots of data. Although using lots of buckets increases the complexity and the memory usage of your program, there are times when it is worth it.

The following figure shows the graphical representation of a simple hash table with 10 buckets. It is not difficult to understand that the `hashFunction` is the modulo operator:

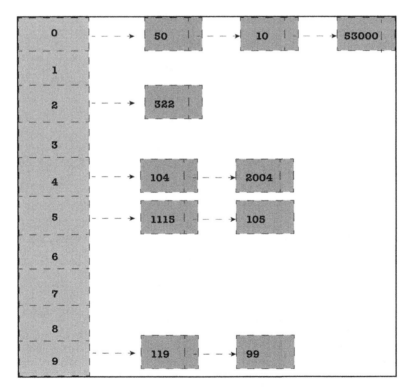

A simple hash table

Although the presented version of a hash table uses numbers because they are a little easier to implement and understand, you can use any data type you want as long as you can find an appropriate `hashFunction` to process your input. The source code of `hash.go` will be presented in three parts.

The first one is the following:

```
package main

import (
    "fmt"
)

type Node struct {
    Value int
    Next   *Node
}

type HashTablestruct {
    Table map[int]*Node


    Size   int
}
```

The `Node struct` definition is taken from the implementation of the linked list you saw earlier. The reason for using a map for the `Table` variable instead of a slice is that the index of a slice can only be a natural number, whereas the key of a map can be anything.

The second part contains the following Go code:

```
func hashFunction(i, size int) int {
    return (i % size)
}

func insert(hash *HashTable, value int) int {
    index := hashFunction(value, hash.Size)
    element := Node{Value: value, Next: hash.Table[index]}
    hash.Table[index] = &element
    return index
}

func traverse(hash *HashTable) {
    for k := range hash.Table {
        if hash.Table[k] != nil {
            t := hash.Table[k]
            for t != nil {
```

```
                fmt.Printf("%d -> ", t.Value)
                t = t.Next
            }
            fmt.Println()
        }
    }
}
```

Note here that the `traverse()` function is using the Go code from `linkedList.go` in order to traverse the elements of each bucket in the hash table. Additionally, note that the `insert` function does not check whether or not a value already exists in the hash table in order to save book space, but this is not usually the case. Also, for reasons of speed and simplicity, new elements are inserted at the beginning of each list.

The last part contains the implementation of the `main()` function:

```
func main() {
    table := make(map[int]*Node, 10)
    hash := &HashTable{Table: table, Size: 10}
    fmt.Println("Number of spaces:", hash.Size)
    for i := 0; i< 95; i++ {
        insert(hash, i)
    }
    traverse(hash)
}
```

Executing `hash.go` will generate the following output, which proves that the hash table is working as expected:

```
$ go run hash.go
Number of spaces: 10
89 -> 79 -> 69 -> 59 -> 49 -> 39 -> 29 -> 19 -> 9 ->
86 -> 76 -> 66 -> 56 -> 46 -> 36 -> 26 -> 16 -> 6 ->
92 -> 82 -> 72 -> 62 -> 52 -> 42 -> 32 -> 22 -> 12 -> 2 ->
94 -> 84 -> 74 -> 64 -> 54 -> 44 -> 34 -> 24 -> 14 -> 4 ->
85 -> 75 -> 65 -> 55 -> 45 -> 35 -> 25 -> 15 -> 5 ->
87 -> 77 -> 67 -> 57 -> 47 -> 37 -> 27 -> 17 -> 7 ->
88 -> 78 -> 68 -> 58 -> 48 -> 38 -> 28 -> 18 -> 8 ->
90 -> 80 -> 70 -> 60 -> 50 -> 40 -> 30 -> 20 -> 10 -> 0 ->
91 -> 81 -> 71 -> 61 -> 51 -> 41 -> 31 -> 21 -> 11 -> 1 ->
93 -> 83 -> 73 -> 63 -> 53 -> 43 -> 33 -> 23 -> 13 -> 3 ->
```

If you execute `hash.go` multiple times, you will see that the order the lines are printed in will vary. This happens because the output of `range hash.Table` found in the`traverse()` function cannot be predicted, which happens because Go has an unspecified return order for hashes.

About Go packages

Packages are for grouping related functions and constants so that you can transfer them easily and use them in your own Go programs. As a result, apart from the main package, packages are not autonomous programs.

There exist many useful Go packages that come with each Go distribution including the following:

- The `net` package: This supports portable TCP and UDP connections
- The `http` package: This is a part of the net package and offers HTTP server and client implementations
- The `math` package: This provides mathematical functions and constants
- The `io` package: This deals with primitive input and output operations
- The `os` package: This gives you a portable interface to the operating system functionality
- The `time` package: This allows you to work with times and dates

For the full list of standard Go packages refer to`https://golang.org/pkg/`. I strongly advise you to look into all the packages that come with Go before you start developing your own functions and packages because there is a realistic chance that the functionality you are looking for is already available in a standard Go package.

Using standard Go packages

You probably already know how to use the standard Go packages. However, what you may not be aware of is the fact that some packages have a structure. So, for example, the `net` package has several sub directories, named `http`, `mail`, `rpc`, `smtp`, `textproto`, and `url`, which should be imported as `net/http`, `net/mail`, `net/rpc`, `net/smtp`, `net/textproto`, and `net/url`, respectively. Go groups packages when this makes sense, but these packages could have also been isolated packages if they were grouped for distribution instead of functionality.

You can find information about a Go standard package with the help of the godoc utility. So, if you are looking for information about the net package, you should execute godoc net.

Creating your own packages

Packages make the design, implementation, and maintenance of large software systems easier and simpler. Moreover, they allow multiple programmers to work on the same project without any overlapping. So, if you find yourselves using the same functions all the time, you should seriously consider including them in your own Go packages.

The source code of a Go package, which can contain multiple files, can be found within a single directory, which is named after the package with the exception of the main package, which can have any name.

The Go code of the aSimplePackage.go file, which will be developed in this section, will be presented in two parts.

The first part is the following:

```
package aSimplePackage

import (
    "fmt"
)
```

There is nothing special here; you just have to define the name of the package and include the necessary import statements because a package can depend on other packages.

The second part contains the following Go code:

```
const Pi = "3.14159"

func Add(x, y int) int {
    return x + y
}

func Println(x int) {
    fmt.Println(x)
}
```

So, the aSimplePackage package offers two functions and one constant.

After you finish writing the code of aSimplePackage.go, you should execute the following commands in order to be able to use the package in other Go programs or packages:

```
$ mkdir ~/go
$ mkdir ~/go/src
$ mkdir ~/go/src/aSimplePackage
$ export GOPATH=~/go
$ vi ~/go/src/aSimplePackage/aSimplePackage.go
$ go install aSimplePackage
```

 You should perform all these actions for every Go package you create, apart from the first two mkdir commands, which should only be executed once.

As you can see, each package needs its own directory inside ~/go/src. After executing the aforementioned commands, the go tool will automatically generate an ar(1) archive of the Go package you have just compiled in the pkg directory:

```
$ ls -lR ~/go
total 0
drwxr-xr-x  3 mtsouk  staff  102 Apr  4 22:35 pkg
drwxr-xr-x  3 mtsouk  staff  102 Apr  4 22:35 src
/Users/mtsouk/go/pkg:
total 0
drwxr-xr-x  3 mtsouk  staff  102 Apr  4 22:35 darwin_amd64
/Users/mtsouk/go/pkg/darwin_amd64:
total 8
-rw-r--r--  1 mtsouk  staff  2918 Apr  4 22:35 aSimplePackage.a
/Users/mtsouk/go/src:
total 0
drwxr-xr-x  3 mtsouk  staff  102 Apr  4 22:35 aSimplePackage
/Users/mtsouk/go/src/aSimplePackage:
total 8
-rw-r--r--  1 mtsouk  staff  148 Apr  4 22:30 aSimplePackage.go
```

Although you are now ready to use the aSimplePackage package, you cannot see the functionality of the package without having an autonomous program.

Private variables and functions

Private variables and functions are different from public ones in that they can be used and called only internally in a package. Controlling which functions and variables are public or not is also known as encapsulation.

Go follows a simple rule which states that functions, variables, types, and so on that begin with an uppercase letter are public, whereas functions, variables, types, and so on that begin with a lowercase letter are private. However, this rule does not affect package names.

 You should understand now why the fmt.Printf() function is named as it is, instead of fmt.printf().

To illustrate this, we will make some changes to the aSimplePackage.go module and add one private variable and one private function. The name of the new separate package will be anotherPackage.go. You can see the changes made to it using the diff(1) command-line utility:

```
$ diff aSimplePackage.go anotherPackage.go
1c1
<packageaSimplePackage
---
>packageanotherPackage
7a8
>const version = "1.1"
15a17,20
>
>func Version() {
>     fmt.Println("The version of the package is", version)
> }
```

The init() function

Every Go package can have a function named init() that is automatically executed at the beginning of the execution. So, let's add the followinginit() function to the code of the anotherPackage.go package:

```
func init() {
    fmt.Println("The init function of anotherPackage")
}
```

The current implementation of the init() function is naïve and does nothing special. However, there are times when you want to perform important initializations before you start using a package such as opening database and network connections—in these relatively rare cases the init() function is invaluable.

Using your own Go packages

This subsection will show you how to use the aSimplePackage and anotherPackage packages in your own Go programs by presenting two small Go programs named usePackage.go and privateFail.go.

In order to use the aSimplePackage package that resides under the GOPATH directory from another Go program, you will need to write the following Go code:

```
package main

import (
    "aSimplePackage"
    "fmt"
)

func main() {
    temp := aSimplePackage.Add(5, 10)
    fmt.Println(temp)

    fmt.Println(aSimplePackage.Pi)
}
```

First of all, if aSimplePackage is not already compiled and located at the expected location, the compilation process will fail with an error message similar to the following:

```
$ go run usePackage.go
usePackage.go:4:2: cannot find package "aSimplePackage" in any of:
        /usr/local/Cellar/go/1.8/libexec/src/aSimplePackage (from $GOROOT)
        /Users/mtsouk/go/src/aSimplePackage (from $GOPATH)
```

However, if aSimplePackage is available, usePackage.go will be executed just fine:

```
$ go run usePackage.go
15
3.14159
```

Now, let's see the Go code of the other small program that uses `anotherPackage`:

```go
package main

import (
    "anotherPackage"
    "fmt"
)

func main() {
    anotherPackage.Version()
    fmt.Println(anotherPackage.version)
    fmt.Println(anotherPackage.Pi)
}
```

If you try to call a private function or use a private variable from `anotherPackage`, your Go program `privateFail.go` will fail to run with the following error message:

```
$ go run privateFail.go
# command-line-arguments
./privateFail.go:10: cannot refer to unexported name anotherPackage.version
./privateFail.go:10: undefined: anotherPackage.version
```

 I really like showing error messages because most books try to hide them as if they were not there. When I was learning Go, it took me about 3 hours of debugging until I found that the reason for an error message I could not explain was the name of a variable!

However, if you remove the call to the private variable from `privateFail.go`, the program will be executed without errors. Additionally, you will see that the `init()` function actually gets executed automatically:

```
$ go run privateFail.go
The init function of anotherPackage
The version of the package is 1.1
3.14159
```

Using external Go packages

Sometimes packages are available on the internet and you would prefer to use them by specifying their internet address. One such example is the Go `MySQL` driver that can be found at `github.com/go-sql-driver/mysql`.

Look at the following Go code, which is saved as useMySQL.go:

```
package main

import (
    "fmt"
    _ "github.com/go-sql-driver/mysql"
)

func main() {
    fmt.Println("Using the MySQL Go driver!")
}
```

The use of _ as the package identifier will make the compiler ignore the fact that the package is not being used—the only sensible reason for bypassing the compiler is when you have an init function in your unused package that you want to be executed. The other sensible reason is for illustrating a Go concept!

If you try to execute useMySQL.go, the compilation process will fail:

```
$ go run useMySQL.go
useMySQL.go:5:2: cannot find package "github.com/go-sql-driver/mysql" in
any of:
        /usr/local/Cellar/go/1.8/libexec/src/github.com/go-sql-driver/mysql
(from $GOROOT)
        /Users/mtsouk/go/src/github.com/go-sql-driver/mysql (from $GOPATH)
```

In order to compile useMySQL.go, you should first perform the following steps:

```
$ go get github.com/go-sql-driver/mysql
$ go run useMySQL.go
Using the MySQL Go driver!
```

After successfully downloading the required package, the contents of the ~/go directory verify that the desired Go package has been downloaded:

```
$ ls -lR ~/go
total 0
drwxr-xr-x  3 mtsouk  staff  102 Apr  4 22:35 pkg
drwxr-xr-x  5 mtsouk  staff  170 Apr  6 21:32 src
/Users/mtsouk/go/pkg:
total 0
drwxr-xr-x  5 mtsouk  staff  170 Apr  6 21:32 darwin_amd64
/Users/mtsouk/go/pkg/darwin_amd64:
total 24
-rw-r--r--  1 mtsouk  staff  2918 Apr  4 23:07 aSimplePackage.a
-rw-r--r--  1 mtsouk  staff  6102 Apr  4 22:50 anotherPackage.a
```

```
drwxr-xr-x  3 mtsouk  staff   102 Apr  6 21:32 github.com
/Users/mtsouk/go/pkg/darwin_amd64/github.com:
total 0
drwxr-xr-x  3 mtsouk  staff   102 Apr  6 21:32 go-sql-driver
/Users/mtsouk/go/pkg/darwin_amd64/github.com/go-sql-driver:
total 728
-rw-r--r--  1 mtsouk  staff   372694 Apr  6 21:32 mysql.a
/Users/mtsouk/go/src:
total 0
drwxr-xr-x  3 mtsouk  staff   102 Apr  4 22:35 aSimplePackage
drwxr-xr-x  3 mtsouk  staff   102 Apr  4 22:50 anotherPackage
drwxr-xr-x  3 mtsouk  staff   102 Apr  6 21:32 github.com
/Users/mtsouk/go/src/aSimplePackage:
total 8
-rw-r--r--  1 mtsouk  staff   148 Apr  4 22:30 aSimplePackage.go
/Users/mtsouk/go/src/anotherPackage:
total 8
-rw-r--r--@ 1 mtsouk  staff   313 Apr  4 22:50 anotherPackage.go
/Users/mtsouk/go/src/github.com:
total 0
drwxr-xr-x  3 mtsouk  staff   102 Apr  6 21:32 go-sql-driver
/Users/mtsouk/go/src/github.com/go-sql-driver:
total 0
drwxr-xr-x  35 mtsouk  staff   1190 Apr  6 21:32 mysql
/Users/mtsouk/go/src/github.com/go-sql-driver/mysql:
total 584
-rw-r--r--  1 mtsouk  staff    2066 Apr  6 21:32 AUTHORS
-rw-r--r--  1 mtsouk  staff    5581 Apr  6 21:32 CHANGELOG.md
-rw-r--r--  1 mtsouk  staff    1091 Apr  6 21:32 CONTRIBUTING.md
-rw-r--r--  1 mtsouk  staff   16726 Apr  6 21:32 LICENSE
-rw-r--r--  1 mtsouk  staff   18610 Apr  6 21:32 README.md
-rw-r--r--  1 mtsouk  staff     470 Apr  6 21:32 appengine.go
-rw-r--r--  1 mtsouk  staff    4965 Apr  6 21:32 benchmark_test.go
-rw-r--r--  1 mtsouk  staff    3339 Apr  6 21:32 buffer.go
-rw-r--r--  1 mtsouk  staff    8405 Apr  6 21:32 collations.go
-rw-r--r--  1 mtsouk  staff    8525 Apr  6 21:32 connection.go
-rw-r--r--  1 mtsouk  staff    1831 Apr  6 21:32 connection_test.go
-rw-r--r--  1 mtsouk  staff    3111 Apr  6 21:32 const.go
-rw-r--r--  1 mtsouk  staff    5036 Apr  6 21:32 driver.go
-rw-r--r--  1 mtsouk  staff    4246 Apr  6 21:32 driver_go18_test.go
-rw-r--r--  1 mtsouk  staff   47090 Apr  6 21:32 driver_test.go
-rw-r--r--  1 mtsouk  staff   13046 Apr  6 21:32 dsn.go
-rw-r--r--  1 mtsouk  staff    7872 Apr  6 21:32 dsn_test.go
-rw-r--r--  1 mtsouk  staff    3798 Apr  6 21:32 errors.go
-rw-r--r--  1 mtsouk  staff     989 Apr  6 21:32 errors_test.go
-rw-r--r--  1 mtsouk  staff    4571 Apr  6 21:32 infile.go
-rw-r--r--  1 mtsouk  staff   31362 Apr  6 21:32 packets.go
-rw-r--r--  1 mtsouk  staff    6453 Apr  6 21:32 packets_test.go
```

```
-rw-r--r--  1 mtsouk   staff     600 Apr  6 21:32 result.go
-rw-r--r--  1 mtsouk   staff    3698 Apr  6 21:32 rows.go
-rw-r--r--  1 mtsouk   staff    3609 Apr  6 21:32 statement.go
-rw-r--r--  1 mtsouk   staff     729 Apr  6 21:32 transaction.go
-rw-r--r--  1 mtsouk   staff   17924 Apr  6 21:32 utils.go
-rw-r--r--  1 mtsouk   staff    5784 Apr  6 21:32 utils_test.go
```

The go clean command

There will be times when you are developing a big Go program that uses lots of nonstandard Go packages and you want to start the compilation process from the beginning. Go allows you to clean up the files of a package in order to recreate it later. The following command cleans up a package without affecting the code of the package:

```
$ go clean -x -i aSimplePackage
cd /Users/mtsouk/go/src/aSimplePackage
rm -f aSimplePackage.test aSimplePackage.test.exe
rm -f /Users/mtsouk/go/pkg/darwin_amd64/aSimplePackage.a
```

Similarly, you can also clean up a package that you have downloaded from the internet, which also requires the use of its full path:

```
$ go clean -x -i github.com/go-sql-driver/mysql
cd /Users/mtsouk/go/src/github.com/go-sql-driver/mysql
rm -f mysql.test mysql.test.exe appengine appengine.exe
rm -f /Users/mtsouk/go/pkg/darwin_amd64/github.com/go-sql-driver/mysql.a
```

 Please note that the `go clean` command is also particularly useful when you want to transfer your projects to another machine without including unnecessary files.

Garbage collection

In this section, we will briefly talk about how Go deals with GC, which tries to free unused memory efficiently. The Go code of `garbageCol.go` can be presented in two parts.

The first part is as follows:

```
package main

import (
    "fmt"
    "runtime"
```

```go
    "time"
)

func printStats(mem runtime.MemStats) {
    runtime.ReadMemStats(&mem)
    fmt.Println("mem.Alloc:", mem.Alloc)
    fmt.Println("mem.TotalAlloc:", mem.TotalAlloc)
    fmt.Println("mem.HeapAlloc:", mem.HeapAlloc)
    fmt.Println("mem.NumGC:", mem.NumGC)
    fmt.Println("-----")
}
```

Every time you want to read the latest memory statistics, you should make a call to the runtime.ReadMemStats() function.

The second part, which contains the implementation of the main() function, has the following Go code:

```go
func main() {
    var memruntime.MemStats
    printStats(mem)

    for i := 0; i< 10; i++ {
        s := make([]byte, 100000000)
        if s == nil {
            fmt.Println("Operation failed!")
        }
    }
    printStats(mem)

    for i := 0; i< 10; i++ {
        s := make([]byte, 100000000)
        if s == nil {
            fmt.Println("Operation failed!")
        }
        time.Sleep(5 * time.Second)
    }
    printStats(mem)


}
```

Here, you try to obtain large amounts of memory in order to trigger the use of the garbage collector.

Executing `garbageCol.go` generates the following output:

```
$ go run garbageCol.go
mem.Alloc: 53944
mem.TotalAlloc: 53944
mem.HeapAlloc: 53944
mem.NumGC: 0
-----
mem.Alloc: 100071680
mem.TotalAlloc: 1000146400
mem.HeapAlloc: 100071680
mem.NumGC: 10
-----
mem.Alloc: 66152
mem.TotalAlloc: 2000230496
mem.HeapAlloc: 66152
mem.NumGC: 20
-----
```

So, the output presents information about properties related to the memory used by the `garbageCol.go` program. If you want to get an even more detailed output, you can execute `garbageCol.go`, as shown here:

```
$ GODEBUG=gctrace=1 go run garbageCol.go
```

This version of the command will give you information in the following format:

```
gc 11 @0.101s 0%: 0.003+0.083+0.020 ms clock, 0.030+0.059/0.033/0.006+0.16
mscpu, 95->95->0 MB, 96 MB goal, 8 P
```

The `95->95->0 MB` part contains information about the various heap sizes that also show how well or how badly the garbage collector is doing. The first value is the heap size when the GC starts, whereas the middle value shows the heap size when the GC ends. The third value is the size of the live heap.

Your environment

In this section, we will show how to find out things about your environment using the `runtime` package—this can be useful when you have to take certain actions depending on the OS and the Go version you are using.

The use of the `runtime` package for finding out about your environment is straightforward and is illustrated in `runTime.go`:

```
package main

import (
    "fmt"
    "runtime"
)

func main() {
    fmt.Print("You are using ", runtime.Compiler, " ")
    fmt.Println("on a", runtime.GOARCH, "machine")
    fmt.Println("with Go version", runtime.Version())
    fmt.Println("Number of Goroutines:", runtime.NumGoroutine())
}
```

As long as you know what you want to call from the runtime package, you can get the information you desire. The last `fmt.Println()` command here displays information about **goroutines**—you will learn more about goroutines in Chapter 9, *Goroutines – Basic Features*.

Executing `runTime.go` on a macOS machine generates the following output:

```
$ go run runTime.go
You are using gc on a amd64 machine
with Go version go1.8
Number of Goroutines: 1
```

Executing `runTime.go` on a Linux machine that uses an older Go version gives the following:

```
$ go run runTime.go
You are using gc on a amd64 machine
with Go version go1.3.3
Number of Goroutines: 4
```

Go gets updated frequently!

As I came to the end of writing this chapter, Go was updated a little. So, I decided to include this information in this book in order to give a better sense of how often Go gets updated:

```
$ date
Sat Apr  8 09:16:46 EEST 2017
$ go version
go version go1.8.1 darwin/amd64
```

Exercises

1. Visit the documentation of the runtime package.
2. Create your own structure, make a slice and use the `sort.Slice()` to sort the elements of the slice you created.
3. Implement the quicksort algorithm in Go and sort some randomly-generated numeric data.
4. Implement a doubly linked list.
5. The implementation of `tree.go` is far from complete! Try to implement a function that checks whether a value can be found in the tree and another function that allows you to delete a tree node.
6. Similarly, the implementation of the `linkedList.go` file is also incomplete. Try to implement a function for deleting a node and another one for inserting a node somewhere inside the linked list.
7. Once again, the hash table implementation of `hash.go` is incomplete as it allows duplicate entries. So, implement a function that searches the hash table for a key before inserting it.

Summary

In this chapter, you learned many things related to algorithms and data structures. You also learned how to use existing Go packages and how to develop your own Go packages. This chapter also talked about garbage collection in Go and how to find information about your environment.

In the next chapter, we will start talking about systems programming and present even more Go code. More precisely, Chapter 5, *Files and Directories*, will talk about how to work with files and directories in Go, how to painlessly traverse directory structures, and how to process command-line arguments using the flag package. But more importantly, we will start developing Go versions of various Unix command-line utilities.

5
Files and Directories

In the previous chapter, we talked about many important topics including developing and using Go packages, Go data structures, algorithms, and GC. However, until now, we have not developed any actual system utility. This will change very soon because starting from this really important chapter, we will begin developing real system utilities in Go by learning how to use Go, to work with the various types of files and directories of a filesystem.

You should always have in mind that Unix considers everything a file including symbolic links, directories, network devices, network sockets, entire hard drives, printers, and plain text files. The purpose of this chapter is to illustrate how the Go standard library allows us to understand if a path exists or not, as well as how to search directory structures to detect the kind of files we want. Additionally, this chapter will prove, using Go code as evidence, that many traditional Unix command-line utilities that work with files and directories do not have a difficult implementation.

In this chapter, you will learn the following topics:

- The Go packages that will help you manipulate directories and files
- Processing command-line arguments and options easilyusing the `flag` package
- Developing a version of the `which(1)` command-line utility in Go
- Developing a version of the `pwd(1)` command-line utility in Go
- Deleting and renaming files and directories
- Traversing directory trees easily
- Writing a version of the `find(1)` utility in Go
- Duplicating a directory structure in another place

Useful Go packages

The single most important package that allows you to manipulate files and directories as entities is the os package, which we will use extensively in this chapter. If you consider files as boxes with contents, the os package allows you to move them, put them into the wastebasket, change their names, visit them, and decide which ones you want to use, whereas the io package, which will be presented in the next chapter, allows you to manipulate the contents of a box without worrying too much about the box itself!

The flag package, which you will see in a while, lets you define and process your own flags and manipulate the command-line arguments of a Go program.

The filepath package is extremely handy as it includes the filepath.Walk() function that allows you to traverse entire directory structures in an easy way.

Command-line arguments revisited!

As we saw in Chapter 2, *Writing Programs in Go*, you cannot work efficiently with multiple command-line arguments and options using if statements. The solution to this problem is to use the flag package, which will be explained here.

Remembering that the flag package is a standard Go packageand that you do not have to search for the functionality of a flag elsewhereis extremely important.

The flag package

The flag package does the dirty work of parsing command-line arguments and options for us; so, there is no need for writing complicated and perplexing Go code. Additionally, it supports various types of parameters, including strings, integers, and Boolean, which saves you time as you do not have to perform any data type conversions.

The usingFlag.go program illustrates the use of the flag Go package and will be presented in three parts. The first part has the following Go code:

```
package main

import (
    "flag"
    "fmt"
)
```

The second part, which has the most important Go code of the program, is as follows:

```
func main() {
    minusO := flag.Bool("o", false, "o")
    minusC := flag.Bool("c", false, "c")
    minusK := flag.Int("k", 0, "an int")

    flag.Parse()
```

In this part, you can see how you can define the flags that interest you. Here, you defined –o, –c, and –k. Although the first two are Boolean flags, the –k flag requires an integer value, which can be given as –k=123.

The last part comes with the following Go code:

```
    fmt.Println("-o:", *minusO)
    fmt.Println("-c:", *minusC)
    fmt.Println("-K:", *minusK)

    for index, val := range flag.Args() {
        fmt.Println(index, ":", val)
    }
}
```

In this part, you can see how you can read the value of an option, which also allows you to tell whether an option has been set or not. Additionally, flag.Args() allows you to access the unused command-line arguments of the program.

The use and the output of usingFlag.go are showcased in the following output:

```
$ go run usingFlag.go
-o: false
-c: false
-K: 0
$ go run usingFlag.go -o a b
-o: true
-c: false
-K: 0
0 : a
1 : b
```

However, if you forget to type the value of a command-line option (-k) or the provided value is of the wrong type, you will get the following messages and the program will terminate:

```
$ ./usingFlag -k
flag needs an argument: -k
Usage of ./usingFlag:
  -c  c
  -k int
       an int
  -o  o

$ ./usingFlag -k=abc
invalid value "abc" for flag -k: strconv.ParseInt: parsing "abc": invalid
syntax
Usage of ./usingFlag:
  -c  c
  -k int
       an int
  -o  o
```

If you do not want your program to exit when there is a parse error, you can use the ErrorHandling type provided by the flag package, which allows you to change the way flag.Parse() behaves on errors with the help of the NewFlagSet() function. However, in systems programming, you usually want your utility to exit when there is an error in one or more command-line options.

Dealing with directories

Directories allow you to create a structure and store your files in a way that is easy for you to organize and search for them. In reality, directories are entries on a filesystem that contain lists of other files and directories. This happens with the help of **inodes**, which are data structures that hold information about files and directories.

As you can see in the following figure, directories are implemented as lists of names assigned to inodes. As a result, a directory contains an entry for itself, its parent directory, and each of its children, which among other things can be regular files or other directories:

 What you should remember is that an inode holds metadata about a file, not the actual data of a file.

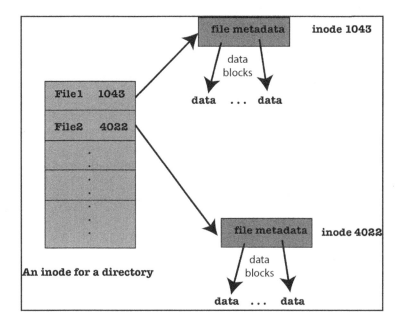

A graphical representation of inodes

About symbolic links

Symbolic links are pointers to files or directories, which are resolved at the time of access. Symbolic links, which are also called **soft links**, are not equal to the file or the directory they are pointing to and are allowed to point to nowhere, which can sometimes complicate things.

The following Go code, saved in `symbLink.go` and presented in two parts, allows you to check whether a path or file is a symbolic link or not. The first part is as follows:

```go
package main

import (
    "fmt"
    "os"
    "path/filepath"
)

func main() {
    arguments := os.Args
    if len(arguments) == 1 {
        fmt.Println("Please provide an argument!")
        os.Exit(1)
    }
    filename := arguments[1]
```

Nothing special is happening here—you just need to make sure that you get one command-line argument in order to have something to test. The second part is the following Go code:

```go
    fileinfo, err := os.Lstat(fil /etcename)
    if err != nil {
        fmt.Println(err)
        os.Exit(1)
    }

    if fileinfo.Mode()&os.ModeSymlink != 0 {
        fmt.Println(filename, "is a symbolic link")
        realpath, err := filepath.EvalSymlinks(filename)
        if err == nil {
            fmt.Println("Path:", realpath)
        }
    }

}
```

The aforementioned code of `symbLink.go` is more cryptic than usual because it uses lower-level functions. The technique for finding out whether a path is a real path or not involves the use of the `os.Lstat()` function that gives you information about a file or directory and the use of the `Mode()` function on the return value of the `os.Lstat()` call in order to compare the outcome with the `os.ModeSymlink` constant, which is the symbolic link bit.

Additionally, there exists the `filepath.EvalSymlinks()` function that allows you to evaluate any symbolic links that exist and return the true path of a file or directory, which is also used in `symbLink.go`. This might make you think that we are using lots of Go code for such a simple task, which is partially true, but when you are developing systems software, you are obliged to consider all possibilities and be cautious.

Executing `symbLink.go`, which only takes one command-line argument, generates the following output:

```
$ go run symbLink.go /etc
/etc is a symbolic link
Path: /private/etc
```

You will also see some of the aforementioned Go code as a part of bigger programs in the rest of this chapter.

Implementing the pwd(1) command

When I start thinking about how to implement a program, so many ideas come to my mind that sometimes it becomes too difficult to decide what to do! The key here is to do something instead of waiting because as you write code, you will be able to tell whether the approach you are taking is good or not, and whether you should try another approach or not.

The `pwd(1)` command-line utility is pretty simplistic, yet it does a pretty good job. If you write lots of shell scripts, you should already know about `pwd(1)` because it is pretty handy when you want to get the full path of a file or a directory that resides in the same directory as the script that is being executed.

The Go code of `pwd.go` will be presented in two parts and will only support the `-P` command-line option, which resolves all symbolic links and prints the physical current working directory. The first part of `pwd.go` is as follows:

```go
package main

import (
    "fmt"
    "os"
    "path/filepath"
)

func main() {
    arguments := os.Args

    pwd, err := os.Getwd()
    if err == nil {
        fmt.Println(pwd)
    } else {
        fmt.Println("Error:", err)
    }
```

The second part is as follows:

```go
    if len(arguments) == 1 {
        return
    }

    if arguments[1] != "-P" {
        return
    }

    fileinfo, err := os.Lstat(pwd)
    if fileinfo.Mode()&os.ModeSymlink != 0 {
        realpath, err := filepath.EvalSymlinks(pwd)
        if err == nil {
            fmt.Println(realpath)
        }
    }
}
```

Note that if the current directory can be described by multiple paths, which can happen if you are using symbolic links, `os.Getwd()` can return any one of them. Additionally, you need to reuse some of the Go code found in `symbLink.go` to discover the physical current working directory in case the `-P` option is given and you are dealing with a directory that is a symbolic link. Also, the reason for not using the flag package in `pwd.go` is that I find the code much simpler the way it is.

Executing `pwd.go` will generate the following output:

```
$ go run pwd.go
/Users/mtsouk/Desktop/goBook/ch/ch5/code
```

On macOS machines, the `/tmp` directory is a symbolic link, which can help us verify that `pwd.go` works as expected:

```
$ go run pwd.go
/tmp
$ go run pwd.go -P
/tmp
/private/tmp
```

Developing the which(1) utility in Go

The `which(1)` utility searches the value of the PATH environment variable in order to find out if an executable file can be found in one of the directories of the PATH variable. The following output shows the way the `which(1)` utility works:

```
$ echo $PATH
/home/mtsouk/bin:/usr/local/bin:/usr/bin:/bin:/usr/local/games:/usr/games
$ which ls
/home/mtsouk/bin/ls
code$ which -a ls
/home/mtsouk/bin/ls
/bin/ls
```

Our implementation of the Unix utility will support the two command-line options supported by the macOS version of `which(1)`, which are `-a` and `-s` with the help of the `flag` package—the Linux version of `which(1)` does not support the `-s` option. The `-a` option lists all the instances of the executable instead of just the first one while the `-s` returns 0 if the executable was found and 1 otherwise—this is not the same as printing 0 or 1 using the `fmt` package.

In order to check the return value of a Unix command-line utility in the shell, you should do the following:

```
$ which -s ls
$ echo $?
0
```

Note that go run prints out nonzero exit codes.

The Go code for which(1) will be saved in which.go and will be presented in four parts. The first part of which.go has the following Go code:

```
package main

import (
    "flag"
    "fmt"
    "os"
    "strings"
)
```

The strings package is needed in order to split the contents of the PATH variable after you read it. The second part of which.go deals with the use of the flag package:

```
func main() {
    minusA := flag.Bool("a", false, "a")
    minusS := flag.Bool("s", false, "s")

    flag.Parse()
    flags := flag.Args()
    if len(flags) == 0 {
        fmt.Println("Please provide an argument!")
        os.Exit(1)
    }
    file := flags[0]
    fountIt := false
```

One very important part of which.go is the part that reads the PATH shell environment variable in order to split it and use it, which is presented in the third part here:

```
path := os.Getenv("PATH")
pathSlice := strings.Split(path, ":")
for _, directory := range pathSlice {
    fullPath := directory + "/" + file
```

The last statement here constructs the full path of the file we are searching for, as if it existed in each separate directory of the PATH variable because if you have the full path of a file, you do not have to search for it!

The last part of `which.go` is as follows:

```
            fileInfo, err := os.Stat(fullPath)
            if err == nil {
                    mode := fileInfo.Mode()
                    if mode.IsRegular() {
                            if mode&0111 != 0 {
                                    fountIt = true
                                    if *minusS == true {
                                            os.Exit(0)
                                    }
                                    if *minusA == true {


                                            fmt.Println(fullPath)
                                    } else {
                                            fmt.Println(fullPath)
                                            os.Exit(0)
                                    }
                            }
                    }
            }
    }
    if fountIt == false {
            os.Exit(1)
    }
}
```

Here, the call to `os.Stat()` tells whether the file we are looking for actually exists or not. In case of success, the `mode.IsRegular()` function checks whether the file is a regular file or not because we are not looking for directories or symbolic links. However, we are not done yet! The `which.go` program performs a test to find out whether the file that was found is indeed an executable file—if it is not an executable file, it will not get printed. So, the `if mode&0111 != 0` statement verifies that the file is actually an executable file using a binary operation.

Next, if the `-s` flag is set to `*minusS == true`, then the `-a` flag does not really matter because the program will terminate as soon as it finds a match.

As you can see, there are lots of tests involved in `which.go`, which is not rare for systems software. Nevertheless, you should always examine all possibilities in order to avoid surprises later. The good thing is that most of these tests will be used later on in the Go implementation of the `find(1)` utility—it is good practice to test some features by writing small programs before putting them all together into bigger programs because by doing so, you learn the technique better and you can detect silly bugs more easily.

Executing `which.go` will produce the following output:

```
$ go run which.go ls
/home/mtsouk/bin/ls
$ go run which.go -s ls
$ echo $?
0
$ go run which.go -s ls123123
exit status 1
$ echo $?
1
$ go run which.go -a ls
/home/mtsouk/bin/ls
/bin/ls
```

Printing the permission bits of a file or directory

With the help of the `ls(1)` command, you can find out the permissions of a file:

```
$ ls -l /bin/ls
-rwxr-xr-x  1 root   wheel  38624 Mar 23 01:57 /bin/ls
```

In this subsection, we will look at how to print the permissions of a file or directory using Go—the Go code will be saved in `permissions.go` and will be presented in two parts. The first part is as follows:

```go
package main

import (
    "fmt"
    "os"
)

func main() {
    arguments := os.Args
    if len(arguments) == 1 {
        fmt.Println("Please provide an argument!")
        os.Exit(1)
    }

    file := arguments[1]
```

The second part contains the important Go code:

```
info, err := os.Stat(file)
if err != nil {
        fmt.Println("Error:", err)
        os.Exit(1)
}
mode := info.Mode()
fmt.Print(file, ": ", mode, "\n")
}
```

Once again, most of the Go code is for dealing with the command-line argument and making sure that you have one! The Go code that does the actual job is mainly the call to the `os.Stat()` function, which returns a `FileInfo` structure that describes the file or directory examined by `os.Stat()`. From the `FileInfo` structure, you can discover the permissions of a file by calling the `Mode()` function.

Executing `permissions.go` produces the following output:

```
$ go run permissions.go /bin/ls
/bin/ls: -rwxr-xr-x
$ go run permissions.go /usr
/usr: drwxr-xr-x
$ go run permissions.go /us
Error: stat /us: no such file or directory
exit status 1
```

Dealing with files in Go

An extremely important task of an operating system is working with files because all data is stored in files. In this section, we will show you how to delete and rename files, and in the next section, *Developing find(1) in Go*, we will teach you how to search directory structures in order to find the files you want.

Deleting a file

In this section, we will illustrate how to delete files and directories using the `os.Remove()` Go function.

When testing programs that delete files and directories be extra careful and use common sense!

The `rm.go` file is a Go implementation of the `rm(1)` tool that illustrates how you can delete files in Go. Although the core functionality of `rm(1)` is there, the options of `rm(1)` are missing—it would be a good exercise to try to implement some of them. Just pay extra attention when implementing the `-f` and `-R` options.

The Go code of `rm.go` is as follows:

```
package main
import (
    "fmt"
    "os"
)

func main() {
    arguments := os.Args
    if len(arguments) == 1 {
        fmt.Println("Please provide an argument!")
        os.Exit(1)
    }

    file := arguments[1]
    err := os.Remove(file)
    if err != nil {
        fmt.Println(err)
        return
    }
}
```

If `rm.go` is executed without any problems, it will create no output according to the Unix philosophy. So, what is interesting here is watching the error messages you can get when the file you are trying to delete does not exist—both when you do not have the necessary permissions to delete it and when a directory is not empty:

```
$ go run rm.go 123
remove 123: no such file or directory
$ ls -l /tmp/AlTest1.err
-rw-r--r--  1 root  wheel  1278 Apr 17 20:13 /tmp/AlTest1.err
$ go run rm.go /tmp/AlTest1.err
remove /tmp/AlTest1.err: permission denied
$ go run rm.go test
remove test: directory not empty
```

Renaming and moving files

In this subsection, we will show you how to rename and move a file using Go code—the Go code will be saved as `rename.go`. Although the same code can be used for renaming or moving directories, `rename.go` is only allowed to work with files.

When performing things that cannot be easily undone, such as overwriting a file, you should be extra careful and maybe inform the user that the destination file already exists in order to avoid unpleasant surprises. Although the default operation of the traditional `mv(1)` utility will automatically overwrite the destination file if it exists, I do not think that this is very safe. Therefore, `rename.go` will not overwrite destination files by default.

When developing systems software, you have to deal with all the details or the details will reveal themselves as bugs when least expected! Extensive testing will allow you to find the details you missed and correct them.

The code of `rename.go` will be presented in four parts. The first part includes the expected preamble as well as the Go code for dealing with the setup of the `flag` package:

```
package main

import (
    "flag"
    "fmt"
    "os"
    "path/filepath"
)

func main() {
    minusOverwrite := flag.Bool("overwrite", false, "overwrite")

    flag.Parse()
    flags := flag.Args()

    if len(flags) < 2 {
        fmt.Println("Please provide two arguments!")
        os.Exit(1)
    }
```

The second part has the following Go code:

```
source := flags[0]
destination := flags[1]
fileInfo, err := os.Stat(source)
if err == nil {
```

```
            mode := fileInfo.Mode()
            if mode.IsRegular() == false {
                    fmt.Println("Sorry, we only support regular files as
    source!")
                    os.Exit(1)
            }
    } else {
            fmt.Println("Error reading:", source)
            os.Exit(1)
    }
```

This part makes sure the source file exists, is a regular file, and is not a directory or something else like a network socket or a pipe. Once again, the trick with os.Stat() you saw in which.go is used here.

The third part of rename.go is as follows:

```
    newDestination := destination
    destInfo, err := os.Stat(destination)
    if err == nil {
            mode := destInfo.Mode()
            if mode.IsDir() {
                    justTheName := filepath.Base(source)
                    newDestination = destination + "/" + justTheName
            }
    }
```

There is another tricky point here; you will need to consider the case where the source is a plain file and the destination is a directory, which is implemented with the help of the newDestination variable.

Another special case that you should consider is when the source file is given in a format that contains an absolute or relative path in it like ./aDir/aFile. In this case, when the destination is a directory, you should get the basename of the path, which is what follows the last / character and in this case is aFile, and add it to the destination directory in order to correctly construct the newDestination variable. This happens with the help of the filepath.Base() function, which returns the last element of a path.

Finally, the last part of rename.go has the following Go code:

```
    destination = newDestination
    destInfo, err = os.Stat(destination)
    if err == nil {
            if *minusOverwrite == false {
                    fmt.Println("Destination file already exists!")
                    os.Exit(1)
```

```
            }
    }

    err = os.Rename(source, destination)
    if err != nil {
            fmt.Println(err)
            os.Exit(1)
    }
}
```

The most important Go code of rename.go has to do with recognizing whether the destination file exists or not. Once again, this is implemented with the support of the os.Stat() function. If os.Stat() returns an error message, this means that the destination file does not exist; so, you are free to call os.Rename(). If os.Stat() returns nil, this means that the os.Stat() call was successful and that the destination file exists. In this case, you should check the value of the overwrite flag to see if you are allowed to overwrite the destination file or not.

When everything is OK, you are free to call os.Rename() and perform the desired task!

If rename.go is executed correctly, it will create no output. However, if there are problems, rename.go will generate some output:

```
$ touch newFILE
$ ./rename newFILE regExpFind.go
Destination file already exists!
$ ./rename -overwrite newFILE regExpFind.go
$
```

Developing find(1) in Go

This section will teach you the necessary things that you need to know in order to develop a simplified version of the find(1) command-line utility in Go. The developed version will not support all the command-line options supported by find(1), but it will have enough options to be truly useful.

What you will see in the following subsections is the entire process in small steps. So, the first subsection will show you the Go way for visiting all files and directories in a given directory tree.

Traversing a directory tree

The most important task that find(1) needs to support is being able to visit all files and sub directories starting from a given directory. So, this section will implement this task in Go. The Go code of traverse.go will be presented in three parts. The first part is the expected preamble:

```
package main

import (
    "fmt"
    "os"
    "path/filepath"
)
```

The second part is about implementing a function named walkFunction() that will be used as an argument to a Go function named filepath.Walk():

```
func walkFunction(path string, info os.FileInfo, err error) error {
    _, err = os.Stat(path)
    if err != nil {
            return err
    }

    fmt.Println(path)
    return nil
}
```

Once again, the os.Stat() function is used because a successful os.Stat() function call means that we are dealing with something (file, directory, pipe, and so on) that actually exists!

 Do not forget that between the time filepath.Walk() is called and the time walkFunction() is called and executed, many things can happen in an active and busy filesystem, which is the main reason for calling os.Stat().

The last part of the code is as follows:

```
func main() {
    arguments := os.Args
    if len(arguments) == 1 {
            fmt.Println("Not enough arguments!")
            os.Exit(1)
    }
```

```
        Path := arguments[1]
        err := filepath.Walk(Path, walkFunction)
        if err != nil {
                fmt.Println(err)
                os.Exit(1)
        }
}
```

All the dirty jobs here are automatically done by the `filepath.Walk()` function with the help of the `walkFunction()` function that was defined previously. The `filepath.Walk()` function takes two parameters—the path of a directory and the walk function it will use.

Executing `traverse.go` will generate the following kind of output:

```
$ go run traverse.go ~/code/C/cUNL
/home/mtsouk/code/C/cUNL
/home/mtsouk/code/C/cUNL/gpp
/home/mtsouk/code/C/cUNL/gpp.c
/home/mtsouk/code/C/cUNL/sizeofint
/home/mtsouk/code/C/cUNL/sizeofint.c
/home/mtsouk/code/C/cUNL/speed
/home/mtsouk/code/C/cUNL/speed.c
/home/mtsouk/code/C/cUNL/swap
/home/mtsouk/code/C/cUNL/swap.c
```

As you can see, the code of `traverse.go` is pretty naïve, as among other things, it cannot differentiate between directories, files, and symbolic links. However, it does the pretty tedious job of visiting every file and directory under a given directory tree, which is the basic functionality of the `find(1)` utility.

Visiting directories only!

Although it is good to be able to visit everything, there are times when you want to visitonlydirectories and not files. So, in this subsection, we will modify `traverse.go` in order to still visit everything but only print the directory names. The name of the new program will be `traverseDir.go`. The only part of `traverse.go` that needs to change is the definition of the `walkFunction()`:

```
func walkFunction(path string, info os.FileInfo, err error) error {
    fileInfo, err := os.Stat(path)
    if err != nil {
            return err
    }

    mode := fileInfo.Mode()
```

```
    if mode.IsDir() {
         fmt.Println(path)
    }
    return nil
}
```

As you can see, here you need to use the information returned by the os.Stat() function call in order to check whether you are dealing with a directory or not. If you have a directory, then you print its path and you are done.

Executing traverseDir.go will generatethe followingoutput:

```
$ go run traverseDir.go ~/code
/home/mtsouk/code
/home/mtsouk/code/C
/home/mtsouk/code/C/cUNL
/home/mtsouk/code/C/example
/home/mtsouk/code/C/sysProg
/home/mtsouk/code/C/system
/home/mtsouk/code/Haskell
/home/mtsouk/code/aLink
/home/mtsouk/code/perl
/home/mtsouk/code/python
```

The first version of find(1)

The Go code in this section is saved as find.go and will be presented in three parts. As you will see, find.go uses a large amount of the code found in traverse.go, which is the main benefit you get when you are developing a program step by step.

The first part of find.go is the expected preamble:

```
package main

import (
    "flag"
    "fmt"
    "os"
    "path/filepath"
)
```

As we already know that we will improve find.go in the near future, the flag package is used here even if this is the first version of find.go and it does not have any flags!

The second part of the Go code contains the implementation of the `walkFunction()`:

```go
func walkFunction(path string, info os.FileInfo, err error) error {

    fileInfo, err := os.Stat(path)
    if err != nil {
        return err
    }

    mode := fileInfo.Mode()
    if mode.IsDir() || mode.IsRegular() {
        fmt.Println(path)
    }
    return nil
}
```

From the implementation of the `walkFunction()` you can easily understand that `find.go` only prints regular files and directories, and nothing else. Is this a problem? Not, if this is what you want. Generally speaking, this is not good. Nevertheless, having a first version of something that works despite some restrictions is a good starting point! The next version, which will be named `improvedFind.go`, will improve `find.go` by adding various command-line options to it.

The last part of `find.go` contains the code that implements the `main()` function:

```go
func main() {
    flag.Parse()
    flags := flag.Args()

    if len(flags) == 0 {
        fmt.Println("Not enough arguments!")
        os.Exit(1)
    }

    Path := flags[0]


    err := filepath.Walk(Path, walkFunction)
    if err != nil {
        fmt.Println(err)
        os.Exit(1)
    }
}
```

Executing `find.go` will create the following output:

```
$ go run find.go ~/code/C/cUNL
/home/mtsouk/code/C/cUNL
/home/mtsouk/code/C/cUNL/gpp
/home/mtsouk/code/C/cUNL/gpp.c
/home/mtsouk/code/C/cUNL/sizeofint
/home/mtsouk/code/C/cUNL/sizeofint.c
/home/mtsouk/code/C/cUNL/speed
/home/mtsouk/code/C/cUNL/speed.c
/home/mtsouk/code/C/cUNL/swap
/home/mtsouk/code/C/cUNL/swap.c
```

Adding some command-line options

This subsection will try to improve the Go version of `find(1)` that you created earlier. Keep in mind that this is the process used for developing real programs because you do not implement every possible command-line option in the first version of a program.

The Go code of the new version is going to be saved as `improvedFind.go`. Among other things, the new version will be able to ignore symbolic links—symbolic links will only be printed when `improvedFind.go` is used with the appropriate command-line option. To do this, we will use some of the Go code of `symbLink.go`.

 The `improvedFind.go` program is a real system tool that you can use on your own Unix machines.

The supported flags will be the following:

- **-s**: This is for printing socket files
- **-p**: This is for printing pipes
- **-sl**: This is for printing symbolic links
- **-d**: This is for printing directories
- **-f**: This is for printing files

As you will see, most of the new Go code is for supporting the flags added to the program. Additionally, by default, `improvedFind.go` prints every type of file or directory, and you are allowed to combine any of the preceding flags in order to print the types of files you want.

Apart from the various changes in the implementation of the `main()` function in order to support all these flags, most of the remaining changes will take place in the code of the `walkFunction()` function. Additionally, the `walkFunction()` function will be defined inside the `main()` function, which happens in order to avoid the use of global variables.

The first part of `improvedFind.go` is as follows:

```
package main

import (
    "flag"
    "fmt"
    "os"
    "path/filepath"
)

func main() {

    minusS := flag.Bool("s", false, "Sockets")
    minusP := flag.Bool("p", false, "Pipes")
    minusSL := flag.Bool("sl", false, "Symbolic Links")
    minusD := flag.Bool("d", false, "Directories")
    minusF := flag.Bool("f", false, "Files")

    flag.Parse()
    flags := flag.Args()

    printAll := false
    if *minusS && *minusP && *minusSL && *minusD && *minusF {
        printAll = true
    }

    if !(*minusS || *minusP || *minusSL || *minusD || *minusF) {
        printAll = true
    }

    if len(flags) == 0 {
        fmt.Println("Not enough arguments!")
        os.Exit(1)
    }

    Path := flags[0]
```

So, if all the flags are unset, the program will print everything, which is handled by the first `if` statement. Similarly, if all the flags are set, the program will also print everything. So, a new Boolean variable named `printAll` is needed.

The second part of improvedFind.go has the following Go code, which is mainly the definition of the walkFunction variable, which in reality is a function:

```
walkFunction := func(path string, info os.FileInfo, err error) error {
    fileInfo, err := os.Stat(path)
    if err != nil {
        return err
    }

    if printAll {
        fmt.Println(path)
        return nil
    }

    mode := fileInfo.Mode()
    if mode.IsRegular() && *minusF {
        fmt.Println(path)
        return nil
    }

    if mode.IsDir() && *minusD {
        fmt.Println(path)
        return nil
    }

    fileInfo, _ = os.Lstat(path)

    if fileInfo.Mode()&os.ModeSymlink != 0 {
        if *minusSL {
            fmt.Println(path)
            return nil
        }
    }

    if fileInfo.Mode()&os.ModeNamedPipe != 0 {
        if *minusP {
            fmt.Println(path)
            return nil
        }
    }

    if fileInfo.Mode()&os.ModeSocket != 0 {
        if *minusS {
            fmt.Println(path)
            return nil
        }
    }
```

```
                    return nil
        }
```

Here, the good thing is that once you find a match and print a file, you do not have to visit the rest of the `if` statements, which is the main reason for putting the `minusF` check first and the `minusD` check second. The call to `os.Lstat()` is used to find out whether we are dealing with a symbolic link or not. This happens because `os.Stat()` follows symbolic links and returns information about the file the link references, whereas `os.Lstat()` does not do so—the same occurs with `stat(2)` and `lstat(2)`.

You should be pretty familiar with the last part of `improvedFind.go`:

```
        err := filepath.Walk(Path, walkFunction)
        if err != nil {
                fmt.Println(err)
                os.Exit(1)
        }
}
```

Executing `improvedFind.go` generates the following output, which is an enriched version of the output of `find.go`:

```
$ go run improvedFind.go -d ~/code/C
/home/mtsouk/code/C
/home/mtsouk/code/C/cUNL
/home/mtsouk/code/C/example
/home/mtsouk/code/C/sysProg
/home/mtsouk/code/C/system
$ go run improvedFind.go -sl ~/code
/home/mtsouk/code/aLink
```

Excluding filenames from the find output

There are times when you do not need to display everything from the output of `find(1)`. So, in this subsection, you will learn a technique that allows you to manually exclude files from the output of `improvedFind.go` based on their filenames.

Note that this version of the program will not support regular expressions and will only exclude filenames that are an exact match.

So, the improved version of improvedFind.go will be named excludeFind.go. The output of the diff(1) utility can reveal the code differences between improvedFind.go and excludeFind.go:

```
$ diff excludeFind.go improvedFind.go
10,19d9
< func excludeNames(name string, exclude string) bool {`
<       if exclude == "" {
<               return false
<       }
<       if filepath.Base(name) == exclude {
<               return true
<       }
<       return false
< }
<
27d16
<       minusX := flag.String("x", "", "Files")
54,57d42
<               if excludeNames(path, *minusX) {
<                       return nil
<               }
<
```

The most significant change is the introduction of a new Go function, named excludeNames(), that deals with filename exclusion and the addition of the -x flag, which is used for setting the filename you want to exclude from the output. All the job is done by the file path. TheBase() function finds the last part of a path, even if the path is not a file but a directory, and compares it against the value of the -x flag.

Note that a more appropriate name for the excludeNames() function could have been isExcluded() or something similar because the -x option accepts a single value.

Executing excludeFind.go with and without the -x flag will prove that the new Go code actually works:

```
$ go run excludeFind.go -x=dT.py ~/code/python
/home/mtsouk/code/python
/home/mtsouk/code/python/dataFile.txt
/home/mtsouk/code/python/python
$ go run excludeFind.go ~/code/python
/home/mtsouk/code/python
/home/mtsouk/code/python/dT.py
/home/mtsouk/code/python/dataFile.txt
/home/mtsouk/code/python/python
```

Excluding a file extension from the find output

A file extension is the part of a filename after the last dot (.) character. So, the file extension of the image.png file is png, which applies to both files and directories.

Once again, you will need a separate command-line option followed by the file extension you want to exclude in order to implement this functionality—the new flag will be named -ext. This version of the find(1) utility will be based on the code of excludeFind.go and will be named finalFind.go. Some of you might say that a more appropriate name for this option would have been -xext and you would be right about that!

Once again, the diff(1) utility will help us spot the code differences between excludeFind.go and finalFind.go—the new functionality is implemented in a Go function named excludeExtensions(), which makes things easier to understand:

```
$ diff finalFind.go excludeFind.go
8d7
<       "strings"
21,34d19
< func excludeExtensions(name string, extension string) bool {
<       if extension == "" {
<               return false
<       }
<       basename := filepath.Base(name)
<       s := strings.Split(basename, ".")
<       length := len(s)
<       basenameExtension := s[length-1]
<       if basenameExtension == extension {
<               return true
<       }
<       return false
< }
<
43d27
<       minusEXT := flag.String("ext", "", "Extensions")
74,77d57
<               if excludeExtensions(path, *minusEXT) {
<                       return nil
<               }
<
```

As we are looking for the string after the last dot in the path, we use strings.Split() to split the path based on the dot characters it contains. Then, we take the last part of the return value of strings.Split() and we compare it against the extension that was given with the -ext flag. Therefore, nothing special here, just some string manipulation code. Once again, a more appropriate name for excludeExtensions() would have been isExcludedExtension().

Executing finalFind.go will generate the following output:

```
$ go run finalFind.go -ext=py ~/code/python
/home/mtsouk/code/python
/home/mtsouk/code/python/dataFile.txt
/home/mtsouk/code/python/python
$ go run finalFind.go ~/code/python
/home/mtsouk/code/python
/home/mtsouk/code/python/dT.py
/home/mtsouk/code/python/dataFile.txt
/home/mtsouk/code/python/python
```

Using regular expressions

This section will illustrate how to add support for regular expressions in finalFind.go—the name of the last version of the tool will be regExpFind.go. The new flag will be called -re and it will require a string value—anything that matches this string value will be included in the output unless it is excluded by another command-line option. Additionally, due to the flexibility that flags offer, we do not need to delete any of the previous options in order to add another one!

Once again, the diff(1) command will tell us the code differences between regExpFind.go and finalFind.go:

```
$ diff regExpFind.go finalFind.go
8d7
<       "regexp"
36,44d34
< func regularExpression(path, regExp string) bool {
<       if regExp == "" {
<               return true
<       }
<       r, _ := regexp.Compile(regExp)
<       matched := r.MatchString(path)
<       return matched
< }
<
```

```
54d43
<        minusRE := flag.String("re", "", "Regular Expression")
71a61
>
75,78d64
<               if regularExpression(path, *minusRE) == false {
<                       return nil
<               }
<
```

In `Chapter 7`, *Working with System Files*, we will talk more about pattern matching and regular expressions in Go—for now, it is enough to understand that `regexp.Compile()` creates a regular expression and `MatchString()` tries to do the matching in the `regularExpression()` function.

Executing `regExpFind.go` will generate the following output:

```
$ go run regExpFind.go -re=anotherPackage /Users/mtsouk/go
/Users/mtsouk/go/pkg/darwin_amd64/anotherPackage.a
/Users/mtsouk/go/src/anotherPackage
/Users/mtsouk/go/src/anotherPackage/anotherPackage.go
$ go run regExpFind.go -ext=go -re=anotherPackage /Users/mtsouk/go
/Users/mtsouk/go/pkg/darwin_amd64/anotherPackage.a
/Users/mtsouk/go/src/anotherPackage
```

The previous output can be verified by using the following command:

```
$ go run regExpFind.go /Users/mtsouk/go | grep anotherPackage
/Users/mtsouk/go/pkg/darwin_amd64/anotherPackage.a
/Users/mtsouk/go/src/anotherPackage
/Users/mtsouk/go/src/anotherPackage/anotherPackage.go
```

Creating a copy of a directory structure

Armed with the knowledge you gained in the previous sections, we will now develop a Go program that creates a copy of a directory structure in another directory—this means that any files in the input directory will not be copied to the destination directory, only the directories will be copied. This can be handy when you want to save useful files from a directory structure somewhere else while keeping the same directory structure or when you want to take a backup of a filesystem manually.

As you are only interested in directories, the code of `cpStructure.go` is based on the code of `traverseDir.go` you saw earlier in this chapter—once again, a small program that was developed for learning purposes helps you implement a bigger program! Additionally, the `test` option will show what the program will do without actually creating any directories.

The code of `cpStructure.go` will be presented in four parts. The first one is as follows:

```
package main

import (
    "flag"
    "fmt"
    "os"
    "path/filepath"
    "strings"
)
```

There is nothing special here, just the expected preamble. The second part is as follows:

```
func main() {
    minusTEST := flag.Bool("test", false, "Test run!")

    flag.Parse()
    flags := flag.Args()

    if len(flags) == 0 || len(flags) == 1 {
        fmt.Println("Not enough arguments!")
        os.Exit(1)
    }

    Path := flags[0]
    NewPath := flags[1]

    permissions := os.ModePerm
    _, err := os.Stat(NewPath)
    if os.IsNotExist(err) {
        os.MkdirAll(NewPath, permissions)
    } else {
        fmt.Println(NewPath, "already exists - quitting...")
        os.Exit(1)
    }
```

The cpStructure.go program demands that the destination directory does not exist in advance in order to avoid unnecessary surprises and errors afterwards.

The third part contains the code of the walkFunction variable:

```
walkFunction := func(currentPath string, info os.FileInfo, err error)
error {
        fileInfo, _ := os.Lstat(currentPath)
        if fileInfo.Mode()&os.ModeSymlink != 0 {
                fmt.Println("Skipping", currentPath)
                return nil
        }

        fileInfo, err = os.Stat(currentPath)
        if err != nil {
                fmt.Println("*", err)
                return err
        }

        mode := fileInfo.Mode()
        if mode.IsDir() {
                tempPath := strings.Replace(currentPath, Path, "", 1)
                pathToCreate := NewPath + "/" + filepath.Base(Path) +
tempPath

                if *minusTEST {
                        fmt.Println(":", pathToCreate)
                        return nil
                }

                _, err := os.Stat(pathToCreate)
                if os.IsNotExist(err) {
                        os.MkdirAll(pathToCreate, permissions)
                } else {
                        fmt.Println("Did not create", pathToCreate, ":", err)
                }
        }
        return nil
}
```

Here, the first if statement makes sure that we will deal with symbolic links because symbolic links can be dangerous and create problems—always try to treat special situations in order to avoid problems and nasty bugs.

The os.IsNotExist() function allows you to make sure that the directory you are trying to create is not already there. So, if the directory is not there, you create it using os.MkdirAll(). The os.MkdirAll() function creates a directory path including all the necessary parents, which makes things simpler for the developer.

Nevertheless, the trickiest part that the code of the walkFunction variable has to deal with is removing the unnecessary parts of the source path and constructing the new path correctly. The strings.Replace() function used in the program replaces the occurrences of its second argument (Path) that can be found in the first argument (currentPath) with its third argument ("") as many times as its last argument (1). If the last argument is a negative number, which is not the case here, then there will be no limit to the number of replacements. In this case, it removes the value of the Path variable, which is the source directory, from the currentPath variable, which is the directory that is being examined.

The last part of the program is as follows:

```
err = filepath.Walk(Path, walkFunction)
if err != nil {
        fmt.Println(err)
        os.Exit(1)
}
}
```

Executing cpStructure.go will generate the following output:

```
$ go run cpStructure.go ~/code /tmp/newCode
Skipping /home/mtsouk/code/aLink
$ ls -l /home/mtsouk/code/aLink
lrwxrwxrwx 1 mtsouk mtsouk 14 Apr 21 18:10 /home/mtsouk/code/aLink ->
/usr/local/bin
```

The following figure shows a graphical representation of the source and destination directory structures used in the aforementioned example:

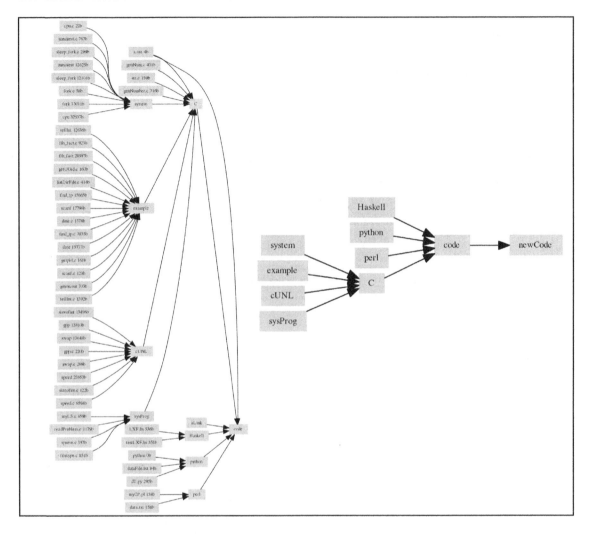

A graphical representation of two directory structures with their files

Exercises

1. Read the documentation page of the os package at https://golang.org/pkg/os/.

2. Visit https://golang.org/pkg/path/filepath/ to learn more about the filepath.Walk() function.

3. Change the code of rm.go in order to support multiple command-line arguments, and then try to implement the -v command-line option of the rm(1) utility.

4. Make the necessary changes to the Go code of which.go in order to support multiple command-line arguments.

5. Start implementing a version of the ls(1) utility in Go. Do not try to support every ls(1) option at once.

6. Change the code of traverseDir.go in order to print regular files only.

7. Check the manual page of find(1) and try to add support for some of its options in regExpFind.go.

Summary

In this chapter, we talked about many things including the use of the flag standard package, Go functions that allow you to work with directories and files, and traverse directory structures, and we developed Go versions of various Unix command-line utilities including pwd(1), which(1), rm(1), and find(1).

In the next chapter, we will continue talking about file operations, but this time you will learn how to read files and write to files in Go—as you will see there are many ways to do this. Although this gives you versatility, it also demands that you should be able to choose the right technique to do your job as efficiently as possible! So, you will start by learning more about the io package as well as the bufio package and by the end of the chapter, you will have Go versions of the wc(1) and dd(1) utilities!

6
File Input and Output

In the previous chapter, we talked about manipulating files and directories as entities without looking at their contents. However, in this chapter, we will take a different approach and look into the contents of files—you might consider this chapter one of the most important chapters in this book because **file input** and **file output** are primary tasks of any operating system.

The main purpose of this chapter is to teach how the Go standard library permits us to open files, read their contents, process them if we like, create new files, and put the desired data into them. There are two main ways to read and write files: using the `io` package and using the functions of the `bufio` package. However, both packages work in a comparative way.

This chapter will tell you about the following:

- Opening files for writing and reading
- Using the `io` package for file input and output
- Using the `io.Writer` and `io.Reader` interfaces
- Using the `bufio` package for buffered input and output
- Copying files in Go
- Implementing a version of the `wc(1)` utility in Go
- Developing a version of the `dd(1)` command in Go
- Creating sparse files
- The importance of byte slices in file input and output—byte slices were first mentioned in Chapter 2, *Writing Programs in Go*
- Storing structured data in files and reading them afterwards
- Converting tabs into space characters and vice versa

This chapter will not talk about appending data to an existing file—you will have to wait until Chapter 7, *Working with System Files*, to learn more about putting data at the end of a file without destroying its existing data.

About file input and output

File input and output includes everything that has to do with reading the data of a file and writing the desired data to a file. There is not a single operating system that does not offer support for files and therefore for file input and output.

As this chapter is pretty big, I will stop talking and start showing you practical Go code that will make things clearer. So, the first thing that you will learn in this chapter is byte slices, which are very important in applications that are concerned with file input and output.

Byte slices

Byte slices are a kind of slices used for file reading and writing. Putting it simply, they are slices of bytes used as a buffer during file reading and writing operations. This section will present a small Go example where a byte slice is used for writing to a file and reading from a file. As you will see byte slices all over this chapter, make sure that you understand the presented example. The related Go code is saved as `byteSlice.go` and will be presented in three parts.

The first part is as follows:

```
package main

import (
    "fmt"
    "io/ioutil"
    "os"
)
```

The second part of `byteSlice.go` is as follows:

```
func main() {
    if len(os.Args) != 2 {
            fmt.Println("Please provide a filename")
            os.Exit(1)
    }
    filename := os.Args[1]

    aByteSlice := []byte("Mihalis Tsoukalos!\n")
    ioutil.WriteFile(filename, aByteSlice, 0644)
```

Here, you use the `aByteSlice` byte slice to save some text into a file that is identified by the `filename` variable. The last part of `byteSlice.go` is the following Go code:

```
    f, err := os.Open(filename)
    if err != nil {
            fmt.Println(err)
            os.Exit(1)
    }
    defer f.Close()

    anotherByteSlice := make([]byte, 100)
    n, err := f.Read(anotherByteSlice)
    fmt.Printf("Read %d bytes: %s", n, anotherByteSlice)


}
```

Here, you define another byte slice named `anotherByteSlice` with 100 places that will be used for reading from the file you created previously. Note that `%s` used in `fmt.Printf()` forces `anotherByteSlice` to be printed as a string—using `Println()` would have produced a totally different output.

 Note that as the file is smaller, the `f.Read()` call will put less data into `anotherByteSlice`.

The size of `anotherByteSlice` denotes the maximum amount of data that can be stored into it after a single call to `Read()` or after any other similar operation that reads data from a file.

Executing `byteSlice.go` will generate the following output:

```
$ go run byteSlice.go usingByteSlices
Read 19 bytes: Mihalis Tsoukalos!
```

Checking the size of the `usingByteSlices` file will verify that the right amount of data was written to it:

```
$ wc usingByteSlices
   1   2  19 usingByteSlices
```

About binary files

There is no difference between reading and writing binary and plain text files in Go. So, when processing a file, Go makes no assumptions about its format. However, Go offers a package named binary that allows you to make translations between different encodings such as **little endian** and **big endian**.

The `readBinary.go` file briefly illustrates how to convert an integer number to a little endian number and to a big endian number, which might be useful when the files you want to process contain certain kinds of data; this mainly happens when we are dealing with raw devices and raw packet manipulation—remember everything is a file! The source code of `readBinary.go` will be presented in two parts.

The first part is as follows:

```go
package main

import (
    "bytes"
    "encoding/binary"
    "fmt"
    "os"
    "strconv"
)

func main() {
    if len(os.Args) != 2 {
        fmt.Println("Please provide an integer")
        os.Exit(1)
    }
    aNumber, _ := strconv.ParseInt(os.Args[1], 10, 64)
```

There is nothing special in this part of the program. The second part is the following:

```
buf := new(bytes.Buffer)
err := binary.Write(buf, binary.LittleEndian, aNumber)
if err != nil {
        fmt.Println("Little Endian:", err)
}

fmt.Printf("%d is %x in Little Endian\n", aNumber, buf)
buf.Reset()
err = binary.Write(buf, binary.BigEndian, aNumber)


if err != nil {
        fmt.Println("Big Endian:", err)
}
fmt.Printf("And %x in Big Endian\n", buf)
}
```

The second part contains all the important Go code—the conversions happen with the help of the `binary.Write()` method and the proper write parameter (`binary.LittleEndian` or `binary.BigEndian`). The `bytes.Buffer` variable is used for the `io.Reader` and `io.Writer` interfaces of the program. Lastly, the `buf.Reset()` statement resets the buffer in order to be used afterwards for storing the big endian.

Executing `readBinary.go` will generate the following output:

```
$ go run readBinary.go 1
1 is 0100000000000000 in Little Endian
And 0000000000000001 in Big Endian
```

You can find more information about the binary package by visiting its documentation page at `https://golang.org/pkg/encoding/binary/`.

Useful I/O packages in Go

The `io` package is for performing primitive file I/O operations, whereas the `bufio` package is for executing buffered I/O.

> In buffered I/O, the operating system uses an intermediate buffer during file read and write operations in order to reduce the number of filesystem calls. As a result, buffered input and output is faster and more efficient.

Additionally, you can use some of the functions of the `fmt` package to write text to a file. Note that the `flag` package will be also used in this chapter as well as in all the forthcoming ones where the developed utilities need to support command-line flags.

The io package

The `io` package offers functions that allow you to write to or read from files. Its use will be illustrated in the `usingIO.go` file, which will be presented in three parts. What the program does is read 8 bytes from a file and write them in a standard output.

The first part is the preamble of the Go program:

```
package main

import (
    "fmt"
    "io"
    "os"
)
```

The second part is the following Go code:

```
func main() {
    if len(os.Args) != 2 {
        fmt.Println("Please provide a filename")
        os.Exit(1)
    }

    filename := os.Args[1]
    f, err := os.Open(filename)
    if err != nil {
        fmt.Printf("error opening %s: %s", filename, err)
        os.Exit(1)
    }
    defer f.Close()
```

The program also uses the handy `defer` command that defers the execution of a function until the surrounding function returns. As a result, `defer` is used very frequently in file I/O operations because it saves you from having to remember to execute the `Close()` call after you are done working with a file or when you leave a function in any number of locations using a `return` statement or `os.Exit()`.

The last part of the program is the following:

```
buf := make([]byte, 8)
if _, err := io.ReadFull(f, buf); err != nil {
        if err == io.EOF {
                err = io.ErrUnexpectedEOF
        }
}
io.WriteString(os.Stdout, string(buf))
fmt.Println()
}
```

The io.ReadFull() function here reads from the reader of an open file and puts the data into a byte slice that has 8 places. You can also see here the use of the io.WriteString() function for printing data to a standard output (os.Stdout) that is also a file. However, this is not a very common practice as you can simply use fmt.Println() instead.

Executing usingIO.go generates the following output:

```
$ go run usingIO.go usingByteSlices
Mihalis
```

The bufio package

The functions of the bufio package allow you to perform buffered file operations, which means that although its operations look similar to the ones found in io, they work in a slightly different way.

What bufio actually does is to wrap an io.Reader or io.Writer object into a new value that implements the required interface while providing buffering to the new value. One of the handy features of the bufio package is that it allows you to read a text file line by line, word by word, and character by character without too much effort.

Once again, an example will try to clarify things—the name of the Go file that showcases the use of bufio is bufIO.go and will be presented in four parts.

The first part is the expected preamble:

```
package main

import (
    "bufio"
    "fmt"
    "os"
)
```

The second part is the following:

```
func main() {
    if len(os.Args) != 2 {
        fmt.Println("Please provide a filename")
        os.Exit(1)
    }

    filename := os.Args[1]
```

Here, you just try to get the name of the file that you are going to use.

The third part of bufIO.go has the following Go code:

```
    f, err := os.Open(filename)
    if err != nil {
        fmt.Printf("error opening %s: %s", filename, err)
        os.Exit(1)
    }
    defer f.Close()

    scanner := bufio.NewScanner(f)
```

The default behavior of bufio.NewScanner is to read its input line by line, which means that each time you call the Scan() method that reads the next token, a new line will be returned. The last part is where you actually call the Scan() method in order to read the full contents of the file:

```
    for scanner.Scan() {
        line := scanner.Text()

        if scanner.Err() != nil {
            fmt.Printf("error reading file %s", err)
            os.Exit(1)
        }
        fmt.Println(line)
    }
}
```

The `Text()` method returns the latest token from the `Scan()` method as a string, which in this case will be a line. However, if you ever get strange results while trying to read a file line by line, it will most likely be the way your file ends a line, which is usually the case with text files coming from Windows machines.

Executing `bufIO.go` and feeding `wc(1)` with its output can help you verify that `bufIO.go` works as expected:

```
$ go run bufIO.go inputFile | wc
      11      12      62
$ wc inputFile
      11      12      62 inputFile
```

File I/O operations

Now that you know the basics of the `io` and `bufio` packages, it is time to learn more detailed information about their usage and how they can help you work with files. But first, we will talk about the `fmt.Fprintf()` function.

Writing to files using fmt.Fprintf()

The use of the `fmt.Fprintf()` function allows you to write formatted text to files in a way that is similar to the way the `fmt.Printf()` function works. Note that `fmt.Fprintf()` can write to any `io.Writer` interface and that our files will satisfy the `io.Writer` interface.

The Go code that illustrates the use of `fmt.Fprintf()` can be found in `fmtF.go`, which will be presented in three parts. The first part is the expected preamble:

```
package main

import (
    "fmt"
    "os"
)
```

The second part has the following Go code:

```
func main() {
    if len(os.Args) != 2 {
        fmt.Println("Please provide a filename")
        os.Exit(1)
    }
```

```
filename := os.Args[1]
destination, err := os.Create(filename)
if err != nil {
        fmt.Println("os.Create:", err)
        os.Exit(1)
}
defer destination.Close()
```

Note that the os.Create() function will truncate the file if it already exists.

The last part is the following:

```
fmt.Fprintf(destination, "[%s]: ", filename)
fmt.Fprintf(destination, "Using fmt.Fprintf in %s\n", filename)
}
```

Here, you write the desired text data to the file that is identified by the destination variable using fmt.Fprintf() as if you were using the fmt.Printf() method.

Executing fmtF.go will generate the following output:

```
$ go run fmtF.go test
$ cat test
[test]: Using fmt.Fprintf in test
```

In other words, you can create plain text files using fmt.Fprintf().

About io.Writer and io.Reader

Both io.Writer and io.Reader are interfaces that embed the io.Write() and io.Read() methods, respectively. The use of io.Writer and io.Reader will be illustrated in readerWriter.go, which will be presented in four parts. The program computes the characters of its input file and writes the number of characters to another file—if you are dealing with Unicode characters that take more than one byte per character, you might consider that the program is reading bytes. The output filename has the name of the original file plus the .Count extension.

The first part is the following:

```
package main

import (
    "fmt"
    "io"
    "os"
)
```

The second part is the following:

```
func countChars(r io.Reader) int {
    buf := make([]byte, 16)
    total := 0
    for {
        n, err := r.Read(buf)
        if err != nil && err != io.EOF {
            return 0
        }
        if err == io.EOF {
            break
        }
        total = total + n
    }
    return total
}
```

Once again, a byte slice is used during reading. The `break` statement allows you to exit the `for` loop. The third part is the following code:

```
func writeNumberOfChars(w io.Writer, x int) {
    fmt.Fprintf(w, "%d\n", x)
}
```

Here you can see how you can write a number to a file using `fmt.Fprintf()`—I did not manage to do the same using a byte slice! Additionally, note that the presented code writes text to a file using an `io.Writer` variable (w).

The last part of `readerWriter.go` has the following Go code:

```
func main() {
    if len(os.Args) != 2 {
        fmt.Println("Please provide a filename")
        os.Exit(1)
    }

    filename := os.Args[1]
```

```
    _, err := os.Stat(filename)


    if err != nil {
            fmt.Printf("Error on file %s: %s\n", filename, err)
            os.Exit(1)
    }

    f, err := os.Open(filename)
    if err != nil {
            fmt.Println("Cannot open file:", err)
            os.Exit(-1)
    }
    defer f.Close()

    chars := countChars(f)
    filename = filename + ".Count"
    f, err = os.Create(filename)
    if err != nil {
            fmt.Println("os.Create:", err)
            os.Exit(1)
    }
    defer f.Close()
    writeNumberOfChars(f, chars)
}
```

The execution of readerWriter.go generates no output; so, it is up to you to check its correctness, which in this case happens with the help of wc(1):

```
$ go run readerWriter.go /tmp/swtag.log
$ wc /tmp/swtag.log
     119      635     7780 /tmp/swtag.log
$ cat /tmp/swtag.log.Count
7780
```

Finding out the third column of a line

Now that you know how to read a file, it is time to present a modified version of the readColumn.go program you saw in Chapter 3, *Advanced Go Features*. The new version is also named readColumn.go, but has two major improvements. The first is that you can provide the desired column as a command-line argument and the second is that it can read multiple files if it gets multiple command-line arguments.

The `readColumn.go` file will be presented in three parts. The first part of `readColumn.go` is the following:

```
package main

import (
    "bufio"
    "flag"
    "fmt"
    "io"
    "os"
    "strings"
)
```

The next part of `readColumn.go` contains the following Go code:

```
func main() {
    minusCOL := flag.Int("COL", 1, "Column")
    flag.Parse()
    flags := flag.Args()

    if len(flags) == 0 {
        fmt.Printf("usage: readColumn <file1> [<file2> [... <fileN]]\n")
        os.Exit(1)
    }

    column := *minusCOL

    if column < 0 {
        fmt.Println("Invalid Column number!")
        os.Exit(1)
    }
```

As you will understand from the definition of the `minusCOL` variable, if the user does not use this flag, the program will print the contents of the first column of each file it reads.

The last part of `readColumn.go` is as follows:

```
    for _, filename := range flags {
        fmt.Println("\t\t", filename)
        f, err := os.Open(filename)
        if err != nil {
            fmt.Printf("error opening file %s", err)
            continue
        }
        defer f.Close()

        r := bufio.NewReader(f)
```

```
        for {
                line, err := r.ReadString('\n')

                if err == io.EOF {
                        break
                } else if err != nil {
                        fmt.Printf("error reading file %s", err)
                }

                data := strings.Fields(line)
                if len(data) >= column {
                        fmt.Println((data[column-1]))
                }
        }
    }
}
```

The preceding code does not do anything that you have not seen before. The `for` loop is used for processing all command-line arguments. However, if a file fails to open for some reason, the program will not stop its execution, but it will continue processing the rest of the files if they exist. However, the program expects that its input files end in a newline and you might see strange results if an input file ends differently.

Executing `readColumn.go` generates the following output, which is abbreviated in order to save some book space:

```
$ go run readColumn.go -COL=3 pF.data isThereAFile up.data
            pF.data
            isThereAFile
error opening file open isThereAFile: no such file or directory
            up.data
0.05
0.05
0.05
0.05
0.05
0.05
```

In this case, there is no file named `isThereAFile` and the `pF.data` file does not have a third column. However, the program did its best and printed what it could!

Copying files in Go

Every operating system allows you to copy files because this is a very important and necessary operation. This section will show you how to copy files in Go now that you know how to read files!

There is more than one way to copy a file!

Most programming languages offer more than one way to create a copy of a file and Go is no exception. It is up to the developer to decide which approach to implement.

 The *there is more than one way to do it* rule applies to almost everything implemented in this book, but file copying is the most characteristic example of this rule because you can copy a file by reading it line by line, byte by byte, or all at once!However, this rule does not apply to the way Go likes to format its code!

Copying text files

There is no point in treating the copying of text files in a special way unless you want to inspect or modify their contents. As a result, the three techniques presented here will not differentiate between plain text and binary file copying.

Chapter 7, *Working with System Files*, will talk about file permissions because there are times that you want to create new files with the file permissions you choose.

Using io.Copy

This subsection will present a technique for copying files that uses the io.Copy() function. What is special about the io.Copy() function is the fact that is does not give you any flexibility in the process. The name of the program will be notGoodCP.go and will be presented in three parts. Note that a more appropriate filename for notGoodCP.go would have been copyEntireFileAtOnce.go or copyByReadingInputFileAllAtOnce.go!

The first part of the Go code of `notGoodCP.go` is the following:

```
package main

import (
    "fmt"
    "io"
    "os"
)
```

The second part is as follows:

```
func Copy(src, dst string) (int64, error) {
    sourceFileStat, err := os.Stat(src)
    if err != nil {
        return 0, err
    }

    if !sourceFileStat.Mode().IsRegular() {
        return 0, fmt.Errorf("%s is not a regular file", src)
    }

    source, err := os.Open(src)
    if err != nil {
        return 0, err
    }
    defer source.Close()

    destination, err := os.Create(dst)
    if err != nil {
        return 0, err
    }
    defer destination.Close()
    nBytes, err := io.Copy(destination, source)
    return nBytes, err


}
```

Here we define our own function that uses `io.Copy()` to make a copy of a file. The `Copy()` function checks whether the source file is a regular file before trying to copy it, which makes perfect sense.

The last part is the implementation of the `main()` function:

```go
func main() {
    if len(os.Args) != 3 {
        fmt.Println("Please provide two command line arguments!")
        os.Exit(1)
    }

    sourceFile := os.Args[1]
    destinationFile := os.Args[2]
    nBytes, err := Copy(sourceFile, destinationFile)

    if err != nil {
        fmt.Printf("The copy operation failed %q\n", err)
    } else {
        fmt.Printf("Copied %d bytes!\n", nBytes)
    }
}
```

The best tool for testing whether a file is an exact copy of another file is the `diff(1)` utility, which also works with binary files. You can learn more about `diff(1)` by reading its main page.

Executing `notGoodCP.go` will generate the following results:

```
$ go run notGoodCP.go testFile aCopy
Copied 871 bytes!
$ diff aCopy testFile
$ wc testFile aCopy
      51     127      871 testFile
      51     127      871 aCopy
     102     254     1742 total
```

Reading a file all at once!

The technique in this section will use the `ioutil.WriteFile()` and `ioutil.ReadFile()` functions. Note that `ioutil.ReadFile()` does not implement the `io.Reader` interface and therefore is a little restrictive.

The Go code for this section is named `readAll.go` and will be presented in three parts.

The first part has the following Go code:

```go
package main

import (
    "fmt"
    "io/ioutil"
    "os"
)
```

The second part is the following:

```go
func main() {
    if len(os.Args) != 3 {
        fmt.Println("Please provide two command line arguments!")
        os.Exit(1)
    }

    sourceFile := os.Args[1]
    destinationFile := os.Args[2]
```

The last part is as follows:

```go
    input, err := ioutil.ReadFile(sourceFile)
    if err != nil {
        fmt.Println(err)
        os.Exit(1)
    }

    err = ioutil.WriteFile(destinationFile, input, 0644)
    if err != nil {
        fmt.Println("Error creating the new file", destinationFile)
        fmt.Println(err)
        os.Exit(1)
    }
}
```

Note that the `ioutil.ReadFile()` function reads the entire file, which might not be efficient when you want to copy huge files. Similarly, the `ioutil.WriteFile()` function writes all the given data to a file that is identified by its first argument.

The execution of `readAll.go` generates the following output:

```
$ go run readAll.go testFile aCopy
$ diff aCopy testFile
$ ls -l testFile aCopy
-rw-r--r--  1 mtsouk  staff  871 May  3 21:07 aCopy
-rw-r--r--@ 1 mtsouk  staff  871 May  3 21:04 testFile
$ go run readAll.go doesNotExist aCopy
open doesNotExist: no such file or directory
exit status 1
```

An even better file copy program

This section will present a program that uses a more traditional approach, where a buffer is used for reading and copying to the new file.

 Although traditional Unix command-line utilities are silent when there are no errors, it is not bad to print some kind of information, such as the number of bytes read, in your own tools. However, the right thing to do is to follow the Unix way.

There exist two main reasons that make `cp.go` better than `notGoodCP.go`. The first is that the developer has more control over the process in exchange for having to write more Go code and the second is that `cp.go` allows you to define the size of the buffer, which is the most important parameter in the copy operation.

The code of `cp.go` will be presented in five parts. The first part is the expected preamble along with a global variable that holds the size of the read buffer:

```go
package main

import (
    "fmt"
    "io"
    "os"
    "path/filepath"
    "strconv"
)


var BUFFERSIZE int64
```

The second part is the following:

```go
func Copy(src, dst string, BUFFERSIZE int64) error {
    sourceFileStat, err := os.Stat(src)
    if err != nil {
        return err
    }

    if !sourceFileStat.Mode().IsRegular() {
        return fmt.Errorf("%s is not a regular file.", src)
    }

    source, err := os.Open(src)
    if err != nil {
        return err
    }
    defer source.Close()
```

As you can see here, the size of the buffer is given to the Copy() function as an argument. The other two command-line arguments are the input filename and the output filename.

The third part has the remaining Go code of the Copy() function:

```go
    _, err = os.Stat(dst)
    if err == nil {
        return fmt.Errorf("File %s already exists.", dst)
    }

    destination, err := os.Create(dst)
    if err != nil {
        return err
    }
    defer destination.Close()

    if err != nil {
        panic(err)
    }

    buf := make([]byte, BUFFERSIZE)
    for {
        n, err := source.Read(buf)
        if err != nil && err != io.EOF {
            return err
        }
        if n == 0 {
            break
        }
```

```
            if _, err := destination.Write(buf[:n]); err != nil {
                    return err
            }
    }
    return err
}
```

There is nothing special here—you just keep calling source, `Read()` until you reach the end of the input file. Each time you read something, you call destination. `Write()` to save it to the output file. The `buf[:n]` notation allows you to read the first n characters from the `buf` slice.

The fourth part contains the following Go code:

```
func main() {
    if len(os.Args) != 4 {
            fmt.Printf("usage: %s source destination BUFFERSIZE\n",
filepath.Base(os.Args[0]))
            os.Exit(1)
    }

    source := os.Args[1]
    destination := os.Args[2]
    BUFFERSIZE, _ = strconv.ParseInt(os.Args[3], 10, 64)
```

The `filepath.Base()` is used for getting the name of the executable file.

The last part is the following:

```
    fmt.Printf("Copying %s to %s\n", source, destination)
    err := Copy(source, destination, BUFFERSIZE)
    if err != nil {
            fmt.Printf("File copying failed: %q\n", err)
    }
}
```

Executing `cp.go` will generate the following output:

```
$ go run cp.go inputFile aCopy 2048
Copying inputFile to aCopy
$ diff inputFile aCopy
```

If there is a problem with the copy operation, you will get a descriptive error message.

So, if the program cannot find the input file, it will print the following:

```
$ go run cp.go A /tmp/myCP 1024
Copying A to /tmp/myCP
File copying failed: "stat A: no such file or directory"
```

If the program cannot read the input file, you will get the following message:

```
$ go run cp.go inputFile /tmp/myCP 1024
Copying inputFile to /tmp/myCP
File copying failed: "open inputFile: permission denied"
```

If the program cannot create the output file, it will print the following error message:

```
$ go run cp.go inputFile /usr/myCP 1024
Copying inputFile to /usr/myCP
File copying failed: "open /usr/myCP: operation not permitted"
```

If the destination file already exists, you will get the following output:

```
$ go run cp.go inputFile outputFile 1024
Copying inputFile to outputFile
File copying failed: "File outputFile already exists."
```

Benchmarking file copying operations

The size of the buffer you use in file operations is really important and affects the performance of your system tools, especially when you are dealing with very big files.

 Although developing reliable software should be your main concern, you should not forget to make your systems software fast and efficient!

So, this section will try to see how the size of the buffer affects the file copying operations by executing cp.go with various buffer sizes and comparing its performance with readAll.go, notGoodCP.go as well as cp(1).

In the old Unix days when the amount of RAM on Unix machines was too small, using a large buffer was not recommended. However, nowadays, using a buffer with a size of 100 MB is not considered bad practice, especially when you know in advance that you are going to copy lots of big files such as the data files of a database server.

We will use three files with different sizes in our testing—these three files will be generated using the dd(1) utility, as shown here:

```
$dd if=/dev/urandom of=100MB count=100000 bs=1024
100000+0 records in
100000+0 records out
102400000 bytes transferred in 6.800277 secs (15058210 bytes/sec)
$ dd if=/dev/urandom of=1GB count=1000000 bs=1024
1000000+0 records in
1000000+0 records out
1024000000 bytes transferred in 68.887482 secs (14864820 bytes/sec)
$ dd if=/dev/urandom of=5GB count=5000000 bs=1024
5000000+0 records in
5000000+0 records out
5120000000 bytes transferred in 339.357738 secs (15087324 bytes/sec)
$ ls -l 100MB 1GB 5GB
-rw-r--r-- 1 mtsouk  staff   102400000 May  4 10:30 100MB
-rw-r--r-- 1 mtsouk  staff  1024000000 May  4 10:32 1GB
-rw-r--r-- 1 mtsouk  staff  5120000000 May  4 10:38 5GB
```

The first file is 100 MB, the second is 1 GB, and the third is 5 GB in size.

Now, it is time for the actual testing using the time(1) utility. First, we will test the performance of notGoodCP.go and readAll.go:

```
$ time ./notGoodCP 100MB copy
Copied 102400000 bytes!
real    0m0.153s
user    0m0.003s
sys     0m0.084s
$ time ./notGoodCP 1GB copy
Copied 1024000000 bytes!
real    0m1.461s
user    0m0.029s
sys     0m0.833s
$ time ./notGoodCP 5GB copy
Copied 5120000000 bytes!
real    0m12.193s
user    0m0.161s
sys     0m5.251s
$ time ./readAll 100MB copy
real    0m0.249s
user    0m0.003s
sys     0m0.138s
$ time ./readAll 1GB copy
real    0m3.117s
user    0m0.639s
sys     0m1.644s
```

```
$ time ./readAll 5GB copy
real   0m28.918s
user   0m8.106s
sys    0m21.364s
```

Now, you will see the results from the cp.go program using four different buffer sizes, 16, 1024, 1048576, and 1073741824. First, let's copy the 100 MB file:

```
$ time ./cp 100MB copy 16
Copying 100MB to copy
real   0m13.240s
user   0m2.699s
sys    0m10.530s
$ time ./cp 100MB copy 1024
Copying 100MB to copy
real   0m0.386s
user   0m0.053s
sys    0m0.303s
$ time ./cp 100MB copy 1048576
Copying 100MB to copy
real   0m0.135s
user   0m0.001s
sys    0m0.075s
$ time ./cp 100MB copy 1073741824
Copying 100MB to copy
real   0m0.390s
user   0m0.011s
sys    0m0.136s
```

Then, we will copy the 1 GB file:

```
$ time ./cp 1GB copy 16
Copying 1GB to copy
real   2m10.054s
user   0m26.497s
sys    1m43.411s
$ time ./cp 1GB copy 1024
Copying 1GB to copy
real   0m3.520s
user   0m0.533s
sys    0m2.944s
$ time ./cp 1GB copy 1048576
Copying 1GB to copy
real   0m1.431s
user   0m0.006s
sys    0m0.749s
$ time ./cp 1GB copy 1073741824
Copying 1GB to copy
```

```
real    0m2.033s
user    0m0.012s
sys     0m1.310s
```

Next, we will copy the 5 GB file:

```
$ time ./cp 5GB copy 16
Copying 5GB to copy
real    10m41.551s
user    2m11.695s
sys     8m29.248s
$ time ./cp 5GB copy 1024
Copying 5GB to copy
real    0m16.558s
user    0m2.415s
sys     0m13.597s
$ time ./cp 5GB copy 1048576
Copying 5GB to copy
real    0m7.172s
user    0m0.028s
sys     0m3.734s
$ time ./cp 5GB copy 1073741824
Copying 5GB to copy
real    0m8.612s
user    0m0.011s
sys     0m4.536s
```

Finally, let's present the results from the cp(1) utility that comes with macOS Sierra:

```
$ time cp 100MB copy
real    0m0.274s
user    0m0.002s
sys     0m0.105s
$ time cp 1GB copy
real    0m2.735s
user    0m0.003s
sys     0m1.014s
$ time cp 5GB copy
real    0m12.199s
user    0m0.012s
sys     0m5.050s
```

The following figure shows a graph with the values of the real fields from the output of the time(1) utility for all the aforementioned results:

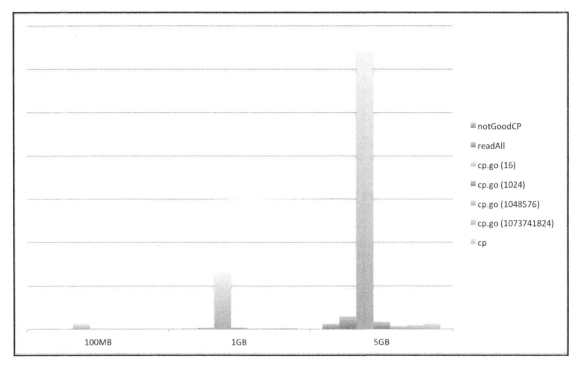

Benchmarking results for the various copy utilities

As you can see from the results, the cp(1) utility does a pretty good job. However, cp.go is more versatile because it allows you to define the size of the buffer. On the other hand, if you use cp.go with a small buffer size (16 bytes), then the entire process will be totally ruined! Additionally, it is interesting that readAll.go does a pretty decent job with relatively small files and it is slow only when copying the 5 GB file, which is not bad for such a small program—you can consider readAll.go as a quick and dirty solution!

Developing wc(1) in Go

The principal idea behind the code of the `wc.go` program is that you can read a text file line by line until there is nothing left to read. For each line you read, you find out the number of characters and the number of words it has. As you need to read your input line by line, the use of `bufio` is preferred instead of the plain `io` because it simplifies the code. However, trying to implement `wc.go` on your own using `io` would be a very educational exercise.

But first, you will see that the `wc(1)` utility generates the following output:

```
$ wc wc.go cp.go
      68       160      1231 wc.go
      45       112       755 cp.go
     113       272      1986 total
```

So, if `wc(1)` has to process more than one file, it automatically generates summary information.

In Chapter 9,*Goroutines – Basic Features*, you will learn how to create a version of `wc.go` using Go routines. However, the core functionality of both versions will be exactly the same!

Counting words

The trickiest part of the code implementation is word counting, which is implemented using regular expressions:

```
r := regexp.MustCompile("[^\\s]+")
for range r.FindAllString(line, -1) {
numberOfWords++
}
```

Here, the provided regular expression separates the words of a line based on whitespace characters in order to count them afterwards!

The wc.go code!

After this little introduction, it is time to see the Go code of `wc.go`, which will be presented in five parts. The first part is the expected preamble:

```
package main
```

```
import (
    "bufio"
    "flag"
    "fmt"
    "io"
    "os"
    "regexp"
)
```

The second part is the implementation of the countLines() function, which includes the core functionality of the program. Note that the name countLines() may have been a poor choice as countLines() also counts the words and the characters of a file:

```
func countLines(filename string) (int, int, int) {
    var err error
    var numberOfLines int
    var numberOfCharacters int
    var numberOfWords int
    numberOfLines = 0


    numberOfCharacters = 0
    numberOfWords = 0

    f, err := os.Open(filename)
    if err != nil {
        fmt.Printf("error opening file %s", err)
        os.Exit(1)
    }
    defer f.Close()

    r := bufio.NewReader(f)
    for {
        line, err := r.ReadString('\n')

        if err == io.EOF {
            break
        } else if err != nil {
            fmt.Printf("error reading file %s", err)
            break
        }

        numberOfLines++
        r := regexp.MustCompile("[^\\s]+")
        for range r.FindAllString(line, -1) {
            numberOfWords++
        }
        numberOfCharacters += len(line)
```

```
    }

    return numberOfLines, numberOfWords, numberOfCharacters
}
```

Lots of interesting things exist here. First of all, you can see the Go code presented in the previous section for counting the words of each line. Counting lines is easy because each time the `bufio` reader reads a new line, the value of the `numberOfLines` variable is increased by one. The `ReadString()` function tells the program to read until the first occurrence of `'\n'` in the input—multiple calls to `ReadString()` mean that you are reading a file line by line.

Next, you can see that the `countLines()` function returns three integer values. Lastly, counting characters is implemented with the help of the `len()` function that returns the number of characters in a given string, which in this case is the line that was read. The `for` loop terminates when you get the `io.EOF` error message, which signifies that there is nothing left to read from the input file.

The third part of `wc.go` starts with the beginning of the implementation of the `main()` function, which also includes the configuration of the `flag` package:

```
func main() {
    minusC := flag.Bool("c", false, "Characters")
    minusW := flag.Bool("w", false, "Words")
    minusL := flag.Bool("l", false, "Lines")

    flag.Parse()
    flags := flag.Args()

    if len(flags) == 0 {
        fmt.Printf("usage: wc <file1> [<file2> [... <fileN]]\n")
        os.Exit(1)
    }

    totalLines := 0
    totalWords := 0
    totalCharacters := 0
    printAll := false

    for _, filename := range flag.Args() {
```

The last `for` statement is for processing all the input files given to the program. The `wc.go` program supports three flags: the `-c` flag is for printing the character count, the `-w` flag is for printing the word count, and the `-l` flag is for printing the line count.

The fourth part is the following:

```
        numberOfLines, numberOfWords, numberOfCharacters :=
countLines(filename)

        totalLines = totalLines + numberOfLines
        totalWords = totalWords + numberOfWords
        totalCharacters = totalCharacters + numberOfCharacters

        if (*minusC && *minusW && *minusL) || (!*minusC && !*minusW &&
!*minusL) {
                fmt.Printf("%d", numberOfLines)
                fmt.Printf("\t%d", numberOfWords)
                fmt.Printf("\t%d", numberOfCharacters)
                fmt.Printf("\t%s\n", filename)
                printAll = true
                continue
        }

        if *minusL {
                fmt.Printf("%d", numberOfLines)
        }

        if *minusW {
                fmt.Printf("\t%d", numberOfWords)
        }

        if *minusC {
                fmt.Printf("\t%d", numberOfCharacters)
        }

        fmt.Printf("\t%s\n", filename)
    }
```

This part deals with printing the information on a per file basis depending on the command-line flags. As you can see, most of the Go code here is for handling the output according to the command-line flags.

The last part is the following:

```
    if (len(flags) != 1) && printAll {
            fmt.Printf("%d", totalLines)
            fmt.Printf("\t%d", totalWords)
            fmt.Printf("\t%d", totalCharacters)
            fmt.Println("\ttotal")
    return
    }
```

```
if (len(flags) != 1) && *minusL {
        fmt.Printf("%d", totalLines)
}

if (len(flags) != 1) && *minusW {
        fmt.Printf("\t%d", totalWords)
}

if (len(flags) != 1) && *minusC {
        fmt.Printf("\t%d", totalCharacters)
}

if len(flags) != 1 {
        fmt.Printf("\ttotal\n")
}
}
```

This is where you print the total number of lines, words, and characters read according to the flags of the program. Once again, most of the Go code here is for modifying the output according to the command-line flags.

Executing `wc.go` will generate the following output:

```
$ go build wc.go
$ ls -l wc
-rwxr-xr-x  1 mtsouk  staff  2264384 Apr 29 21:10 wc
$ ./wc wc.go sparse.go notGoodCP.go
120    280    2319   wc.go
44     98     697    sparse.go
27     61     418    notGoodCP.go
191    439    3434   total
$ ./wc -l wc.go sparse.go
120    wc.go
44     sparse.go
164    total
$ ./wc -w -l wc.go sparse.go
120    280    wc.go
44     98     sparse.go
164    378    total
```

There is a subtle point here: using Go source files as command-line arguments to the `go run wc.go` command will fail. This will happen because the compiler will try to compile the Go source files instead of treating them as command-line arguments to the `go run wc.go` command. The following output proves this:

```
$ go run wc.go sparse.go
# command-line-arguments
```

```
./sparse.go:11: main redeclared in this block
      previous declaration at ./wc.go:49
$ go run wc.go wc.go
package main: case-insensitive file name collision:
"wc.go" and "wc.go"
$ go run wc.go cp.go sparse.go
# command-line-arguments
./cp.go:35: main redeclared in this block
      previous declaration at ./wc.go:49
./sparse.go:11: main redeclared in this block
      previous declaration at ./cp.go:35
```

Additionally, trying to execute wc.go on a Linux system with Go version 1.3.3 will fail with the following error message:

```
$ go version
go version go1.3.3 linux/amd64
$ go run wc.go
# command-line-arguments
./wc.go:40: syntax error: unexpected range, expecting {
./wc.go:46: non-declaration statement outside function body
./wc.go:47: syntax error: unexpected }
```

Comparing the performance of wc.go and wc(1)

In this subsection, we will compare the performance of our version of wc(1) with the wc(1) version that comes with macOS Sierra 10.12.6. First, we will execute wc.go:

```
$ file wc
wc: Mach-O 64-bit executable x86_64
$ time ./wc *.data
672320        3361604       9413057       connections.data
269123        807369        4157790       diskSpace.data
672040        1344080       8376070       memory.data
1344533       2689066       5378132       pageFaults.data
269465        792715        4068250       uptime.data
3227481       8994834       31393299      total
real   0m17.467s
user   0m22.164s
sys    0m3.885s
```

Then, we will execute the macOS version of wc(1) to process the same files:

```
$ file `which wc`
/usr/bin/wc: Mach-O 64-bit executable x86_64
$ time wc *.data
672320 3361604 9413057 connections.data
269123  807369 4157790 diskSpace.data
672040 1344080 8376070 memory.data
1344533 2689066 5378132 pageFaults.data
269465  792715 4068250 uptime.data
3227481 8994834 31393299 total
real  0m0.086s
user  0m0.076s
sys   0m0.007s
```

Let's look at the good news here first; the two utilities generated exactly the same output, which means that our Go version of wc(1) works great and can process big text files!

Now, the bad news; wc.go is slow! It took wc(1) less than a second to process all five files, whereas it took wc.go nearly 18 seconds to perform the same task!

The general idea when developing software of any kind, on any platform, using any programming language, is that you should try to have a working version of it, which does not contain any bugs before trying to optimize it and not the other way round!

Reading a text file character by character

Although reading a text file character by character is not needed for the development of the wc(1) utility, it would be good to know how to implement it in Go. The name of the file will be charByChar.go and will be presented in four parts.

The first part is the following Go code:

```
package main

import (
    "bufio"
    "fmt"
    "io/ioutil"
    "os"
    "strings"
)
```

Although `charByChar.go` does not have many lines of Go code, it needs lots of Go standard packages, which is a naïve indication that the task it implements is not trivial. The second part is as follows:

```go
func main() {
    arguments := os.Args
    if len(arguments) == 1 {
        fmt.Println("Not enough arguments!")
        os.Exit(1)
    }
    input := arguments[1]
```

The third part is the following:

```go
    buf, err := ioutil.ReadFile(input)
    if err != nil {
        fmt.Println(err)
        os.Exit(1)
    }
```

The last part has the following Go code:

```go
    in := string(buf)
    s := bufio.NewScanner(strings.NewReader(in))
    s.Split(bufio.ScanRunes)

    for s.Scan() {
        fmt.Print(s.Text())
    }
}
```

Here, `ScanRunes` is a split function that returns each character (rune) as a token. Then, the call to `Scan()` allows us to process each character one by one. There also exist `ScanWords` and `ScanLines` for getting words and lines, respectively. If you use `fmt.Println(s.Text())` as the last statement in the program instead of `fmt.Print(s.Text())`, then each character will be printed on its own line and the task of the program will be more obvious.

Executing `charByChar.go` generates the following output:

```
$ go run charByChar.go test
package main
...
```

The wc(1) command can verify the correctness of the Go code of charByChar.go by comparing the input file with the output generated by charByChar.go:

```
$ go run charByChar.go test | wc
      32        54       439
$ wc test
      32        54       439 test
```

Doing some file editing!

This section will present a Go program that converts tab characters to space characters in files and vice versa! This is the job that is usually done by a text editor, but it is good to know how to perform it on your own.

The code will be saved in tabSpace.go and will be presented in four parts.

 Note that tabSpace.go reads text files line by line, but you can also develop a version that reads text file character by character.

In the current implementation, all the work is done with the help of regular expressions, pattern matching, and search and replace operations.

The first part is the expected preamble:

```go
package main

import (
    "bufio"
    "fmt"
    "io"
    "os"
    "path/filepath"
    "strings"
)
```

The second part contains the following Go code:

```go
func main() {
    if len(os.Args) != 3 {
        fmt.Printf("Usage: %s [-t|-s] filename!\n",
filepath.Base(os.Args[0]))
        os.Exit(1)
    }
    convertTabs := false
```

```go
convertSpaces := false
newLine := ""

option := os.Args[1]
filename := os.Args[2]
if option == "-t" {
        convertTabs = true
} else if option == "-s" {
        convertSpaces = true
} else {
        fmt.Println("Unknown option!")
        os.Exit(1)
}
```

The third part contains the following Go code:

```go
f, err := os.Open(filename)
if err != nil {
        fmt.Printf("error opening %s: %s", filename, err)
        os.Exit(1)
}
defer f.Close()

r := bufio.NewReader(f)
for {
        line, err := r.ReadString('\n')

        if err == io.EOF {
            break
        } else if err != nil {
            fmt.Printf("error reading file %s", err)
            os.Exit(1)
        }
```

The last part is the following:

```go
        if convertTabs == true {
            newLine = strings.Replace(line, "\t", "    ", -1)
        } else if convertSpaces == true {
            newLine = strings.Replace(line, "    ", "\t", -1)
        }

        fmt.Print(newLine)
    }
}
```

This part is where the magic happens using the appropriate `strings.Replace()` call. In its current implementation, each tab is replaced by four space characters and vice versa, but you can change that by modifying the Go code.

Once again, a big part of `tabSpace.go` relates to error handling because many strange things can happen when you try to open a file for reading!

According to the Unix philosophy, the output of `tabSpace.go` will be printed on the screen and will not be saved in a new text file. Using `tabSpace.go` with `wc(1)` can prove its correctness:

```
$ go run tabSpace.go -t cp.go > convert
$ wc convert cp.go
      76     192    1517 convert
      76     192    1286 cp.go
     152     384    2803 total
$ go run tabSpace.go -s convert | wc
      76     192    1286
```

Interprocess communication

Interprocess communication (IPC), putting it simply, is allowing Unix processes to talk to each other. Various techniques exist that allow processes and programs to talk to each other. The single most popular technique used in Unix systems is the pipe, which exists since the early Unix days. `Chapter 8`, *Processes and Signals*, will talk more about implementing Unix pipes in Go. Another form of IPC is Unix domain sockets, which will also be discussed in `Chapter 8`, *Processes and Signals*.

`Chapter 12`, *Network Programming*, will talk about another form of Interprocess communication, which is network sockets. Shared memory also exists, but Go is against the use of shared memory as a means of communication. `Chapter 9`, *Goroutines – Basic Features*, and `Chapter 10`, *Goroutines - Advanced Features*, will show various techniques that allow goroutines to communicate with others and share and exchange data.

Sparse files in Go

Large files that are created with the `os.Seek()` function may have holes in them and occupy fewer disk blocks than files with the same size, but without holes in them; such files are called sparse files. This section will develop a program that creates sparse files.

The Go code of `sparse.go` will be presented in three parts. The first part is the following:

```go
package main

import (
    "fmt"
    "log"
    "os"
    "path/filepath"
    "strconv"
)
```

The second part of `sparse.go` has the following Go code:

```go
func main() {
    if len(os.Args) != 3 {
        fmt.Printf("usage: %s SIZE filename\n", filepath.Base(os.Args[0]))
        os.Exit(1)
    }

    SIZE, _ := strconv.ParseInt(os.Args[1], 10, 64)
    filename := os.Args[2]

    _, err := os.Stat(filename)
    if err == nil {
        fmt.Printf("File %s already exists.\n", filename)
        os.Exit(1)
    }
```

The `strconv.ParseInt()` function is used for converting the command-line argument that defines the size of the sparse file from its string value to its integer value. Additionally, the `os.Stat()` call makes sure that you will not accidentally overwrite an existing file.

The last part is where the action takes place:

```go
    fd, err := os.Create(filename)
    if err != nil {
        log.Fatal("Failed to create output")
    }

    _, err = fd.Seek(SIZE-1, 0)
    if err != nil {
        fmt.Println(err)
        log.Fatal("Failed to seek")
    }

    _, err = fd.Write([]byte{0})
    if err != nil {
```

```
                fmt.Println(err)
                log.Fatal("Write operation failed")
        }

        err = fd.Close()
        if err != nil {
                fmt.Println(err)
                log.Fatal("Failed to close file")
        }
}
```

First, you try to create the desired sparse file using os.Create(). Then, you call fd.Seek() in order to make the file bigger without adding actual data. Lastly, you write a byte to it using fd.Write(). As you do not have anything more to do with the file, you call fd.Close() and you are done.

Executing sparse.go generates the following output:

```
$ go run sparse.go 1000 test
$ go run sparse.go 1000 test
File test already exists.
exit status 1
```

How can you tell whether a file is a sparse file or not? You will learn this in a while, but first, let's create some files:

```
$ go run sparse.go 100000 testSparse
$ dd if=/dev/urandom  bs=1 count=100000 of=noSparseDD
100000+0 records in
100000+0 records out
100000 bytes (100 kB) copied, 0.152511 s, 656 kB/s
$ dd if=/dev/urandom seek=100000 bs=1 count=0 of=sparseDD
0+0 records in
0+0 records out
0 bytes (0 B) copied, 0.000159399 s, 0.0 kB/s
$ ls -l noSparseDD sparseDD testSparse
-rw-r--r-- 1 mtsouk mtsouk 100000 Apr 29 21:43 noSparseDD
-rw-r--r-- 1 mtsouk mtsouk 100000 Apr 29 21:43 sparseDD
-rw-r--r-- 1 mtsouk mtsouk 100000 Apr 29 21:40 testSparse
```

Note that some Unix variants will not create sparse files—the first such Unix variant that comes to mind is macOS that uses the HFS filesystem. Therefore, for better results, you can execute all these commands on a Linux machine.

So, how can you tell if any of these three files is a sparse file or not? The -s flag of the ls(1) utility shows the number of filesystem blocks actually used by a file. So, the output of the ls -ls command allows you to detect if you are dealing with a sparse file or not:

```
$ ls -ls noSparseDD sparseDD testSparse
104 -rw-r--r-- 1 mtsouk mtsouk 100000 Apr 29 21:43 noSparseDD
  0 -rw-r--r-- 1 mtsouk mtsouk 100000 Apr 29 21:43 sparseDD
  8 -rw-r--r-- 1 mtsouk mtsouk 100000 Apr 29 21:40 testSparse
```

Now look at the first column of the output. The noSparseDD file, which was generated using the dd(1) utility, is not a sparse file. The sparseDD file is a sparse file generated using the dd(1) utility. Lastly, the testSparse is also a sparse file that was created using sparse.go.

Reading and writing data records

This section will teach you how to deal with writing and reading data records. What differentiates a record from other kinds of text data is that a record has a given structure with a specific number of fields—think of it as a row from a table in a relational database. Actually, records can be very useful for storing data in tables in case you want to develop your own database server in Go!

The Go code of records.go will save data in the CSV format and will be presented in four parts. The first part contains the following Go code:

```go
package main

import (
    "encoding/csv"
    "fmt"
    "os"
)
```

So, this is where you have to declare that you are going to read or write data in the CSV format. The second part is the following:

```
func main() {
    if len(os.Args) != 2 {
            fmt.Println("Need just one filename!")
            os.Exit(-1)
    }

    filename := os.Args[1]
    _, err := os.Stat(filename)
    if err == nil {
            fmt.Printf("File %s already exists.\n", filename)
            os.Exit(1)
    }
```

The third part of the program is as follows:

```
    output, err := os.Create(filename)
    if err != nil {
            fmt.Println(err)
            os.Exit(-1)
    }
    defer output.Close()

    inputData := [][]string{{"M", "T", "I."}, {"D", "T", "I."},
{"M", "T", "D."}, {"V", "T", "D."}, {"A", "T", "D."}}
    writer := csv.NewWriter(output)
    for _, record := range inputData {
            err := writer.Write(record)
            if err != nil {
                    fmt.Println(err)
                    os.Exit(-1)
            }
    }
    writer.Flush()
```

You should be familiar with the operations in this part; the biggest difference from what you have seen so far in this chapter is that the writer is from the csv package.

The last part of `records.go` has the following Go code:

```
f, err := os.Open(filename)
if err != nil {
        fmt.Println(err)
        return
}
defer f.Close()

reader := csv.NewReader(f)
reader.FieldsPerRecord = -1
allRecords, err := reader.ReadAll()
if err != nil {
        fmt.Println(err)
        os.Exit(1)
}

for _, rec := range allRecords {
        fmt.Printf("%s:%s:%s\n", rec[0], rec[1], rec[2])
}
}
```

The `reader` reads the entire file at once to make the whole operation faster. However, if you are dealing with huge data files, you might need to read smaller parts of the file each time until you have read the complete file. The used `reader` is from the `csv` package.

Executing `records.go` will create the following output:

```
$ go run records.go recordsDataFile
M:T:I.
D:T:I.
M:T:D.
V:T:D.
A:T:D.
$ ls -l recordsDataFile
-rw-r--r--  1 mtsouk  staff  35 May  2 19:20 recordsDataFile
```

The CSV file, which is named `recordsDataFile`, contains the following data:

```
$ cat recordsDataFile
M,T,I.
D,T,I.
M,T,D.
V,T,D.
A,T,D.
```

File locking in Go

There are times that you do not want any other child of the same process to change a file or even access it because you are changing its data and you do not want the other processes to read incomplete or inconsistent data. Although you will learn more about file locking and go routines in Chapter 9, *Goroutines – Basic Features* and Chapter 10, *Goroutines - Advanced Features*, this chapter will present a small Go example without a detailed explanation in order to give you an idea about how things work—you should wait until Chapter 9, *Goroutines – Basic Features* and Chapter 10, *Goroutines - Advanced Features*, to learn more.

The presented technique will use Mutex, which is a general synchronization mechanism. The Mutex lock will allow us to lock a file from within the same Go process. As a result, this technique has nothing to do with the use of the flock(2) system call.

 Various techniques exist for file locking. One of them is by creating an additional file that signifies that another program or process is using a given resource. The presented technique is more suitable for programs that use multiple go routines.

The file locking technique for writing will be illustrated in fileLocking.go, which will be presented in four parts. The first part is the following:

```go
package main

import (
    "fmt"
    "math/rand"
    "os"
    "sync"
    "time"
)

var mu sync.Mutex

func random(min, max int) int {
    return rand.Intn(max-min) + min
}
```

The second part is the following:

```go
func writeDataToFile(i int, file *os.File, w *sync.WaitGroup) {
    mu.Lock()
    time.Sleep(time.Duration(random(10, 1000)) * time.Millisecond)
    fmt.Fprintf(file, "From %d, writing %d\n", i, 2*i)
    fmt.Printf("Wrote from %d\n", i)
    w.Done()
mu.Unlock()
}
```

The locking of the file is done using the mu.Lock() statement and the unlocking of the file with the mu.Unlock() statement.

The third part is the following:

```go
func main() {
    if len(os.Args) != 2 {
        fmt.Println("Please provide one command line argument!")
        os.Exit(-1)
    }

    filename := os.Args[1]
    number := 3

    file, err := os.OpenFile(filename, os.O_CREATE|os.O_WRONLY|os.O_TRUNC,
0644)
    if err != nil {
        fmt.Println(err)
        os.Exit(1)
    }
```

The last part is the following Go code:

```go
    var w *sync.WaitGroup = new(sync.WaitGroup)
    w.Add(number)

    for r := 0; r < number; r++ {
        go writeDataToFile(r, file, w)
    }

    w.Wait()
}
```

Executing `fileLocking.go` will create the following output:

```
$ go run fileLocking.go 123
Wrote from 0
Wrote from 2
Wrote from 1
$ cat /tmp/swtag.log
From 0, writing 0
From 2, writing 4
From 1, writing 2
```

The correct version of `fileLocking.go` has a call to `mu.Unlock()` at the end of the
`writeDataToFile()` function, which allows all goroutines to use the file. If you remove
that call to `mu.Unlock()` from the `writeDataToFile()` function, and execute
`fileLocking.go`, you will get the following output:

```
$ go run fileLocking.go 123
Wrote from 2
fatal error: all goroutines are asleep - deadlock!
goroutine 1 [semacquire]:
sync.runtime_Semacquire(0xc42001024c)
        /usr/local/Cellar/go/1.8.1/libexec/src/runtime/sema.go:47 +0x34
sync.(*WaitGroup).Wait(0xc420010240)
        /usr/local/Cellar/go/1.8.1/libexec/src/sync/waitgroup.go:131 +0x7a
main.main()
        /Users/mtsouk/Desktop/goBook/ch/ch6/code/fileLocking.go:47 +0x172
goroutine 5 [semacquire]:
sync.runtime_SemacquireMutex(0x112dcbc)
        /usr/local/Cellar/go/1.8.1/libexec/src/runtime/sema.go:62 +0x34
sync.(*Mutex).Lock(0x112dcb8)
        /usr/local/Cellar/go/1.8.1/libexec/src/sync/mutex.go:87 +0x9d
main.writeDataToFile(0x0, 0xc42000c028, 0xc420010240)
        /Users/mtsouk/Desktop/goBook/ch/ch6/code/fileLocking.go:18 +0x3f
created by main.main
        /Users/mtsouk/Desktop/goBook/ch/ch6/code/fileLocking.go:44 +0x151
goroutine 6 [semacquire]:
sync.runtime_SemacquireMutex(0x112dcbc)
        /usr/local/Cellar/go/1.8.1/libexec/src/runtime/sema.go:62 +0x34
sync.(*Mutex).Lock(0x112dcb8)
        /usr/local/Cellar/go/1.8.1/libexec/src/sync/mutex.go:87 +0x9d
main.writeDataToFile(0x1, 0xc42000c028, 0xc420010240)
        /Users/mtsouk/Desktop/goBook/ch/ch6/code/fileLocking.go:18 +0x3f
created by main.main
        /Users/mtsouk/Desktop/goBook/ch/ch6/code/fileLocking.go:44 +0x151
exit status 2
$ cat 123
From 2, writing 4
```

The reason for getting this output is that apart from the first goroutine that will be able to execute the mu.Lock() statement, the rest of them cannot get Mutex. Therefore, they cannot write to the file, which means that they will never finish their jobs and wait forever, which is the reason that Go is generating the aforementioned error messages.

If you do not completely understand this example, you should wait until Chapter 9, *Goroutines – Basic Features* and Chapter 10, *Goroutines - Advanced Features*.

A simplified Go version of the dd utility

The dd(1) tool can do many things, but this section will implement a small part of its functionality. Our version of dd(1) will include support for two command-line flags: one for specifying the block size in bytes (-bs) and the other for specifying the total number of blocks that will be written (-count). Multiplying these two values will give you the size of the generated file in bytes.

The Go code is saved as ddGo.go and will be presented to you in four parts. The first part is the expected preamble:

```
package main

import (
    "flag"
    "fmt"
    "math/rand"
    "os"
    "time"
)
```

The second part contains the Go code of two functions:

```
func random(min, max int) int {
    return rand.Intn(max-min) + min
}

func createBytes(buf *[]byte, count int) {
    if count == 0 {
        return
    }
    for i := 0; i < count; i++ {
        intByte := byte(random(0, 9))
        *buf = append(*buf, intByte)
    }
}
```

The first function is for getting random numbers and the second one is for creating a byte slice with the desired size filled with random numbers.

The third part of ddGo.go is the following:

```go
func main() {
    minusBS := flag.Int("bs", 0, "Block Size")
    minusCOUNT := flag.Int("count", 0, "Counter")
    flag.Parse()
    flags := flag.Args()

    if len(flags) == 0 {
        fmt.Println("Not enough arguments!")
        os.Exit(-1)
    }

    if *minusBS < 0 || *minusCOUNT < 0 {
        fmt.Println("Count or/and Byte Size < 0!")
        os.Exit(-1)
    }

    filename := flags[0]
    rand.Seed(time.Now().Unix())

    _, err := os.Stat(filename)
    if err == nil {
        fmt.Printf("File %s already exists.\n", filename)
        os.Exit(1)
    }

    destination, err := os.Create(filename)
    if err != nil {
        fmt.Println("os.Create:", err)
        os.Exit(1)
    }
}
```

Here, you mainly deal with the command-line arguments of the program.

The last part is the following:

```
buf := make([]byte, *minusBS)
buf = nil
for i := 0; i < *minusCOUNT; i++ {
    createBytes(&buf, *minusBS)
    if _, err := destination.Write(buf); err != nil {
        fmt.Println(err)
        os.Exit(-1)
    }
    buf = nil
}
}
```

The reason for emptying the `buf` byte slice each time you want to call `createBytes()` is that you do not want the `buf` byte slice to get bigger and bigger each time you call the `createBytes()` function. This happens because the `append()` function adds data at the end of a slice without touching the existing data.

In the first version of `ddGo.go` that I wrote, I forgot to empty the `buf` byte slice before each call to `createBytes()`. Consequently, the generated files were bigger than expected! It took me a while and a couple of `fmt.Println(buf)` statements to find out the reason for this unforeseen behavior!

The execution of `ddGo.go` will generate the files you want quite fast:

```
$ time go run ddGo.go -bs=10000 -count=5000 test3
real    0m1.655s
user    0m1.576s
sys     0m0.104s
$ ls -l test3
-rw-r--r-- 1 mtsouk  staff  50000000 May  6 15:27 test3
```

Additionally, the use of random numbers makes the generated files of the same size different from each other:

```
$ go run ddGo.go -bs=100 -count=50 test1
$ go run ddGo.go -bs=100 -count=50 test2
$ ls -l test1 test2
-rw-r--r-- 1 mtsouk  staff  5000 May  6 15:26 test1
-rw-r--r-- 1 mtsouk  staff  5000 May  6 15:26 test2
$ diff test1 test2
Binary files test1 and test2 differ
```

Exercises

1. Visit the documentation page of the `bufio` package that can be found at `https://golang.org/pkg/bufio/`.
2. Visit the documentation of the `io` package at `https://golang.org/pkg/io/`.
3. Try to make `wc.go` faster.
4. Implement the functionality of `tabSpace.go`, but try to read your input text files character by character instead of line by line.
5. Change the code of `tabSpace.go` in order to be able to get the number of spaces that will replace a tab as a command-line argument.
6. Learn more information about the little endian and the big endian representations.

Summary

In this chapter, we talked about file input and output in Go. Among other things, we developed Go versions of the `wc(1)`, `dd(1)`, and `cp(1)` Unix command-line utilities while learning more about the `io` and `bufio` packages of the Go standard library, which allow you to read from and write to files.

In the next chapter, we will talk about another important subject, which is the Go way of working with the system files of a Unix machine. Additionally, you will learn how to read and change the Unix file permissions as well as how to find the owner and the group of a file. Also, we will talk about log files and how you can use pattern matching to acquire the information you want from log files.

7
Working with System Files

In the previous chapter, we talked about file input and output in Go, and created Go versions of the wc(1), dd(1), and cp(1) utilities.

While the main subject of this chapter is Unix system files and log files, you will also learn many other things, including pattern matching, file permissions, working with users and groups, and dealing with dates and times in Go. For all these subjects, you will see handy Go codes that will explain the presented techniques, and these can be used in your own Go programs without requiring too many changes.

So, this chapter will talk about the following topics:

- Appending data to an existing file
- Reading a file and altering each one of its lines
- Regular expressions and pattern matching in Go
- Sending information to Unix log files
- Working with dates and times in Go
- Working with Unix file permissions
- Working with user IDs and group IDs
- Learning more information about files and directories
- Processing log files and extracting useful information from them
- Generating difficult to guess passwords using random numbers

Which files are considered system files?

Each Unix operation system contains files that are responsible for the configuration of the system as well as its various services. Most of these files are located in the /etc directory. I also like to consider log files as system files, although some people might disagree. Usually, most system log files can be found inside /var/log. However, the log files of the Apache and the nginx web server can be found elsewhere, depending on their configuration.

Logging in Go

The log package provides a general way to log information on your Unix machine, whereas the log/syslog Go package allows you to send information to the system logging service using the logging level and the logging facility you want. Also, the time package can help you work with dates and times.

Putting data at the end of a file

As discussed in Chapter 6, *File Input and Output*, in this chapter, we will talk about opening a file for writing without destroying its existing data.

The Go program that will illustrate the technique, appendData.go, will accept two command-line arguments—the message you want to append and the name of the file that will store the text. This program will be presented in three parts.

The first part of appendData.go contains the following Go code:

```
package main

import (
    "fmt"
    "os"
    "path/filepath"
)
```

As expected, the first part of the program contains the Go packages that will be used in the program.

The second part is the following:

```
func main() {
    arguments := os.Args
    if len(arguments) != 3 {
        fmt.Printf("usage: %s message filename\n",
filepath.Base(arguments[0]))
        os.Exit(1)
    }
    message := arguments[1]
    filename := arguments[2]

    f, err := os.OpenFile(filename,
os.O_RDWR|os.O_APPEND|os.O_CREATE, 0660)
```

The desired task is done by the os.O_APPEND flag of the os.OpenFile() function that tells Go to write at the end of the file. Additionally, the os.O_CREATE flag will make os.OpenFile() to create the file if it does not exist, which is pretty handy because it saves you from having to write Go code that tests whether the file is already there or not.

The last part of the program is the following:

```
    if err != nil {
        fmt.Println(err)
        os.Exit(-1)
    }
    defer f.Close()

    fmt.Fprintf(f, "%s\n", message)
}
```

The fmt.Fprintf() function is used here in order to write the message to the file as plain text. As you can see, appendData.go is a relatively small Go program that does not contain any surprises.

Executing appendData.go will create no output, but it will do its job, as you can see from the output of the cat(1) utility before and after the execution of appendData.go:

```
$ cat test
[test]: test
: test
$ go run appendData.go test test
$ cat test
[test]: test
: test
test
```

Altering existing data

This section will teach you how to modify the contents of a file. The program that will be developed does a pretty convenient job: it adds a line number in front of each line of a text file. This means that you will need to read the input file line by line, keep a variable that will hold the line number value, and save it using the original name. Additionally, the initial value of the variable that holds the line number value can be defined when you start the program. The name of the Go program will be insertLineNumber.go, and it will be presented in four parts.

First, you will see the expected preamble:

```
package main

import (
    "flag"
    "fmt"
    "io/ioutil"
    "os"
    "strings"
)
```

The second part is mainly the configuration of the flag package:

```
func main() {
    minusINIT := flag.Int("init", 1, "Initial Value")
    flag.Parse()
    flags := flag.Args()

    if len(flags) == 0 {
        fmt.Printf("usage: insertLineNumber <files>\n")
        os.Exit(1)
    }

    lineNumber := *minusINIT
    for _, filename := range flags {
        fmt.Println("Processing:", filename)
```

The lineNumber variable is initiated by the value of the minusINIT flag. Additionally, the utility can process multiple files using a for loop.

The third part of the program is the following:

```
input, err := ioutil.ReadFile(filename)
if err != nil {
        fmt.Println(err)
        os.Exit(-1)
}


lines := strings.Split(string(input), "\n")
```

As you can see, insertLineNumber.go reads its input file all at once using ioutil.ReadFile(), which might not be so efficient when processing huge text files. However, with today's computers, this should not be a problem. A better approach would be to read the input file line by line, write each altered line to a temporary file, and then replace the original file with the temporary one.

The last part of the utility is the following:

```
for i, line := range lines {
        lines[i] = fmt.Sprintf("%d: %s ", lineNumber, line)
        lineNumber = lineNumber + 1
}

lines[len(lines)-1] = ""
output := strings.Join(lines, "\n")
err = ioutil.WriteFile(filename, []byte(output), 0644)
if err != nil {
        fmt.Println(err)
        os.Exit(-1)
}
    }
    fmt.Println("Processed", lineNumber-*minusINIT, "lines!")
}
```

As the range loop will introduce an extra line at the end of the file, you have to delete the last line in the lines slice using the lines[len(lines)-1] = "" statement, which means that the program assumes that all the files it processes end with a new line. If your text files do not do that, then you might want to change the code of insertLineNumber.go or add a new line at the end of your text files.

The running of `insertLineNumber.go` generates no visible output apart from the filename of each file it processes and the total number of processed lines. However, you can see the results of its execution by looking at the contents of the files you processed:

```
$ cat test
a
b
$ go run insertLineNumber.go -init=10 test
Processing: test
Processed 4 lines!
$ cat test
10: a
11:
12: b
```

If you try to process the same input file multiple times, as in the following example, an interesting thing will happen:

```
$ cat test
a
b
$ go run insertLineNumber.go -init=10 test test test
Processing: test
Processing: test
Processing: test
Processed 12 lines!
$ cat test
18: 14: 10: a
19: 15: 11:
20: 16: 12: b
```

About log files

This part will teach you how to send information from a Go program to the logging service and therefore to system log files. Despite the obvious fact that it is good to keep information stored, log files are necessary for server processes because there is no other way for a server process to send information to the outside world, as it has no Terminal to send any output.

Log files are important and you should not underestimate the value of the information stored in them. Log files should be the first place to look for help when strange things start happening on a Unix machine.

Generally speaking, using a log file is better than displaying the output on the screen for two reasons: first, the output does not get lost, as it is stored on a file, and second, you can search and process log files using Unix tools, such as grep(1), awk(1), and sed(1), which cannot be done when messages are printed on a Terminal window.

About logging

All Unix machines have a separate server process for logging log files. On macOS machines, the name of the process is syslogd(8). On the other hand, most Linux machines use rsyslogd(8), which is an improved and more reliable version of syslogd(8), which was the original Unix system utility for message logging.

However, despite the Unix variant you are using, or the name of the server process used for logging, logging works the same way on every Unix machine and therefore does not affect the Go code that you will write.

The best way to watch one or more log files is with the help of the tail(1) utility, followed by the -f flag and the name of the log file you want to watch. The -f flag tells tail(1) to wait for additional data. You will need to terminate such a tail(1) command by pressing *Ctrl + C*.

Logging facilities

A logging facility is like a category used for logging information. The value of the logging facility part can be any one of *auth, authpriv, cron, daemon, kern, lpr, mail, mark, news, syslog, user, UUCP, local0, local1, local2, local3, local4, local5, local6,* and *local7*; this is defined inside /etc/syslog.conf, /etc/rsyslog.conf, or another appropriate file depending on the server process used for system logging on your Unix machine. This means that if a logging facility is not defined and therefore handled, the log messages you send to it might get lost.

Logging levels

A **logging level** or **priority** is a value that specifies the severity of the log entry. There exist various logging levels including *debug, info, notice, warning, err, crit, alert,* and *emerg,* in reverse order of severity.

Look at the /etc/rsyslog.conf file of a Linux machine to learn more about how to control logging facilities and logging levels.

The syslog Go package

This subsection will present a Go program that works on all Unix machines and sends data to the logging service in various ways. The name of the program is useSyslog.go, and it will be presented in four parts.

First, you will see the expected preamble:

```
package main

import (
    "fmt"
    "log"
    "log/syslog"
    "os"
    "path/filepath"
)
```

You have to use the log package for logging and the log/syslog package for defining the logging facility and the logging level of your program.

The second part is the following:

```
func main() {
    programName := filepath.Base(os.Args[0])
    sysLog, e := syslog.New(syslog.LOG_INFO|syslog.LOG_LOCAL7, programName)
    if e != nil {
        log.Fatal(e)
    }
    sysLog.Crit("Crit: Logging in Go!")
```

The syslog.New() function call, which returns a writer, tells your program where to direct all log messages. The good thing is that you already know how to use a writer!

 Note that the developer should define both the priority and the facility that a program uses.

However, even with a defined priority and facility, the log/syslog package allows you to send direct log messages to other priorities using functions such as sysLog.Crit().

The third part of the program is the following:

```
    sysLog, e = syslog.New(syslog.LOG_ALERT|syslog.LOG_LOCAL7, "Some
program!")
    if e != nil {
        log.Fatal(sysLog)
    }
sysLog.Emerg("Emerg: Logging in Go!")
```

This part shows that you can call `syslog.New()` multiple times in the same program. Once again, calling the `Emerg()` function allows you to bypass what was defined by the `syslog.New()` function.

The last part is the following:

```
    fmt.Fprintf(sysLog, "log.Print: Logging in Go!")
}
```

This is the only call that uses the logging priority and the logging facility that were defined by `syslog.New()`, by directly writing to the `sysLog` writer.

Executing `useLog.go` will generate some output on the screen, but it will also write data to the appropriate log files. On a macOS Sierra or a Mac OS X machine, you will see the following:

```
$ go run useSyslog.go
Broadcast Message from _iconservices@iMac.local
        (no tty) at 18:01 EEST...
Emerg: Logging in Go!
$ grep "Logging in Go" /var/log/* 2>/dev/null
/var/log/system.log:May 19 18:01:31 iMac useSyslog[22608]: Crit: Logging in
Go!
/var/log/system.log:May 19 18:01:31 iMac Some program![22608]: Emerg:
Logging in Go!
/var/log/system.log:May 19 18:01:31 iMac Some program![22608]: log.Print:
Logging in Go!
```

On a Debian Linux machine, you will see the following results:

```
$ go run useSyslog.go
Message from syslogd@mail at May 19 18:03:00 ...
Some program![1688]: Emerg: Logging in Go!
$
Broadcast message from systemd-journald@mail (Fri 2017-05-19 18:03:00
EEST):
useSyslog[1688]: Some program![1688]: Emerg: Logging in Go!
$ tail -5 /var/log/syslog
May 19 18:03:00 mail useSyslog[1688]: Crit: Logging in Go!
May 19 18:03:00 mail Some program![1688]: Emerg: Logging in Go!
May 19 18:03:00 mail Some program![1688]: log.Print: Logging in Go!
$ grep "Logging in Go" /var/log/* 2>/dev/null
/var/log/cisco.log:May 19 18:03:00 mail useSyslog[1688]: Crit: Logging in
Go!
/var/log/cisco.log:May 19 18:03:00 mail Some program![1688]: Emerg: Logging
in Go!
/var/log/cisco.log:May 19 18:03:00 mail Some program![1688]: log.Print:
Logging in Go!
/var/log/syslog:May 19 18:03:00 mail useSyslog[1688]: Crit: Logging in Go!
/var/log/syslog:May 19 18:03:00 mail Some program![1688]: Emerg: Logging in
Go!
/var/log/syslog:May 19 18:03:00 mail Some program![1688]: log.Print:
Logging in Go!
```

The output from the two machines shows that the Linux machine has a different `syslog` configuration, which is the reason that the messages from `useLog.go` were also written to `/var/log/cisco.log`.

However, your main concern should not be whether the log messages will be written to too many files or not; rather if you will be able to find them or not!

Processing log files

This subsection will process a log file that contains client IP addresses in order to create a summary of them. The name of the Go file will be `countIP.go`, and it will be presented in four parts. Note that `countIP.go` requires two parameters: the name of the log file and the field that contains the desired information. As `countIP.go` does not check whether the given field contains an IP address or not, it can also be used for other kinds of data if you remove some of its code.

First, you will see the expected preamble of the program:

```
package main

import (
    "bufio"
    "flag"
    "fmt"
    "io"
    "net"
    "os"
    "path/filepath"
    "strings"
)
```

The second part comes with the following Go code, which is the beginning of the implementation of the `main()` function:

```
func main() {
    minusCOL := flag.Int("COL", 1, "Column")
    flag.Parse()
    flags := flag.Args()

    if len(flags) == 0 {
            fmt.Printf("usage: %s <file1> [<file2> [... <fileN]]\n",
filepath.Base(os.Args[0]))
            os.Exit(1)
    }

    column := *minusCOL
    if column < 0 {
            fmt.Println("Invalid Column number!")
            os.Exit(1)
    }
```

The `countIP.go` utility uses the `flag` package and can process multiple files.

The third part of the program is the following:

```
    myIPs := make(map[string]int)
    for _, filename := range flags {
            fmt.Println("\t\t", filename)
            f, err := os.Open(filename)
            if err != nil {
                    fmt.Printf("error opening file %s\n", err)
                    continue
            }
            defer f.Close()
```

```
        r := bufio.NewReader(f)
        for {
                line, err := r.ReadString('\n')

                if err == io.EOF {
                        break
                } else if err != nil {
                        fmt.Printf("error reading file %s", err)
                        continue
                }
```

Each input file is read line by line, whereas the myIPs map variable is used for holding the count of each IP address.

The last part of countIP.go is as follows:

```
                data := strings.Fields(line)
                ip := data[column-1]
                trial := net.ParseIP(ip)
                if trial.To4() == nil {
                        continue
                }

                _, ok := myIPs[ip]
                if ok {
                        myIPs[ip] = myIPs[ip] + 1
                } else {
                        myIPs[ip] = 1
                }
        }
}

for key, _ := range myIPs {
        fmt.Printf("%s %d\n", key, myIPs[key])
}
}
```

Here is where the magic happens: first, you extract the desired field from the working line. Then, you use the net.ParseIP() function to make sure that you are dealing with a valid IP address—if you want the program to process other kinds of data, you should delete the Go code that uses the net.ParseIP() function. After that, you update the contents of the myIPs map based on whether the current IP address can be found in the map or not—you saw that code back in Chapter 2, *Writing Programs in Go*. Finally, you print the contents of the myIPs map on the screen, and you are done!

Executing `countIP.go` generates the following output:

```
$ go run countIP.go /tmp/log.1 /tmp/log.2
             /tmp/log.1
             /tmp/log.2
164.132.161.85 4
66.102.8.135 17
5.248.196.10 15
180.76.15.10 12
66.249.69.40 142
51.255.65.35 7
95.158.53.56 1
64.183.178.218 31
$ go run countIP.go /tmp/log.1 /tmp/log.2 | wc
    1297    2592    21266
```

However, it would be better if the output was sorted by the count associated with each IP address, which you can easily do with the help of the `sort(1)` Unix utility:

```
$ go run countIP.go /tmp/log.1 /tmp/log.2 | sort -rn -k2
45.55.38.245 979
159.203.126.63 976
130.193.51.27 698
5.9.63.149 370
77.121.238.13 340
46.4.116.197 308
51.254.103.60 302
51.255.194.31 277
195.74.244.47 201
61.14.225.57 179
69.30.198.242 152
66.249.69.40 142
2.86.9.124 140
2.86.27.46 127
66.249.69.18 125
```

If you want the first 10 IP addresses, you can filter the previous output with the head(1) utility as follows:

```
$ go run countIP.go /tmp/log.1 /tmp/log.2 | sort -rn -k2 | head
45.55.38.245 979
159.203.126.63 976
130.193.51.27 698
5.9.63.149 370
77.121.238.13 340
46.4.116.197 308
51.254.103.60 302
51.255.194.31 277
195.74.244.47 201
61.14.225.57 179
```

File permissions revisited

There are times that we need to find detailed information about the Unix permissions of a file. The filePerm.go Go utility will teach you how to read the Unix file permissions of a file or a directory and print them as a binary number, a decimal number, and a string. The program will be presented in three parts. The first part is the following:

```go
package main

import (
    "fmt"
    "os"
    "path/filepath"
)
```

The second part is as follows:

```go
func tripletToBinary(triplet string) string {
    if triplet == "rwx" {
        return "111"
    }
    if triplet == "-wx" {
        return "011"
    }
    if triplet == "--x" {
        return "001"
    }
    if triplet == "---" {
        return "000"
    }
    if triplet == "r-x" {
```

```
                return "101"
        }
        if triplet == "r--" {
                return "100"
        }
        if triplet == "--x" {
                return "001"
        }
        if triplet == "rw-" {
                return "110"
        }
        if triplet == "-w-" {
                return "010"
        }
        return "unknown"
}

func convertToBinary(permissions string) string {
        binaryPermissions := permissions[1:]
        p1 := binaryPermissions[0:3]
        p2 := binaryPermissions[3:6]
        p3 := binaryPermissions[6:9]
        return tripletToBinary(p1) + tripletToBinary(p2) + tripletToBinary(p3)
}
```

Here, you implement two functions that will help you convert a string with nine characters that hold the permissions of a file into a binary number. As an example, the `rwxr-x---` string will be converted to `111101000`. The initial string is extracted from the `os.Stat()` function call.

The last part contains the following Go code:

```
func main() {
        arguments := os.Args
        if len(arguments) == 1 {
                fmt.Printf("usage: %s filename\n", filepath.Base(arguments[0]))
                os.Exit(1)
        }

        filename := arguments[1]
        info, _ := os.Stat(filename)
        mode := info.Mode()

        fmt.Println(filename, "mode is", mode)
        fmt.Println("As string is", mode.String()[1:10])
        fmt.Println("As binary is", convertToBinary(mode.String()))
}
```

Executing `filePerm.go` will generate the following output:

```
$ go run filePerm.go .
. mode is drwxr-xr-x
As string is rwxr-xr-x
As binary is 111101101
$ go run filePerm.go /tmp/swtag.log
/tmp/swtag.log mode is -rw-rw-rw-
As string is rw-rw-rw-
As binary is 110110110
```

Changing file permissions

This section will explain how to change the Unix permissions of a file or a directory to the desired value; however, it will not deal with the sticky bit, the set user ID bit, or the set group ID bit—not because they are difficult to implement, but because you usually do not need any of these when dealing with system files.

The name of the utility will be `setFilePerm.go`, and it will be presented in four parts. The new file permissions will be given as a string with nine characters such as `rwxrw-rw-`.

The first part of `setFilePerm.go` contains the expected preamble Go code:

```go
package main

import (
    "fmt"
    "os"
    "path/filepath"
    "strconv"
)
```

The second part is the implementation of the `tripletToBinary()` function that you saw in the previous section:

```go
func tripletToBinary(triplet string) string {
    if triplet == "rwx" {
        return "111"
    }
    if triplet == "-wx" {
        return "011"
    }
    if triplet == "--x" {
        return "001"
    }
    if triplet == "---" {
```

```
            return "000"
    }
    if triplet == "r-x" {
            return "101"
    }
    if triplet == "r--" {
            return "100"
    }
    if triplet == "--x" {
            return "001"
    }
    if triplet == "rw-" {
            return "110"
    }
    if triplet == "-w-" {
            return "010"
    }
    return "unknown"
}
```

The third part contains the following Go code:

```
func convertToBinary(permissions string) string {
    p1 := permissions[0:3]
    p2 := permissions[3:6]
    p3 := permissions[6:9]

    p1 = tripletToBinary(p1)
    p2 = tripletToBinary(p2)
    p3 = tripletToBinary(p3)

    p1Int, _ := strconv.ParseInt(p1, 2, 64)
    p2Int, _ := strconv.ParseInt(p2, 2, 64)
    p3Int, _ := strconv.ParseInt(p3, 2, 64)

    returnValue := p1Int*100 + p2Int*10 + p3Int
    tempReturnValue := int(returnValue)
    returnString := "0" + strconv.Itoa(tempReturnValue)
    return returnString
}
```

Here, the name of the function is misleading, as it does not return a binary number—this is my fault.

The last part contains the following Go code:

```go
func main() {
    arguments := os.Args
    if len(arguments) != 3 {
        fmt.Printf("usage: %s filename permissions\n",
filepath.Base(arguments[0]))
        os.Exit(1)
    }

    filename, _ := filepath.EvalSymlinks(arguments[1])
    permissions := arguments[2]
    if len(permissions) != 9 {
        fmt.Println("Permissions should be 9 characters
(rwxrwxrwx):", permissions)
        os.Exit(-1)
    }

    bin := convertToBinary(permissions)
    newPerms, _ := strconv.ParseUint(bin, 0, 32)
    newMode := os.FileMode(newPerms)
    os.Chmod(filename, newMode)
}
```

Here, you get the return value of `convertToBinary()` and convert it to an `os.FileMode()` variable in order to use it with the `os.Chmod()` function.

Running `setFilePerm.go` generates the following results:

```
$ go run setFilePerm.go /tmp/swtag.log rwxrwxrwx
$ ls -l /tmp/swtag.log
-rwxrwxrwx  1 mtsouk  wheel  7066 May 22 19:17 /tmp/swtag.log
$ go run setFilePerm.go /tmp/swtag.log rwxrwx---
$ ls -l /tmp/swtag.log
-rwxrwx---  1 mtsouk  wheel  7066 May 22 19:17 /tmp/swtag.log
```

Finding other kinds of information about files

The most important information about a Unix file is its owner and its group, and this section will teach you how to find both of them using Go code. The `findOG.go` utility accepts a list of files as its command-line arguments and returns the owner and the group of each one of them. Its Go code will be presented in three parts.

The first part is the following:

```
package main

import (
    "fmt"
    "os"
    "path/filepath"
    "syscall"
)
```

The second part is the following:

```
func main() {
    arguments := os.Args
    if len(arguments) == 1 {
        fmt.Printf("usage: %s <files>\n", filepath.Base(arguments[0]))
        os.Exit(1)
    }

    for _, filename := range arguments[1:] {
        fileInfo, err := os.Stat(filename)
        if err != nil {
            fmt.Println(err)
            continue
        }
```

In this part, you make a call to the `os.Stat()` function to make sure that the file you want to process exists.

The last part of `findOG.go` comes with the following Go code:

```
        fmt.Printf("%+v\n", fileInfo.Sys())
        fmt.Println(fileInfo.Sys().(*syscall.Stat_t).Uid)
        fmt.Println(fileInfo.Sys().(*syscall.Stat_t).Gid)
    }
}
```

Yes, this is the most cryptic code you have seen so far in this book that uses the return value of `os.Stat()` to extract the desired information. Additionally, it is neither portable, which means that it might not work on your Unix variant, nor you can be sure that it will continue to work in forthcoming versions of Go!

Sometimes tasks that look easy might take you more time than expected. One of these tasks is the `findOG.go` program. This mainly happens because Go does not have an easy and portable way to find out the owner and the group of a file. Hopefully, this will change in the future.

Executing `findOG.go` on macOS Sierra or Mac OS X will generate the following output:

```
$ go run findOG.go /tmp/swtag.log
&{Dev:16777218 Mode:33206 Nlink:1 Ino:50547755 Uid:501 Gid:0 Rdev:0
Pad_cgo_0:[0 0 0 0] Atimespec:{Sec:1495297106 Nsec:0}
Mtimespec:{Sec:1495297106 Nsec:0} Ctimespec:{Sec:1495297106 Nsec:0}
Birthtimespec:{Sec:1495044975 Nsec:0} Size:2586 Blocks:8 Blksize:4096
Flags:0 Gen:0 Lspare:0 Qspare:[0 0]}
501
0
$ ls -l /tmp/swtag.log
-rw-rw-rw-  1 mtsouk  wheel  2586 May 20 19:18 /tmp/swtag.log
$ grep wheel /etc/group
wheel:*:0:root
```

Here, you can see that the `fileInfo.Sys()` call returns a plethora of information from the file in a somehow puzzling format—the information is analogous to the information from a C call to `stat(2)`. The first line of output is the contents of the `os.Stat.Sys()` call, whereas the second line is the user ID (`501`) of the owner of the file and the third line is the group ID (`0`) of the owner of the file.

Executing `findOG.go` on a Debian Linux machine will generate the following output:

```
$ go run findOG.go /home/mtsouk/connections.data
&{Dev:2048 Ino:1196167 Nlink:1 Mode:33188 Uid:1000 Gid:1000 X__pad0:0
Rdev:0 Size:9626800 Blksize:4096 Blocks:18840 Atim:{Sec:1412623801 Nsec:0}
Mtim:{Sec:1495307521 Nsec:929812185} Ctim:{Sec:1495307521 Nsec:929812185}
X__unused:[0 0 0]}
1000
1000
$ ls -l /home/mtsouk/connections.data
-rw-r--r-- 1 mtsouk mtsouk 9626800 May 20 22:12
/home/mtsouk/connections.data
code$ grep ^mtsouk /etc/group
mtsouk:x:1000:
```

The good news here is that `findOG.go` worked on both macOS Sierra and Debian Linux, even though macOS Sierra was using Go version 1.8.1 and Debian Linux was using Go version 1.3.3!

Most of the presented Go code will be used later in this chapter for the implementation of the `userFiles.go` utility.

More pattern matching examples

This section will present regular expressions that match more difficult patterns than the ones you have seen so far in this book. Just remember that regular expressions and pattern matching are practical subjects that you should learn by experimenting and sometimes failing, not by reading about them.

 If you are very careful with regular expressions in Go, you can easily read or change almost all the system files of a Unix system that are in plain text format. Just be extra careful when modifying system files!

A simple pattern matching example

The example of this section will improve the functionality of the countIP.go utility, by developing a program that automatically detects the field with the IP address; therefore, it will not require the user to define the field of each log entry that contains the IP address. To make things simpler, the created program will only process the first IP address of each line—findIP.go takes a single command-line argument, which is the name of the log file you want to process. The program will be presented in four parts.

The first part of findIP.go is the following:

```
package main

import (
    "bufio"
    "fmt"
    "io"
    "net"
    "os"
    "path/filepath"
    "regexp"
)
```

The second part is where most of the magic happens with the help of a function:

```
func findIP(input string) string {
    partIP := "(25[0-5]|2[0-4][0-9]|1[0-9][0-9]|[1-9]?[0-9])"
    grammar := partIP + "\\." + partIP + "\\." + partIP + "\\." + partIP
    matchMe := regexp.MustCompile(grammar)
    return matchMe.FindString(input)
}
```

The regular expression is pretty complex considering that we just want to match four decimal numbers in the 0-255 range that are separated by dots, which mainly shows that regular expressions can be pretty complicated when you want to be methodical.

But let me explain this to you in more detail. An IP address has four parts separated by dots. Each one of these parts can have a value between 0 and 255, which means that number 257 is not an acceptable value—this is the main reason that the regular expression is so complex. The first case is for numbers between 250 and 255. The second case is for numbers between 200 and 249, and the third case is for numbers between 100 and 199. The last case is for catching values between 0 and 99.

The third part of `findIP.go` is the following:

```
func main() {
    if len(os.Args) != 2 {
        fmt.Printf("usage: %s logFile\n", filepath.Base(os.Args[0]))
        os.Exit(1)
    }
    filename := os.Args[1]

    f, err := os.Open(filename)
    if err != nil {
        fmt.Printf("error opening file %s\n", err)
        os.Exit(-1)
    }
    defer f.Close()

    myIPs := make(map[string]int)
    r := bufio.NewReader(f)
    for {
        line, err := r.ReadString('\n')
        if err == io.EOF {
            break
        } else if err != nil {
            fmt.Printf("error reading file %s", err)
            break
        }
```

Here, you read the input log file line by line using `bufio.NewReader()`.

The last part has the following Go code, which deals with processing the matches of the regular expression:

```go
ip := findIP(line)
trial := net.ParseIP(ip)
if trial.To4() == nil {
        continue
} else {
        _, ok := myIPs[ip]
        if ok {
                myIPs[ip] = myIPs[ip] + 1
        } else {
                myIPs[ip] = 1
        }
}
}
for key, _ := range myIPs {
        fmt.Printf("%s %d\n", key, myIPs[key])
}
}
```

As you can see, `findIP.go` executes an additional checking on the IP that was found by the function that performed the pattern matching operation, using `net.ParseIP()`; this mainly happens because IP addresses are pretty tricky, and it is considered good practice to double check them! Additionally, this catches the case where `findIP()` returns nothing because a valid IP was not found in the processed line. The last thing the program does before exiting is to print the contents of the `myIPs` map.

 Consider how many incredible and useful utilities you can develop with a small amount of Go code: it is really amazing!

Executing `findIP.go` on a Linux machine in order to process the `/var/log/auth.log` log file will create the following output:

```
$ wc /var/log/auth.log
  1499647  20313719 155224677 /var/log/auth.log
$ go run findIP.go /var/log/auth.log
39.114.101.107 1003
111.224.233.41 10
189.41.147.179 306
55.31.112.181 1
5.141.131.102 10
171.60.251.143 30
218.237.65.48 1
```

```
24.16.210.120 8
199.115.116.50 3
139.160.113.181 1
```

You can sort the previous output by the number of times an IP was found and display the 10 most popular IP addresses, as shown here:

```
$ go run findIP.go /var/log/auth.log | sort -nr -k2 | head
218.65.30.156 102533
61.177.172.27 37746
218.65.30.43 34640
109.74.11.18 32870
61.177.172.55 31968
218.65.30.124 31649
59.63.188.3 30970
61.177.172.28 30023
116.31.116.30 29314
61.177.172.14 28615
```

So, in this case, the findIP.go utility is used for checking the security of your Linux machine!

An advanced example of pattern matching

In this section, you will learn how to swap the values of two fields of each line of a text file, provided they are in the correct format. This mainly happens in log files or other text files where you want to scan a line for certain types of data, and if the data is found, you might need to do something with them—in this case, you will change the place of the two values.

The name of the program will be swapRE.go, and it will be presented in four parts. Once again, the program will read a text file line by line and try to match the desired strings before swapping them. The utility will print the contents of the new file on the screen; it is the responsibility of the user to save the results to a new file. The format of the log entries that swapRE.go expects to process are similar to the following:

```
127.0.0.1 - - [24/May/2017:06:41:11 +0300] "GET /contact HTTP/1.1" 200 6048
"http://www.mtsoukalos.eu/" "Mozilla/5.0 (Windows NT 6.3; WOW64;
Trident/7.0; rv:11.0) like Gecko" 132953
```

The entries from the previous line that the program will swap are [24/May/2017:06:41:11 +0300] and 132953, which are the date and time and the time it took the browser to get the desired information, respectively; the program expects to find this at the end of each line. However, the regular expression also checks that the date and time are in the correct format and that the last field of each log entry is indeed a number.

> As you will see, using regular expressions in Go, can be perplexing sometimes, mainly because regular expressions are relatively difficult to build, in general.

The first part of swapRE.go will be the expected preamble:

```
package main

import (
    "bufio"
    "flag"
    "fmt"
    "io"
    "os"
    "regexp"
)
```

The second part comes with the following Go code:

```
func main() {
    flag.Parse()
    if flag.NArg() != 1 {
        fmt.Println("Please provide one log file to process!")
        os.Exit(-1)
    }
    numberOfLines := 0
    numberOfLinesMatched := 0

    filename := flag.Arg(0)
    f, err := os.Open(filename)
    if err != nil {
        fmt.Printf("error opening file %s", err)
        os.Exit(1)
    }
    defer f.Close()
```

There is nothing particularly interesting or new here.

The third part is the following:

```
r := bufio.NewReader(f)
for {
        line, err := r.ReadString('\n')
        if err == io.EOF {
                break
        } else if err != nil {
                fmt.Printf("error reading file %s", err)
        }
```

Here is the Go code that allows you to process the input file line by line.

The last part of swapRE.go is the following:

```
        numberOfLines++
        r := regexp.MustCompile(`(.*)
(\[\d\d\/(\w+)/\d\d\d\d:\d\d:\d\d:\d\d(.*)\]) (.*) (\d+)`)
        if r.MatchString(line) {
                numberOfLinesMatched++
                match := r.FindStringSubmatch(line)
                fmt.Println(match[1], match[6], match[5], match[2])
        }
    }
    fmt.Println("Line processed:", numberOfLines)
    fmt.Println("Line matched:", numberOfLinesMatched)
}
```

As you can imagine, complex regular expressions, such as the one presented here, are built step by step, not all at once. Even in that case, you may still fail many times in the process because even the tiniest mistake in a complex regular expression will cause it to not do what you expect—extensive testing is the key here!

The parentheses used inside a regular expression allow you to reference each match afterwards and are very handy when you want to process what you have matched. What you want here is to find a [character, then two digits that will be the day of the month, then a word, which will be the name of the month, and then four digits that will be the year. Next, you match anything else until you find a] character. Then you match all the digits at the end of each line.

 Note that there might exist alternative ways to write the same regular expression. The general advice here is to write it in a way that is clear and that you can understand.

Executing swapRE.gowith, a small test log file will generate the following output:

```
$ go run swapRE.go /tmp/log.log
127.0.0.1 - - 28787 "GET /taxonomy/term/35/feed HTTP/1.1" 200 2360 "-"
"Mozilla/5.0 (compatible; Baiduspider/2.0;
+http://www.baidu.com/search/spider.html)" [24/May/2017:07:04:48 +0300]
- - 32145 HTTP/1.1" 200 2616 "http://www.mtsoukalos.eu/" "Mozilla/5.0
(compatible; inoreader.com-like FeedFetcher-Google)" [24/May/2017:07:09:24
+0300]
Line processed: 3
Line matched: 2
```

Renaming multiple files using regular expressions

The last section on pattern matching and regular expressions will work on filenames and will allow you to rename multiple files. As you can guess, a walk function will be used in the program while a regular expression will match the filenames you want to rename.

 When dealing with files, you should be extra careful because you might accidentally destroy things! Putting it simply, do not test such utilities on a production server.

The name of the utility will be multipleMV.go, and it will be presented in three parts. What multipleMV.go will do is insert a string in front of every filename that is a match to the given regular expression.

The first part is the expected preamble:

```
package main

import (
    "flag"
    "fmt"
    "os"
    "path/filepath"
    "regexp"
)

var RE string
var renameString string
```

The two global variables save you from having to use many parameters in your functions. Additionally, as the signature of the walk() function, presented in a while, cannot change, it will not be possible to pass them as parameters to walk(). So, in this case, having two global parameters makes things easier and simpler.

The second part contains the following Go code:

```
func walk(path string, f os.FileInfo, err error) error {
    regex, err := regexp.Compile(RE)
    if err != nil {
        fmt.Printf("Error in RE: %s\n", RE)
        return err
    }

    if path == "." {
        return nil
    }
    nameOfFile := filepath.Base(path)
    if regex.MatchString(nameOfFile) {
        newName := filepath.Dir(path) + "/" + renameString + "_" +
nameOfFile
        os.Rename(path, newName)
    }
    return nil
}
```

All the functionality of the program is embedded in the walk() function. After a successful match, the new filename is stored in the newName variable before executing the os.Rename() function.

The last part of multipleMV.go is the implementation of the main() function:

```
func main() {
    flag.Parse()
    if flag.NArg() != 3 {
        fmt.Printf("Usage: %s REGEXP RENAME Path",
filepath.Base(os.Args[0]))
        os.Exit(-1)
    }

    RE = flag.Arg(0)
    renameString = flag.Arg(1)
    Path := flag.Arg(2)
    Path, _ = filepath.EvalSymlinks(Path)
    filepath.Walk(Path, walk)
}
```

Here, there isnothing you have not seen before—the only interesting thing is the call to `filepath.EvalSymlinks()` in order to not have to deal with symbolic links.

Using `multipleMV.go` is as simple as running the following commands:

```
$ ls -l /tmp/swtag.log
-rw-rw-rw-  1 mtsouk  wheel  446 May 22 09:18 /tmp/swtag.log
$ go run multipleMV.go 'log$' new /tmp
$ ls -l /tmp/new_swtag.log
-rw-rw-rw-  1 mtsouk  wheel  446 May 22 09:18 /tmp/new_swtag.log
$ go run multipleMV.go 'log$' new /tmp
$ ls -l /tmp/new_new_swtag.log
-rw-rw-rw-  1 mtsouk  wheel  446 May 22 09:18 /tmp/new_new_swtag.log
$ go run multipleMV.go 'log$' new /tmp
$ ls -l /tmp/new_new_new_swtag.log
-rw-rw-rw-  1 mtsouk  wheel  446 May 22 09:18 /tmp/new_new_new_swtag.log
```

Searching files revisited

This section will teach you how to find files using criteria such as user ID, group ID, and file permissions. Although this section could have been included in Chapter 5,*Files and Directories*, I decided to put it here, because there are times when you will want to use this kind of information in order to inform a system administrator that there is something wrong with the system.

Finding the user ID of a user

This subsection will present a program that shows the user ID of a user, given their username, which is more or less the output of the `id -u` utility:

```
$ id -u
33
$ id -u root
0
```

The fact that there exists a Go package named `user`, whichcan be found under the `os` package that can help you implement the desired task,should not come as surprise to you. The name of the program will be `userID.go`, and it will be presented in two parts. If you give no command-line arguments to `userID.go`, it will print the user ID of the current user; otherwise, it will print the user ID of the given username.

The first part of `userID.go` is the following:

```
package main

import (
    "fmt"
    "os"
    "os/user"
)

func main() {
    arguments := os.Args
    if len(arguments) == 1 {
            uid := os.Getuid()
            fmt.Println(uid)
            return
    }
```

The `os.Getuid()` function returns the user ID of the current user.

The second part of `userID.go` comes with the following Go code:

```
    username := arguments[1]
    u, err := user.Lookup(username)
    if err != nil {
            fmt.Println(err)
            return
    }
    fmt.Println(u.Uid)
}
```

Given a username, the `user.Lookup()` function returns a `user.User` compound value. We will only use the `Uid` field of that compound value to find the user ID of the given username.

Executing `userID.go` will generate the following output:

```
$ go run userID.go
501
$ go run userID.go root
0
$ go run userID.go doesNotExist
user: unknown user doesNotExist
```

Finding all the groups a user belongs to

Each user can belong to more than one group—this section will show how to find out the list of groups a user belongs to, given their username.

The name of the utility will be listGroups.go, and it will be presented in four parts. The first part of listGroups.go is the following:

```
package main

import (
    "fmt"
    "os"
    "os/user"
)
```

The second part has the following Go code:

```
func main() {
    arguments := os.Args
    var u *user.User
    var err error
    if len(arguments) == 1 {
        u, err = user.Current()
        if err != nil {
            fmt.Println(err)
            return
        }
```

The approach that listGroups.go takes when there are no command-line arguments is similar to the one found in userID.go. However, there is a big difference, as this time you do not need the user ID of the current user, but the username of the current user; so you call user.Current(), which returns a user.User value.

The third part contains the following Go code:

```
    } else {
        username := arguments[1]
        u, err = user.Lookup(username)
        if err != nil {
            fmt.Println(err)
            return
        }
    }
```

So, if a command-line argument is given to the program, it is handled by the previous code with the help of the `user.Lookup()` function that also returns a `user.User` value.

The last part contains the following Go code:

```
gids, _ := u.GroupIds()
for _, gid := range gids {
        group, err := user.LookupGroupId(gid)
        if err != nil {
                fmt.Println(err)
                continue
        }
        fmt.Printf("%s(%s) ", group.Gid, group.Name)
}
fmt.Println()
}
```

Here, you get the list of the group IDs that the user—signified by the `u` variable—is a member of, by calling the `u.GroupIds()` function. Then, you will need a `for` loop to iterate over all the list elements and print them. It should be made clear that this list is stored in `u`; that is, a `user.User` value.

Executing `listGroups.go` will generate the following output:

```
$ go run listGroups.go
    20(staff) 701(com.apple.sharepoint.group.1) 12(everyone)
61(localaccounts) 79(_appserverusr) 80(admin) 81(_appserveradm)
98(_lpadmin) 33(_appstore) 100(_lpoperator) 204(_developer)
395(com.apple.access_ftp) 398(com.apple.access_screensharing)
399(com.apple.access_ssh)
$ go run listGroups.go www
70(_www) 12(everyone) 61(localaccounts) 701(com.apple.sharepoint.group.1)
100(_lpoperator)
```

The output of `listGroups.go` is much more enriched than the output of both the `id -G -n` and `groups` commands:

```
$ id -G -n
staff com.apple.sharepoint.group.1 everyone localaccounts _appserverusr
admin _appserveradm _lpadmin _appstore _lpoperator _developer
com.apple.access_ftp com.apple.access_screensharing com.apple.access_ssh
$ groups
staff com.apple.sharepoint.group.1 everyone localaccounts _appserverusr
admin _appserveradm _lpadmin _appstore _lpoperator _developer
com.apple.access_ftp com.apple.access_screensharing com.apple.access_ssh
```

Finding files that belong or do not belong to a given user

This subsection will create a Go program that scans a directory tree and presents files that belong or do not belong to a given user. The name of the program will be userFiles.go. In its default mode of operation, userFiles.go will display all files that belong to a given username; when used with the -no flag, it will only display the files that do not belong to the given username.

The code of userFiles.go will be presented in four parts.

The first one is the following:

```
package main

import (
    "flag"
    "fmt"
    "os"
    "os/user"
    "path/filepath"
    "strconv"
    "syscall"
)


var uid int32 = 0
var INCLUDE bool = true
```

The reason for declaring INCLUDE and uid as global variables is that you want both of them to be accessible from every point of the program. Additionally, as the signature of walkFunction() cannot change—only its name can change—using global variables makes things easier for the developer.

The second part comes with the following Go code:

```
func userOfFIle(filename string) int32 {
    fileInfo, err := os.Stat(filename)
    if err != nil {
        fmt.Println(err)
        return 1000000
    }
    UID := fileInfo.Sys().(*syscall.Stat_t).Uid
    return int32(UID)
}
```

The use of a local variable named UID might be a poor choice, given that there is a global variable named uid! A better name for the global variable would have been gUID. Note that for an explanation of the way that the call that returns the UID variable works, you should search for the interfaces and type conversions in Go, because talking about it is beyond the scope of this book.

The third part contains the following Go code:

```go
func walkFunction(path string, info os.FileInfo, err error) error {
    _, err = os.Lstat(path)
    if err != nil {
        return err
    }

    if userOfFIle(path) == uid && INCLUDE {
        fmt.Println(path)
    } else if userOfFIle(path) != uid && !(INCLUDE) {
        fmt.Println(path)
    }

    return err
}
```

Here you can see the implementation of a walk function that will access every file and directory in a given directory tree, in order to print the desired filenames only.

The last part of the utility contains the following Go code:

```go
func main() {
    minusNO := flag.Bool("no", true, "Include")
    minusPATH := flag.String("path", ".", "Path to Search")
    flag.Parse()
    flags := flag.Args()

    INCLUDE = *minusNO
    Path := *minusPATH

    if len(flags) == 0 {
        uid = int32(os.Getuid())
    } else {
        u, err := user.Lookup(flags[0])
        if err != nil {
            fmt.Println(err)
            os.Exit(1)
        }
        temp, err := strconv.ParseInt(u.Uid, 10, 32)
        uid = int32(temp)
```

```
        }

        err := filepath.Walk(Path, walkFunction)
        if err != nil {
                fmt.Println(err)
        }
}
```

Here you deal with the configuration of the `flag` package before calling the `filepath.Walk()` function.

Executing `userFiles.go` generates the following output:

```
$ go run userFiles.go -path=/tmp www-data
/tmp/.htaccess
/tmp/update-cache-2a113cac
/tmp/update-extraction-2a113cac
```

If you do not give any command-line arguments or flags, the `userFiles.go` utility will assume that you want to search the current directory for files that belong to the current user:

```
$ go run userFiles.go
.
appendData.go
countIP.go
```

So, in order to find all the files in the `/srv/www/www.highiso.net` directory that do not belong to the `www-data` user, you should execute the following command:

```
$ go run userFiles.go -no=false -path=/srv/www/www.highiso.net www-data
/srv/www/www.highiso.net/list.files
/srv/www/www.highiso.net/public_html/wp-content/.htaccess
/srv/www/www.highiso.net/public_html.UnderCon/.htaccess
```

Finding files based on their permissions

Now that you know how to find the Unix permissions of a file, you can improve the `regExpFind.go` utility from the previous chapter in order to support searching based on file permissions; however, in order to avoid presenting a really big Go program here without any practical reason, the presented program will be autonomous and only support finding files based on their permissions. The name of the new utility will be `findPerm.go`, and it will be presented in four parts. The permissions will be given in the command line as a string using the format returned by the `ls(1)` command (`rwxr-xr--`).

The first part of the utility is the following:

```
package main

import (
    "fmt"
    "os"
    "path/filepath"
)

var PERMISSIONS string
```

The `PERMISSIONS` variable is made global in order to be accessible from anywhere in the program, and because the signature of `walkFunction()` cannot change.

The second part of `findPerm.go` contains the following code:

```
func permissionsOfFIle(filename string) string {
    info, err := os.Stat(filename)
    if err != nil {
        return "-1"
    }
    mode := info.Mode()
    return mode.String()[1:10]
}
```

The third part is the implementation of `walkFunction()`:

```
func walkFunction(path string, info os.FileInfo, err error) error {
    _, err = os.Lstat(path)
    if err != nil {
        return err
    }

    if permissionsOfFIle(path) == PERMISSIONS {
        fmt.Println(path)
    }
    return err
}
```

The last part of `findPerm.go` is the following:

```
func main() {
    arguments := os.Args
    if len(arguments) != 3 {
        fmt.Printf("usage: %s RootDirectory permissions\n",
filepath.Base(arguments[0]))
        os.Exit(1)
    }

    Path := arguments[1]
    Path, _ = filepath.EvalSymlinks(Path)
    PERMISSIONS = arguments[2]

    err := filepath.Walk(Path, walkFunction)
    if err != nil {
        fmt.Println(err)
    }
}
```

Executing `findPerm.go` will generate the following output:

```
$ go run findPerm.go /tmp rw-------
/private/tmp/.adobeLockFile
$ ls -l /private/tmp/.adobeLockFile
-rw-------  1 mtsouk  wheel  0 May 19 14:36 /private/tmp/.adobeLockFile
```

Date and time operations

This section will show you how to work with dates and times in Go. This task might look insignificant, but it can be very important when you want to synchronize things such as log entries and error messages. We will start by illustrating some of the functionality of the time package.

Playing with dates and times

This section will present a small Go program named dateTime.go that shows how to work with times and dates in Go. The code of dateTime.go will be presented in three parts. The first part is the following:

```
package main

import (
    "fmt"
    "time"
)

func main() {

    fmt.Println("Epoch time:", time.Now().Unix())
    t := time.Now()
    fmt.Println(t, t.Format(time.RFC3339))
    fmt.Println(t.Weekday(), t.Day(), t.Month(), t.Year())
    time.Sleep(time.Second)
    t1 := time.Now()
    fmt.Println("Time difference:", t1.Sub(t))

    formatT := t.Format("01 January 2006")
    fmt.Println(formatT)
    loc, _ := time.LoadLocation("Europe/London")
    londonTime := t.In(loc)
    fmt.Println("London:", londonTime)
```

In this part, you can see how you can change a date from one format to another, and also, how to find the date and time in a different time zone. The time.Now() function used at the beginning of the main() function returns the current time.

The second part is the following:

```
myDate := "23 May 2017"
d, _ := time.Parse("02 January 2006", myDate)
fmt.Println(d)

myDate1 := "23 May 2016"
d1, _ := time.Parse("02 February 2006", myDate1)
fmt.Println(d1)
```

The list of constants that can be used for creating your own parse format can be found at https://golang.org/src/time/format.go. Go does not define the format of a date or a time in a form like DDYYYYMM or %D %Y %M as the rest of the programming languages do, but uses its own approach.

Here, you see how you can read a string and try to convert it to a valid date, both successfully (d) and unsuccessfully (d1). The problem with the d1 variable is the use of February in the format string—you should have used January instead.

The last part of dateTime.go comes with the following Go code:

```
myDT := "Tuesday 23 May 2017 at 23:36"
dt, _ := time.Parse("Monday 02 January 2006 at 15:04", myDT)
fmt.Println(dt)
}
```

This part also shows how to convert a string into a date and a time, provided that it is in the expected format.

Executing dateTime.go will generate the following output:

```
$ go run dateTime.go
Epoch time: 1495572122
2017-05-23 23:42:02.459713551 +0300 EEST 2017-05-23T23:42:02+03:00
Tuesday 23 May 2017
Time difference: 1.001749054s
05 May 2017
London: 2017-05-23 21:42:02.459713551 +0100 BST
2017-05-23 00:00:00 +0000 UTC
0001-01-01 00:00:00 +0000 UTC
2017-05-23 23:36:00 +0000 UTC
```

Reformatting the times in a log file

This section will show how to implement a program that reads a log file that contains date and time information, in order to convert the time format found in each log entry. This operation might be needed when you have log files from different servers that are in several time zones, and you want to synchronize their times in order to create reports from their data or store them into a database to process them some other time.

The name of the presented program will be `dateTimeLog.go`, and it will be presented in four parts.

The first part is the following:

```
package main

import (
    "bufio"
    "flag"
    "fmt"
    "io"
    "os"
    "regexp"
    "strings"
    "time"
)
```

The second part contains the following Go code:

```
func main() {
    flag.Parse()
    if flag.NArg() != 1 {
        fmt.Println("Please provide one log file to process!")
        os.Exit(-1)
    }

    filename := flag.Arg(0)
    f, err := os.Open(filename)
    if err != nil {
        fmt.Printf("error opening file %s", err)
        os.Exit(1)
    }
    defer f.Close()
```

Here, you just configure the `flag` package and open the input file for reading.

The third part of the program is the following:

```
r := bufio.NewReader(f)
for {
        line, err := r.ReadString('\n')
        if err == io.EOF {
                break
        } else if err != nil {
                fmt.Printf("error reading file %s", err)
        }
}
```

Here you read the input file line by line.

The last part is the following:

```
        r :=
regexp.MustCompile(`.*\[(\d\d/\w+/\d\d\d\d:\d\d:\d\d:\d\d.*)\] .*`)
        if r.MatchString(line) {
                match := r.FindStringSubmatch(line)
                d1, err := time.Parse("02/Jan/2006:15:04:05 -0700",
match[1])

                if err != nil {
                        fmt.Println(err)
                }
                newFormat := d1.Format(time.RFC3339)
                fmt.Print(strings.Replace(line, match[1], newFormat, 1))
        }
    }
}
```

The general idea here is that once you have a match, you parse the date and time you found using `time.Parse()` and then convert it to the desired format using the `time.Format()` function. Also, you replace the initial match with the output of the `time.Format()` function before you print it using `strings.Replace()`.

Executing `dateTimeLog.go` will generate the following output:

```
$ go run dateTimeLog.go /tmp/log.log
127.0.0.1 - - [2017-05-24T07:04:48+03:00] "GET /taxonomy/term/35/feed
HTTP/1.1" 200 2360 "-" "Mozilla/5.0 (compatible; Baiduspider/2.0;
+http://www.baidu.com/search/spider.html)" 28787
- - [2017-05-24T07:09:24+03:00] HTTP/1.1" 200 2616
"http://www.mtsoukalos.eu/" "Mozilla/5.0 (compatible; inoreader.com-like
FeedFetcher-Google)" 32145
[2017-05-24T07:38:08+03:00] "GET /tweets?page=181 HTTP/1.1" 200 8605 "-"
"Mozilla/5.0 (compatible; Baiduspider/2.0;
+http://www.baidu.com/search/spider.html)" 100531
```

Rotating log files

Log files tend to get bigger and bigger all the time because data is written to them all the time; it would be good to have a technique for rotating them. This section will present such a technique. The name of the Go program will be `rotateLog.go`, and it will be presented in three parts. Note that for a process to rotate a log file, the process must be the one that opened that log file for writing. Trying to rotate a log that you do not own might create problems on your Unix machine, and should be avoided!

What you will also see here is another technique where you use your own log file for storing your log entries, with the help of `log.SetOutput()`—after a successful call to `log.SetOutput()`, each function call to `log.Print()` will make the output go to the log file used as the parameter of `log.SetOutput()`.

The first part of `rotateLog.go` is the following:

```
package main

import (
    "fmt"
    "log"
    "os"
    "strconv"
    "time"
)

var TOTALWRITES int = 0
var ENTRIESPERLOGFILE int = 100
var WHENTOSTOP int = 230
var openLogFile os.File
```

Using hard coded variables that define when the program will stop is considered good practice—this happens because you do not have any other way to tell `rotateLog.go` to stop. However, if you use the functionality of the `rotateLog.go` utility in a compiled program, then such variables should be given as command-line arguments, because you should not have to recompile the program in order to change the way the program behaves!

The second part of `rotateLog.go` is the following:

```
func rotateLogFile(filename string) error {
    openLogFile.Close()
    os.Rename(filename, filename+"."+strconv.Itoa(TOTALWRITES))
    err := setUpLogFile(filename)
    return err
}

func setUpLogFile(filename string) error {
    openLogFile, err := os.OpenFile(filename,
os.O_RDWR|os.O_CREATE|os.O_APPEND, 0644)
    if err != nil {
        return err
    }
    log.SetOutput(openLogFile)
    return nil
}
```

Here, you define the Go function named `rotateLogFile()` for rotating the desired log file, which is the most important part of the program. The `setUpLogFile()` function helps you restart the log file after you rotate it. What is also illustrated here is the use of `log.SetOutput()` to tell the program where to write the log entries. Note that you should open your log file using `os.OpenFile()`, because `os.Open()` will not work for `log.SetOutput()`, and `os.Open()` does open files for writing!

The last part is the following:

```
func main() {
    numberOfLogEntries := 0
    filename := "/tmp/myLog.log"
    err := setUpLogFile(filename)
    if err != nil {
        fmt.Println(err)
        os.Exit(-1)
    }

    for {
        log.Println(numberOfLogEntries, "This is a test log entry")
        numberOfLogEntries++
        TOTALWRITES++
        if numberOfLogEntries > ENTRIESPERLOGFILE {
            rotateLogFile(filename)
            numberOfLogEntries = 0
        }
        if TOTALWRITES > WHENTOSTOP {
            rotateLogFile(filename)
```

```
            break
        }
        time.Sleep(time.Second)
    }
    fmt.Println("Wrote", TOTALWRITES, "log entries!")
}
```

In this part, the `main()` function keeps writing data to a log file while counting the number of entries that have been written so far. When the defined number of entries have been reached (`ENTRIESPERLOGFILE`), the `main()` function will call the `rotateLogFile()` function, which will do the dirty work for us. On a real program, you will most likely not need to call `time.Sleep()` to delay the execution of the program. For this particular program, `time.Sleep()` will give you time to examine your log file using `tail -f`, should you choose to do so.

Running `rotateLog.go` will generate the following output on the screen and inside the `/tmp` directory:

```
$ go run rotateLog.go
Wrote 231 log entries!
$ wc /tmp/myLog.log*
    0      0       0 /tmp/myLog.log
  101    909    4839 /tmp/myLog.log.101
  101    909    4839 /tmp/myLog.log.202
   29    261    1382 /tmp/myLog.log.231
  231   2079   11060 total
```

`Chapter 8`, *Processes and Signals*, will present a much better approach on log rotating that will be based on Unix signals.

Creating good random passwords

This section will illustrate how to create good random passwords in Go, in order to protect the security of your Unix machines. The main reason for including it here instead of another chapter is because the presented Go program will use the /dev/random device, which is a file defined by your Unix system, for getting the seed of the random number generator. The name of the Go program will be goodPass.go, and it will require just one optional parameter, which will be the length of the generated password—the default size of the generated password will be 10 characters. Additionally, the program will generate ASCII characters starting from ! up to z. The ASCII code of the exclamation mark is 33, whereas the ASCII code of small z is 122.

The first part of goodPass.go is the required preamble:

```
package main

import (
    "encoding/binary"
    "fmt"
    "math/rand"
    "os"
    "path/filepath"
    "strconv"
)
```

The second part of the program is as follows:

```
var MAX int = 90
var MIN int = 0
var seedSize int = 10

func random(min, max int) int {
    return rand.Intn(max-min) + min
}
```

You have already seen the random() function back in Chapter 2, *Writing Programs in Go*, so there is nothing particularly interesting here.

The third part of `goodPass.go` is where the implementation of the `main()` function begins:

```
func main() {
    if len(os.Args) != 2 {
        fmt.Printf("usage: %s length\n", filepath.Base(os.Args[0]))
        os.Exit(1)
    }

    LENGTH, _ := strconv.ParseInt(os.Args[1], 10, 64)
    f, _ := os.Open("/dev/random")
    var seed int64
    binary.Read(f, binary.LittleEndian, &seed)
    rand.Seed(seed)
    f.Close()
    fmt.Println("Seed:", seed)
```

Here, apart from reading the command-line argument, you also open the `/dev/random` device for reading, which happens by calling the `binary.Read()` function and storing what you read in the `seed` variable. The reason for using `binary.Read()` is that you need to specify the byte order used (`binary.LittleEndian`) and that you need to build an int64 instead of a series of bytes. This is an example of having to read from a binary file into Go types.

The last part of the program contains the following Go code:

```
    startChar := "!"
    var i int64
    for i = 0; i < LENGTH; i++ {
        anInt := int(random(MIN, MAX))
        newChar := string(startChar[0] + byte(anInt))
        if newChar == " " {
            i = i - i
            continue
        }
        fmt.Print(newChar)
    }
    fmt.Println()
}
```

As you can see, Go has a strange way of dealing with ASCII characters because Go supports Unicode characters by default. However, you can still convert an integer number into an ASCII character as can be seen in the way you define the `newChar` variable.

Executing `goodPass.go` will generate the following output:

```
$ go run goodPass.go 1
Seed: -5195038511418503382
b
$ go run goodPass.go 10
Seed: 8492864627151568776
k43Ve`+YD)
$ go run goodPass.go 50
Seed: -4276736612056007162
!=Gy+;XV>6eviuR=ST\u:Mk4Q875Y4YZiZhq&q_4Ih/]''`2:x
```

Another Go update

As I was writing this chapter, Go got updated. The following output shows the related information:

```
$ date
Wed May 24 13:35:36 EEST 2017
$ go version
go version go1.8.2 darwin/amd64
```

Exercises

1. Find and read the documentation of the `time` package.
2. Try to change the Go code of `userFiles.go` in order to support multiple users.
3. Change the Go code of `insertLineNumber.go` in order to read the input file line by line, write each line to a temporary file, and then, replace the original file with the temporary one. If you do not know how and where to create a temporary file, you can use a random number generator to get a temporary filename and the `/tmp` directory to temporarily save it.
4. Make the necessary changes to `multipleMV.go` in order to print the files that are a match to the given regular expression without actually renaming them.
5. Try to create a regular expression that matches PNG files and use it to process the contents of a log file.
6. Create a regular expression that catches a date and a time string in order to print just the date part and delete the time part.

Summary

In this chapter, we talked about many things, including working with log files, dealing with Unix file permissions, users, and groups, creating regular expressions, and processing text files.

In the next chapter, we will talk about Unix signals, which allow you to communicate with a running program from the outside world, in an asynchronous way. Furthermore, we will tell you how to plot in Go.

8
Processes and Signals

In the previous chapter, we talked about many interesting topics including working with Unix system files, dealing with dates and times in Go, finding information about file permissions and usersas well asregular expressions and pattern matching.

The central subject of this chapter is developing Go applications that can handle the Unix signals that can be caught and handled. Go offers the `os/signal` package for dealing with signals, which uses Go channels. Although channels are fully explored in the next chapter, this will not stop you from learning how to work with Unix signals in Go programs.

Furthermore, you will learn how to create Go command-line utilities that can work with Unix pipes, how to draw bar charts in Go, and how to implement a Go version of the `cat(1)` utility.So, in this chapter you will learn about the following topics:

- Listing the processes of a Unix machine
- Signal handling in Go
- The signals that a Unix machine supports as well as how to use the `kill(1)` command to send these signals
- Making signals do the work you want
- Implementing a simple version of the `cat(1)` utility in Go
- Plotting data in Go
- Using pipes in order to send the output of one program to another
- Converting a big program into two smaller ones that will cooperate with the help of Unix pipes
- Creating a client for a Unix socket

About Unix processes and signals

Strictly speaking, a **process** is an execution environment that contains instructions, user-data and system-data parts, and other kinds of resources that are obtained during runtime, whereas a **program** is a file that contains instructions and data, which are used for initializing the instruction and user-data parts of a process.

Process management

Go is not that good at dealing with processes and process management in general. Nevertheless, this section will present a small Go program that lists all the processes of a Unix machine by executing a Unix command and getting its output. The name of the program will be `listProcess.go`. It works on both Linux and macOS systems, and will be presented in three parts.

The first part of the program is the following:

```
package main

import (
    "fmt"
    "os"
    "os/exec"
    "syscall"
)
```

The second part of `listProcess.go` has the following Go code:

```
func main() {

    PS, err := exec.LookPath("ps")
    if err != nil {
            fmt.Println(err)
    }
fmt.Println(PS)

    command := []string{"ps", "-a", "-x"}
    env := os.Environ()
    err = syscall.Exec(PS, command, env)
```

As you can see, you first need to get the path of the executable file using `exec.LookPath()` to make sure that you are not going to accidentally execute another binary file and then define the command you want to execute, including the parameters of the command, using a slice. Next, you will have to read the Unix environment using `os.Environ()`. Also, you execute the desired command using `syscall.Exec()`, which will automatically print its output, which is not a very elegant way to execute commands because you have no control over the task and because you are calling processes at the lowest level instead of using a higher level library such as `os/exec`.

The last part of the program is for printing the error message of the previous code, in case there is one:

```
if err != nil {
        fmt.Println(err)
}
}
```

Executing `listProcess.go` will generate the following output—the `head(1)` utility is used to get a smaller output:

```
$ go run listProcess.go | head -3
/bin/ps
  PID TTY           TIME CMD
    1 ??         0:30.72 /sbin/launchd
signal: broken pipe
```

About Unix signals

Have you ever pressed *Ctrl + C* in order to stop a program from running? If yes, then you are already familiar with signals because *Ctrl + C* sends the `SIGINT` signal to the program.

Strictly speaking, Unix **signals** are software interrupts that can be accessed either by a name or number and offer a way of handling asynchronous events such as when a child process exits or a process is told to pause on a Unix system.

A program cannot handle all signals; some of them are non-catchable and non-ignorable. The `SIGKILL` and `SIGSTOP` signals cannot be caught, blocked, or ignored. The reason for this is that they provide the kernel and the root user a way of stopping any process. The `SIGKILL` signal, which is also known by the number 9, is usually called in extreme conditions where you need to act fast; so, it is the only signal that is usually called by number because it is quicker to do so. The most important thing to remember here is that not all Unix signals can be handled!

Unix signals in Go

Go provides the `os/signal` package to programmers to help them handle incoming signals. However, we will start the discussion about handling by presenting the `kill(1)` utility.

The kill(1) command

The `kill(1)` command is used for either terminating a process or sending a less cruel signal to it. Keep in mind that the fact that you can send a signal to a process does not mean that the process can or has code to handle this signal.

By default, `kill(1)` sends the `SIGTERM` signal. If you want to find out all the supported signals of your Unix machine, you should execute the `kill -l` command. On a macOS Sierra machine, the output of `kill -l` is the following:

```
$ kill -1
1) SIGHUP    2) SIGINT     3) SIGQUIT   4) SIGILL
5) SIGTRAP   6) SIGABRT    7) SIGEMT    8) SIGFPE
9) SIGKILL  10) SIGBUS    11) SIGSEGV 12) SIGSYS
13) SIGPIPE 14) SIGALRM    15) SIGTERM 16) SIGURG
17) SIGSTOP 18) SIGTSTP    19) SIGCONT 20) SIGCHLD
21) SIGTTIN 22) SIGTTOU    23) SIGIO   24) SIGXCPU
25) SIGXFSZ 26) SIGVTALRM  27) SIGPROF 28) SIGWINCH
29) SIGINFO 30) SIGUSR1    31) SIGUSR2
```

If you execute the same command on a Debian Linux machine, you will get a more enriched output:

```
$ kill -1
 1) SIGHUP     2) SIGINT    3) SIGQUIT  4) SIGILL    5) SIGTRAP
 6) SIGABRT    7) SIGBUS    8) SIGFPE   9) SIGKILL  10) SIGUSR1
11) SIGSEGV  12) SIGUSR2  13) SIGPIPE 14) SIGALRM  15) SIGTERM
16) SIGSTKFLT   17) SIGCHLD
18) SIGCONT     19) SIGSTOP 20) SIGTSTP
21) SIGTTIN     22) SIGTTOU
23) SIGURG      24) SIGXCPU 25) SIGXFSZ
26) SIGVTALRM   27) SIGPROF 28) SIGWINCH
29) SIGIO       30) SIGPWR
31) SIGSYS      34) SIGRTMIN
35) SIGRTMIN+1  36) SIGRTMIN+2    37) SIGRTMIN+3
38) SIGRTMIN+4  39) SIGRTMIN+5
40) SIGRTMIN+6  41) SIGRTMIN+7    42) SIGRTMIN+8
43) SIGRTMIN+9  44) SIGRTMIN+10
```

```
45) SIGRTMIN+11   46) SIGRTMIN+12   47) SIGRTMIN+13
48) SIGRTMIN+14   49) SIGRTMIN+15
50) SIGRTMAX-14   51) SIGRTMAX-13   52) SIGRTMAX-12
53) SIGRTMAX-11   54) SIGRTMAX-10
55) SIGRTMAX-9    56) SIGRTMAX-8    57) SIGRTMAX-7
58) SIGRTMAX-6    59) SIGRTMAX-5
60) SIGRTMAX-4    61) SIGRTMAX-3    62) SIGRTMAX-2
63) SIGRTMAX-1    64) SIGRTMAX
```

If you try to kill or send another signal to the process of another user without having the required permissions, which most likely will happen if you are not the *root* user, kill(1) will not do the job and you will get an error message similar to the following:

```
$ kill 2908
-bash: kill: (2908) - Operation not permitted
```

A simple signal handler in Go

This subsection will present a naïve Go program that handles only the SIGTERM and SIGINT signals. The Go code of h1s.go will be presented in three parts; the first part is the following:

```go
package main

import (
    "fmt"
    "os"
    "os/signal"
    "syscall"
    "time"
)

func handleSignal(signal os.Signal) {
    fmt.Println("Got", signal)
}
```

Apart from the preamble of the program, there is also a function named handleSignal() that will be called when the program receives any of the two supported signals.

The second part of h1s.go contains the following Go code:

```go
func main() {
    sigs := make(chan os.Signal, 1)
    signal.Notify(sigs, os.Interrupt, syscall.SIGTERM)
    go func() {
        for {
```

```
                    sig := <-sigs
                    fmt.Println(sig)
                    handleSignal(sig)
            }
        }()
```

The previous code uses a **goroutine** and a Go **channel**, which are Go features that have not been discussed in this book. Unfortunately, you will have to wait until Chapter 9, *Goroutines – Basic Features*, to learn more about both of them. Note that although os.Interrupt and syscall.SIGTERM belong to different Go packages, they are both signals.

For now, understanding the technique is important; it includes three steps:

1. The definition of a channel, which acts as a way of passing data around, that is required for the technique (sigs).
2. Calling signal.Notify() in order to define the list of signals you want to be able to catch.
3. The definition of an anonymous function that runs in a goroutine (go func()) right after signal.Notify(), which is used for deciding what you are going to do when you get any of the desired signals.

In this case, the handleSignal() function will be called. The for loop inside the anonymous function is used to make the program to keep handling all signals and not stop after receiving its first signal.

The last part of h1s.go is the following:

```
    for {
            fmt.Printf(".")
            time.Sleep(10 * time.Second)
    }
}
```

This is an endless for loop that delays the ending of the program forever—in its place you would most likely put the actual code of your program. Executing h1s.go and sending signals to it from another Terminal will make h1s.go generate the following output:

```
$ ./h1s
....................^Cinterrupt
Got interrupt
^Cinterrupt
Got interrupt
.Hangup: 1
```

The bad thing here is that h1s.go will stop when it receives the SIGHUP signal because the default action for SIGHUP when it is not being specifically handled by a program is to kill the process! The next subsection will show how to handle three signals in a better way, and the subsection after that will teach you how to handle all signals that can be handled.

Handling three different signals!

This subsection will teach you how to create a Go application that can handle three different signals—the name of the program will be h2s.go, and it will handle the SIGTERM, SIGINT, and SIGHUP signals.

The Go code of h2s.go will be presented in four parts.

The first part of the program contains the expected preamble:

```
package main

import (
    "fmt"
    "os"
    "os/signal"
    "syscall"
    "time"
)
```

The second part has the following Go code:

```
func handleSignal(signal os.Signal) {
    fmt.Println("* Got:", signal)
}

func main() {
    sigs := make(chan os.Signal, 1)
    signal.Notify(sigs, os.Interrupt, syscall.SIGTERM, syscall.SIGHUP)
```

Here, the last statement tells you that the program will only handle the os.Interrupt, syscall.SIGTERM, and syscall.SIGHUP signals.

The third part of h2s.go is the following:

```
go func() {
    for {
        sig := <-sigs
        switch sig {
        case os.Interrupt:
```

```
                        handleSignal(sig)
            case syscall.SIGTERM:
                        handleSignal(sig)
            case syscall.SIGHUP:
                        fmt.Println("Got:", sig)
                        os.Exit(-1)
            }

        }
    }()
```

Here, you can see that it is not compulsory to call a separate function when a given signal is caught; it is also allowed to handle it inside the `for` loop as it happens with `syscall.SIGHUP`. However, I find the use of a named function better because it makes the Go code easier to read and modify. The good thing is that Go has a central place for handling all signals, which makes it easy to find out what is going on with your program.

Additionally, `h2s.go` specifically handles the `SIGHUP` signal, although a `SIGHUP` signal will still terminate the program; however, this time this is our decision.

 Keep in mind that it is considered good practice to make one of the signal handlers to stop the program because otherwise you will have to terminate it by issuing a `kill -9` command.

The last part of `h2s.go` is the following:

```
    for {
            fmt.Printf(".")
            time.Sleep(10 * time.Second)
    }
}
```

Executing `h2s.go` and sending four signals to it (`SIGINT`, `SIGTERM`, `SIGHUP`, and `SIGKILL`) from another shell will generate the following output:

```
$ go build h2s.go
$ ./h2s
..* Got: interrupt
* Got: terminated
.Got: hangup
.Killed: 9
```

The reason for building h2s.go is that it is easier to find the process ID of an autonomous program—the go run command builds a temporary executable program behind the scenes, which in this case offers less flexibility. If you want to improve h2s.go, you can make it call os.Getpid() in order to print its process ID, which will save you from having to find it on your own.

The program handles three signals before getting a SIGKILL that cannot be handled and therefore terminates it!

Catching every signal that can be handled

This subsection will present a simple technique that allows you to catch every signal that can be handled—once again, you should keep in mind that you cannot handle all signals! The program will stop once it gets a SIGTERM signal.

The name of the program will be catchAll.go and will be presented in three parts.

The first part is the following:

```
package main

import (
    "fmt"
    "os"
    "os/signal"
    "syscall"
    "time"
)

func handleSignal(signal os.Signal) {
    fmt.Println("* Got:", signal)
}
```

The second part of the program is the following:

```
func main() {
    sigs := make(chan os.Signal, 1)
    signal.Notify(sigs)
    go func() {
            for {
                    sig := <-sigs
                    switch sig {
                    case os.Interrupt:
                            handleSignal(sig)
                    case syscall.SIGTERM:
```

```
                    handleSignal(sig)
                    os.Exit(-1)
            case syscall.SIGUSR1:
                    handleSignal(sig)
            default:
                    fmt.Println("Ignoring:", sig)
            }
        }
    }()
```

In this case, all the difference is made by the way you call `signal.Notify()` in your code. As you do not define any particular signals, the program will be able to handle any signal that can be handled. However, the `for` loop inside the anonymous function only takes care of three signals while ignoring the remaining ones! Note that I believe that this is the best way to handle signals in Go: catch everything while processing only the signals that interest you. However, some people believe that being explicit about what you handle is a better approach. There is no right or wrong here.

The `catchAll.go` program will not terminate when it gets `SIGHUP` because the `default` case of the `switch` block handles it.

The last part is the expected call to the `time.Sleep()` function:

```
    for {
            fmt.Printf(".")
            time.Sleep(10 * time.Second)
    }
}
```

Executing `catchAll.go` will create the following output:

```
$ ./catchAll
.Ignoring: hangup
.....................................* Got: interrupt
* Got: user defined signal 1
.Ignoring: user defined signal 2
Ignoring: hangup
.* Got: terminated
$
```

Rotating log files revisited!

As I told you back in Chapter 7, *Working with System Files*, this chapter will present you with a technique that will allow you to end the program and rotate log files in a more conventional way with the help of signals and signal handling.

The name of the new version of `rotateLog.go` will be `rotateSignals.go` and will be presented in four parts. Moreover, when the utility receives `os.Interrupt`, it will rotate the current log file, whereas when it receives `syscall.SIGTERM`, it will terminate its execution. Every other signal that can be handled will create a log entry without any other action.

The first part of the `rotateSignals.go` is the expected preamble:

```
package main

import (
    "fmt"
    "log"
    "os"
    "os/signal"
    "strconv"
    "syscall"
    "time"
)

var TOTALWRITES int = 0
var openLogFile os.File
```

The second part of `rotateSignals.go` has the following Go code:

```
func rotateLogFile(filename string) error {
    openLogFile.Close()
    os.Rename(filename, filename+"."+strconv.Itoa(TOTALWRITES))
    err := setUpLogFile(filename)
    return err
}

func setUpLogFile(filename string) error {
    openLogFile, err := os.OpenFile(filename,
os.O_RDWR|os.O_CREATE|os.O_APPEND, 0644)
    if err != nil {
        return err
    }
    log.SetOutput(openLogFile)
    return nil
}
```

You have just defined two functions here that perform two tasks. The third part of
rotateSignals.go contains the following Go code:

```go
func main() {
    filename := "/tmp/myLog.log"
    err := setUpLogFile(filename)
    if err != nil {
            fmt.Println(err)
            os.Exit(-1)
    }

    sigs := make(chan os.Signal, 1)
    signal.Notify(sigs)
```

Once again, all signals will be caught. The last part of rotateSignals.go is the following:

```go
    go func() {
            for {
                    sig := <-sigs
                    switch sig {
                    case os.Interrupt:
                            rotateLogFile(filename)
                            TOTALWRITES++
                    case syscall.SIGTERM:
                            log.Println("Got:", sig)
                            openLogFile.Close()
                            TOTALWRITES++
                            fmt.Println("Wrote", TOTALWRITES, "log entries in
total!")
                            os.Exit(-1)
                    default:
                            log.Println("Got:", sig)
                            TOTALWRITES++
                    }
            }
    }()

    for {
            time.Sleep(10 * time.Second)
    }
}
```

As you can see, rotateSignals.go records information about the signals it has received by writing one log entry for each signal. Although presenting the entire code of rotateSignals.go is good, it would be very educational to see the output of the diff(1) utility to show the code differences between rotateLog.go and rotateSignals.go:

```
$ diff rotateLog.go rotateSignals.go
6a7
>       "os/signal"
7a9
>       "syscall"
12,13d13
< var ENTRIESPERLOGFILE int = 100
< var WHENTOSTOP int = 230
33d32
<       numberOfLogEntries := 0
41,51c40,59
<       for {
<               log.Println(numberOfLogEntries, "This is a test log entry")
<               numberOfLogEntries++
<               TOTALWRITES++
<               if numberOfLogEntries > ENTRIESPERLOGFILE {
<                       _ = rotateLogFile(filename)
<                       numberOfLogEntries = 0
<               }
<               if TOTALWRITES > WHENTOSTOP {
<                       _ = rotateLogFile(filename)
<                       break
---
>       sigs := make(chan os.Signal, 1)
>       signal.Notify(sigs)
>
>       go func() {
>               for {
>                       sig := <-sigs
>                       switch sig {
>                       case os.Interrupt:
>                               rotateLogFile(filename)
>                               TOTALWRITES++
>                       case syscall.SIGTERM:
>                               log.Println("Got:", sig)
>                               openLogFile.Close()
>                               TOTALWRITES++
>                               fmt.Println("Wrote", TOTALWRITES, "log entries in
total!")
>                               os.Exit(-1)
>                       default:
>                               log.Println("Got:", sig)
```

```
>                        TOTALWRITES++
>                    }
53c61,64
<            time.Sleep(time.Second)
---
>      }()
>
>      for {
>           time.Sleep(10 * time.Second)
55d65
<      fmt.Println("Wrote", TOTALWRITES, "log entries!")
```

The good thing here is that the use of signals in rotateSignals.go makes most of the global variables used in rotateLog.go unnecessary because you can now control the utility by sending signals. Additionally, the design and the structure of rotateSignals.go are simpler than rotateLog.go because you only have to understand what the anonymous function does.

After executing rotateSignals.go and sending some signals to it, the contents of /tmp/myLog.log will look like the following:

```
$ cat /tmp/myLog.log
2017/06/03 14:53:33 Got: user defined signal 1
2017/06/03 14:54:08 Got: user defined signal 1
2017/06/03 14:54:12 Got: user defined signal 2
2017/06/03 14:54:19 Got: terminated
```

Additionally, you will have the following files inside /tmp:

```
$ ls -l /tmp/myLog.log*
-rw-r--r--  1 mtsouk  wheel  177 Jun  3 14:54 /tmp/myLog.log
-rw-r--r--  1 mtsouk  wheel  106 Jun  3 13:42 /tmp/myLog.log.0
```

Improving file copying

The original cp(1) utility prints useful information when it receives a SIGINFO signal, as shown in the following output:

```
$ cp FileToCopy /tmp/copy
FileToCopy -> /tmp/copy  26%
FileToCopy -> /tmp/copy  29%
FileToCopy -> /tmp/copy  31%
```

So, the rest of this section will implement the same functionality to the Go implementation of the cp(1) command. The Go code in this section will be based on the cp.go program because it can be very slow when used with a small buffer size giving us time for testing. The name of the new copy utility will be cpSignal.go and will be presented in four parts.

The fundamental difference between cpSignal.go and cp.go is that cpSignal.go should find the size of the input file and keep the number of bytes that have been written at a given point. Apart from those modifications there is nothing else that you should worry about because the core functionality of the two versions, which is copying a file, is exactly the same.

The first part of the program is the following:

```
package main

import (
    "fmt"
    "io"
    "os"
    "os/signal"
    "path/filepath"
    "strconv"
    "syscall"
)

var BUFFERSIZE int64
var FILESIZE int64
var BYTESWRITTEN int64
```

In order to make things simpler for the developer, the program introduces two global variables called FILESIZE and BYTESWRITTEN and these keep the size of the input file and the number of bytes that have been written, respectively. Both variables are used by the function that handles the SIGINFO signal.

The second part is as follows:

```
func Copy(src, dst string, BUFFERSIZE int64) error {
    sourceFileStat, err := os.Stat(src)
    if err != nil {
        return err
    }

    FILESIZE = sourceFileStat.Size()

    if !sourceFileStat.Mode().IsRegular() {
        return fmt.Errorf("%s is not a regular file.", src)
```

```
        }

        source, err := os.Open(src)
        if err != nil {
                return err
        }
        defer source.Close()

        _, err = os.Stat(dst)
        if err == nil {
                return fmt.Errorf("File %s already exists.", dst)
        }

        destination, err := os.Create(dst)
        if err != nil {
                return err
        }
        defer destination.Close()

        if err != nil {
                panic(err)
        }

        buf := make([]byte, BUFFERSIZE)
        for {
                n, err := source.Read(buf)
                if err != nil && err != io.EOF {
                        return err
                }
                if n == 0 {
                        break
                }
                if _, err := destination.Write(buf[:n]); err != nil {
                        return err
                }
                BYTESWRITTEN = BYTESWRITTEN + int64(n)
        }
        return err
}
```

Here, you use the `sourceFileStat.Size()` function to get the size of the input file and set the value of the `FILESIZE` global variable.

The third part is where you define the signal handling:

```
func progressInfo() {
    progress := float64(BYTESWRITTEN) / float64(FILESIZE) * 100
    fmt.Printf("Progress: %.2f%%\n", progress)
}

func main() {
    if len(os.Args) != 4 {
        fmt.Printf("usage: %s source destination BUFFERSIZE\n",
filepath.Base(os.Args[0]))
        os.Exit(1)
    }

    source := os.Args[1]
    destination := os.Args[2]
    BUFFERSIZE, _ = strconv.ParseInt(os.Args[3], 10, 64)
    BYTESWRITTEN = 0

    sigs := make(chan os.Signal, 1)
    signal.Notify(sigs)
```

Here, you choose to catch all signals. However, the Go code of the anonymous function will only call `progressInfo()` after receiving a `syscall.SIGINFO` signal.

If you want to have a way of gracefully terminating the program, you might want to use the `SIGINT` signal because when capturing all signals, gracefully terminating a program is no longer possible—you will need to send a `SIGKILL` in order to terminate your program, which is a little cruel.

The last part of `cpSignal.go` is the following:

```
    go func() {
        for {
            sig := <-sigs
            switch sig {
            case syscall.SIGINFO:
                progressInfo()
            default:
                fmt.Println("Ignored:", sig)
            }
        }
    }()

    fmt.Printf("Copying %s to %s\n", source, destination)
    err := Copy(source, destination, BUFFERSIZE)
    if err != nil {
```

```
                    fmt.Printf("File copying failed: %q\n", err)
        }
    }
```

Executing `cpSignal.go` and sending two `SIGINFO` signals to it will generate the following output:

```
$ ./cpSignal FileToCopy /tmp/copy 2
Copying FileToCopy to /tmp/copy
Ignored: user defined signal 1
Progress: 21.83%
^CIgnored: interrupt
Progress: 29.78%
```

Plotting data

The utility that will be developed in this section will read multiple log files and will create a graphical image with as many bars as the number of log files read. Each bar will represent the number of times a given IP address has been found in a log file.

However, the Unix philosophy tells us that instead of developing a single utility, we should make two distinct utilities: one for processing the log files and creating a report and another for plotting the data generated by the first utility—the two utilities will communicate using Unix pipes. Although this section will implement the first approach, you will see the implementation of the second approach later in *The* `plotIP.go` *utility revisited* section of this chapter.

 The idea for the presented utility came from a tutorial that I wrote for a magazine where I developed a small Go program that did some plotting—even small and naïve programs can inspire you to develop bigger things, so do not underestimate their power.

The name of the utility will be `plotIP.go`, and it will be presented in seven parts—the good thing is that `plotIP.go` will reuse some of the code of `countIP.go` and `findIP.go`. The only thing that `plotIP.go` does not do is writing text to the image, so you can only plot the bars without knowing the actual values or the corresponding log file of a particular bar—you can try to add text capabilities to the program as an exercise.

Also, plotIP.go will require at least three parameters, which are the width and height of the image and the name of the log file that will be used—in order to make plotIP.go smaller, plotIP.go will not use the flag package and assume that you will give its parameters in the correct order. If you give it more parameters , it will consider them as log files.

The first part of plotIP.go is the following:

```
package main

import (
    "bufio"
    "fmt"
    "image"
    "image/color"
    "image/png"
    "io"
    "os"
    "path/filepath"
    "regexp"
    "strconv"
)

var m *image.NRGBA
var x int
var y int
var barWidth int
```

These global variables related to the dimensions of the image (x and y), the image as a Go variable (m), and the width of one of its bars (barWidth) that depends on the size of the image and the number of the bars that will be plotted. Note that using x and y as variable names instead of something like IMAGEWIDTH and IMAGEHEIGHT might be a little wrong and dangerous here.

The second part is the following:

```
func findIP(input string) string {
    partIP := "(25[0-5]|2[0-4][0-9]|1[0-9][0-9]|[1-9]?[0-9])"
    grammar := partIP + "\\." + partIP + "\\." + partIP + "\\." + partIP
    matchMe := regexp.MustCompile(grammar)
    return matchMe.FindString(input)
}

func plotBar(width int, height int, color color.RGBA) {
    xx := 0
    for xx < barWidth {
```

```
        yy := 0
        for yy < height {
                m.Set(xx+width, y-yy, color)
                yy = yy + 1
        }
        xx = xx + 1
    }
}
```

Here, you implement a Go function named `plotBar()` that does the plotting of each bar, given its height, its width, and its color of the bar. This function is the most challenging part of `plotIP.go`.

The third part has the following Go code:

```
func getColor(x int) color.RGBA {
    switch {

    case x == 0:
            return color.RGBA{0, 0, 255, 255}
    case x == 1:
            return color.RGBA{255, 0, 0, 255}
    case x == 2:
            return color.RGBA{0, 255, 0, 255}
    case x == 3:
            return color.RGBA{255, 255, 0, 255}
    case x == 4:
            return color.RGBA{255, 0, 255, 255}
    case x == 5:
            return color.RGBA{0, 255, 255, 255}
    case x == 6:
            return color.RGBA{255, 100, 100, 255}
    case x == 7:
            return color.RGBA{100, 100, 255, 255}
    case x == 8:
            return color.RGBA{100, 255, 255, 255}
    case x == 9:
            return color.RGBA{255, 255, 255, 255}
    }
    return color.RGBA{0, 0, 0, 255}
}
```

This function lets you define the colors that will be present in the output—you can change them if you want.

The fourth part contains the following Go code:

```go
func main() {
    var data []int
    arguments := os.Args
    if len(arguments) < 4 {
            fmt.Printf("%s X Y IP input\n", filepath.Base(arguments[0]))
            os.Exit(0)
    }

    x, _ = strconv.Atoi(arguments[1])
    y, _ = strconv.Atoi(arguments[2])
    WANTED := arguments[3]
    fmt.Println("Image size:", x, y)
```

Here, you read the desired IP address, which is saved in the WANTED variable and you read the dimensions of the generated PNG image.

The fifth part contains the following Go code:

```go
    for _, filename := range arguments[4:] {
            count := 0
            fmt.Println(filename)
            f, err := os.Open(filename)
            if err != nil {
                    fmt.Fprintf(os.Stderr, "Error: %s\n", err)
                    continue
            }
            defer f.Close()

            r := bufio.NewReader(f)
            for {
                    line, err := r.ReadString('\n')
                    if err == io.EOF {
                        break
                    }

    if err != nil {
                        fmt.Fprintf(os.Stderr, "Error in file: %s\n", err)
                        continue
                    }
                    ip := findIP(line)
                    if ip == WANTED {
                        count++
```

```
                }
        }
        data = append(data, count)
}
```

Here, you process the input log files one by one and store the values you calculate in the data slice. Error messages are printed to os.Stderr—the main advantage you get from printing error messages to os.Stderr is that you can easily redirect error messages to a file while using data written to os.Stdout in a different way.

The sixth part of plotIP.go contains the following Go code:

```
fmt.Println("Slice length:", len(data))
if len(data)*2 > x {
        fmt.Println("Image size (x) too small!")
        os.Exit(-1)
}

maxValue := data[0]
for _, temp := range data {
        if maxValue < temp {
                maxValue = temp
        }
}

if maxValue > y {
        fmt.Println("Image size (y) too small!")
        os.Exit(-1)
}
fmt.Println("maxValue:", maxValue)
barHeighPerUnit := int(y / maxValue)
fmt.Println("barHeighPerUnit:", barHeighPerUnit)
PNGfile := WANTED + ".png"
OUTPUT, err := os.OpenFile(PNGfile, os.O_CREATE|os.O_WRONLY, 0644)
if err != nil {
        fmt.Println(err)
        os.Exit(-1)
}
m = image.NewNRGBA(image.Rectangle{Min: image.Point{0, 0}, Max:
image.Point{x, y}})
```

Here, you calculate things about the plot and create the output image file using `os.OpenFile()`. The PNG file generated by the `plotIP.go` utility is named after the given IP address to make things simpler.

The last part of the Go code of `plotIP.go` is the following:

```
i := 0
barWidth = int(x / len(data))
fmt.Println("barWidth:", barWidth)
for _, v := range data {
        c := getColor(v % 10)
        yy := v * barHeighPerUnit
        plotBar(barWidth*i, yy, c)
        fmt.Println("plotBar", barWidth*i, yy)
        i = i + 1
}
png.Encode(OUTPUT, m)
}
```

Here, you read the values of the `data` slice and create a bar for each one of them by calling the `plotBar()` function.

Executing `plotIP.go` will generate the following output:

```
$ go run plotIP.go 1300 1500 127.0.0.1 /tmp/log.*
Image size: 1300 1500
/tmp/log.1
/tmp/log.2
/tmp/log.3
Slice length: 3
maxValue: 1500
barHeighPerUnit: 1
barWidth: 433
plotBar 0 1500
plotBar 433 1228
plotBar 866 532
$  ls -l 127.0.0.1.png
-rw-r--r-- 1 mtsouk mtsouk 11023 Jun  5 18:36 127.0.0.1.png
```

However, apart from the generated text output, what is important is the produced PNG file that can be seen in the following figure:

The output generated by the plotIP.go utility

If you want to save the error messages to a different file, you can use a variation of the following command:

```
$ go run plotIP.go 130 150 127.0.0.1 doNOTExist 2> err
Image size: 130 150
doNOTExist
Slice length: 0
$ cat err
Error: open doNOTExist: no such file or directory
panic: runtime error: index out of range
goroutine 1 [running]:
main.main()
        /Users/mtsouk/Desktop/goBook/ch/ch8/code/plotIP.go:112 +0x12de
exit status 2
```

The following command discards all error messages by sending them to `/dev/null`:

```
$ go run plotIP.go 1300 1500 127.0.0.1 doNOTExist 2>/dev/null
Image size: 1300 1500
doNOTExist
Slice length: 0
```

Unix pipes in Go

We first talked about pipes in `Chapter 6`, *File Input and Output*. Pipes have two serious limitations: first, they usually communicate in one direction, and second, they can only be used between processes that have a common ancestor.

The general idea behind pipes is that if you do not have a file to process, you should wait to get your input from standard input. Similarly, if you are not told to save your output to a file, you should write your output to standard output, either for the user to see it or for another program to process it. As a result, pipes can be used for streaming data between two processes without creating any temporary files.

This section will present some simple utilities written in Go that use Unix pipes for clarity.

Reading from standard input

The first thing that you need to know in order to develop Go applications that support Unix pipes is how to read from standard input.

The developed program is named `readSTDIN.go` and will be presented in three parts.

The first part of the program is the expected preamble:

```
package main

import (
    "bufio"
    "fmt"
    "os"
)
```

The second part of `readSTDIN.go` has the following Go code:

```
func main() {
    filename := ""
    var f *os.File
    arguments := os.Args
    if len(arguments) == 1 {
        f = os.Stdin
    } else {
        filename = arguments[1]
        fileHandler, err := os.Open(filename)
        if err != nil {
            fmt.Printf("error opening %s: %s", filename, err)
            os.Exit(1)
        }
        f = fileHandler
    }
    defer f.Close()
```

Here, you resolve whether you have an actual file to process, which can be determined by the number of the command-line arguments of your program. If you do not have a file to process, you will try to read data from `os.Stdin`. Make sure that you understand the presented technique because it will be used many times in this chapter.

The last part of readSTDIN.go is the following:

```
scanner := bufio.NewScanner(f)
for scanner.Scan() {
        fmt.Println(">", scanner.Text())
}
}
```

This code is the same whether you are processing an actual file or os.Stdin, which happens because everything in Unix is a file. Note that the program output begins with the > character.

Executing readSTDIN.go will generate the following output:

```
$ cat /tmp/testfile
1
2
$ go run readSTDIN.go /tmp/testFile
> 1
> 2
$ cat /tmp/testFile | go run readSTDIN.go
> 1
> 2
$ go run readSTDIN.go
3
> 3
2
> 2
1
> 1
```

In the last case, readSTDIN.go echoes each line it reads because the input is read line by line—the cat (1) utility works the same way.

Sending data to standard output

This subsection will show you how to send data to standard output in a better way than just using fmt.Println() or any other function from the fmt standard Go package. The Go program will be named writeSTDOUT.go and will be presented to you in three parts.

The first part is the following:

```
package main

import (
    "io"
    "os"
)
```

The second part of writeSTDOUT.go has the following Go code:

```
func main() {
    myString := ""
    arguments := os.Args
    if len(arguments) == 1 {
        myString = "You did not give an argument!"
    } else {
        myString = arguments[1]
    }
```

The last part of writeSTDOUT.go is the following:

```
    io.WriteString(os.Stdout, myString)
    io.WriteString(os.Stdout, "\n")
}
```

The only subtle thing is that you need to put your text into a slice before using io.WriteString() to write data to os.Stdout.

Executing writeSTDOUT.go will generate the following output:

```
$ go run writeSTDOUT.go 123456
123456
$ go run writeSTDOUT.go
You do not give an argument!
```

Implementing cat(1) in Go

This subsection will present a Go version of the cat(1) command-line utility. If you give one or more command-line arguments to cat(1), then cat(1) will print their contents on the screen. However, if you just type cat(1) on your Unix shell, then cat(1) will wait for your input, which will be terminated when you type *Ctrl + D*.

The name of the Go implementation will be cat.go and will be presented in three parts.

The first part of cat.go is the following:

```
package main

import (
    "bufio"
    "fmt"
    "io"
    "os"
)
```

The second part is the following:

```
func catFile(filename string) error {
    f, err := os.Open(filename)
    if err != nil {
        return err
    }
    defer f.Close()
    scanner := bufio.NewScanner(f)
    for scanner.Scan() {
        fmt.Println(scanner.Text())
    }
    return nil
}
```

The catFile() function is called when the cat.go utility has to process real files. Having a function to do your job makes the design of the program better.

The last part has the following Go code:

```
func main() {
    filename := ""
    arguments := os.Args
    if len(arguments) == 1 {
        io.Copy(os.Stdout, os.Stdin)
        os.Exit(0)
    }
```

```
        filename = arguments[1]
        err := catFile(filename)
        if err != nil {
                fmt.Println(err)
        }
    }
```

So, if the program has no arguments, then it assumes that it has to read `os.Stdin`. In that case, it just echoes each line you give to it. If the program has arguments, then it processes the first argument as a file using the `catFile()` function.

Executing `cat.go` will generate the following output:

```
$ go run cat.go /tmp/testFile  |  go run cat.go
1
2
$ go run cat.go
Mihalis
Mihalis
Tsoukalos
Tsoukalos
$ echo "Mihalis Tsoukalos" | go run cat.go
Mihalis Tsoukalos
```

The plotIP.go utility revisited

As promised in a previous section of this chapter, this section will create two separate utilities, which when combined will implement the functionality of `plotIP.go`. Personally, I prefer to have two separate utilities and combine them when needed than having just one utility that does two or more tasks.

The names of the two utilities will be `extractData.go` and `plotData.go`. As you can easily understand, only the second utility would have to be able to get input from standard input as long as the first utility prints its output on standard output either using `os.Stdout`, which is the correct way, or using `fmt.Println()`, which usually does the job.

I think that I should now tell you my little secret: I created `extractData.go` and `plotData.go` first and then developed `plotIP.go` because it is easier to develop two separate utilities than a bigger one that does everything! Additionally, the use of two different utilities allows you to filter the output of `extractData.go` using standard Unix utilities such as `tail(1)`, `sort(1)`, and `head(1)`, which means that you can modify your data in different ways without the need for writing any extra Go code.

Taking two command-line utilities and creating one utility that implements the functionality of both utilities is easier than taking one big utility and dividing its functionality into two or more distinct utilities because the latter usually requires more variables and more error checking.

The extractData.go utility will be presented in four parts; the first part is the following:

```
package main

import (
    "bufio"
    "fmt"
    "io"
    "os"
    "path/filepath"
    "regexp"
)
```

The second part of extractData.go has the following Go code:

```
func findIP(input string) string {
    partIP := "(25[0-5]|2[0-4][0-9]|1[0-9][0-9]|[1-9]?[0-9])"
    grammar := partIP + "\\." + partIP + "\\." + partIP + "\\." + partIP
    matchMe := regexp.MustCompile(grammar)
    return matchMe.FindString(input)
}
```

You should be familiar with the findIP() function, which you saw in findIP.go in Chapter 7, *Working with System files*.

The third part of extractData.go is the following:

```
func main() {
    arguments := os.Args
    if len(arguments) < 3 {
        fmt.Printf("%s IP <files>\n", filepath.Base(os.Args[0]))
        os.Exit(-1)
    }

    WANTED := arguments[1]
    for _, filename := range arguments[2:] {
        count := 0
        buf := []byte(filename)
        io.WriteString(os.Stdout, string(buf))
        f, err := os.Open(filename)
        if err != nil {
```

```
            fmt.Fprintf(os.Stderr, "Error: %s\n", err)
            continue
    }
    defer f.Close()
```

The use of the `buf` variable is redundant here because `filename` is a string and `io.WriteString()` expects a string—it is just my habit to put the value of `filename` into a byte slice. You can remove it if you want.

Once again, most of the Go code is from the `plotIP.go` utility. The last part of `extractData.go` is the following:

```
    r := bufio.NewReader(f)
    for {
            line, err := r.ReadString('\n')
            if err == io.EOF {
                    break
            } else if err != nil {
                    fmt.Fprintf(os.Stderr, "Error in file: %s\n", err)
                    continue
            }

            ip := findIP(line)
            if ip == WANTED {
                    count = count + 1
            }
    }
    buf = []byte(strconv.Itoa(count))
    io.WriteString(os.Stdout, " ")
    io.WriteString(os.Stdout, string(buf))
    io.WriteString(os.Stdout, "\n")
    }
}
```

Here, `extractData.go` writes its output to standard output (`os.Stdout`) instead of using the functions of the `fmt` package in order to be more compatible with pipes. The `extractData.go` utility requires at least two parameters—an IP address and a log file, but it can process as many log files as you wish.

You might want to move the printing of the `filename` value from the third part here in order to have all printing commands at the same place.

Executing `extractData.go` will generate the following output:

```
$ ./extractData 127.0.0.1 access.log{,.1}
access.log 3099
access.log.1 6333
```

Although `extractData.go` prints two values in each line, only the second field will be used by `plotData.go`. The best way to do that is filter the output of `extractData.go` using `awk(1)`:

```
$ ./extractData 127.0.0.1 access.log{,.1} | awk '{print $2}'
3099
6333
```

As you can understand, `awk(1)` allows you to do many more things with the generated values.

The `plotData.go` utility will also be presented in six parts; its first part is the following:

```
package main

import (
    "bufio"
    "fmt"
    "image"
    "image/color"
    "image/png"
    "os"
    "path/filepath"
    "strconv"
)

var m *image.NRGBA
var x int
var y int
var barWidth int
```

Once again, the use of global variables is for avoiding the passing of too many arguments to some of the functions of the utility.

The second part of `plotData.go` contains the following Go code:

```go
func plotBar(width int, height int, color color.RGBA) {
    xx := 0
    for xx < barWidth {
        yy := 0
        for yy < height {
            m.Set(xx+width, y-yy, color)
            yy = yy + 1
        }
        xx = xx + 1
    }
}
```

The third part of `plotData.go` has the following Go code:

```go
func getColor(x int) color.RGBA {
    switch {
    case x == 0:
        return color.RGBA{0, 0, 255, 255}
    case x == 1:
        return color.RGBA{255, 0, 0, 255}
    case x == 2:
        return color.RGBA{0, 255, 0, 255}
    case x == 3:
        return color.RGBA{255, 255, 0, 255}
    case x == 4:
        return color.RGBA{255, 0, 255, 255}
    case x == 5:
        return color.RGBA{0, 255, 255, 255}
    case x == 6:
        return color.RGBA{255, 100, 100, 255}
    case x == 7:
        return color.RGBA{100, 100, 255, 255}
    case x == 8:
        return color.RGBA{100, 255, 255, 255}
    case x == 9:
        return color.RGBA{255, 255, 255, 255}
    }
    return color.RGBA{0, 0, 0, 255}
}
```

The fourth part of `plotData.go` contains the following Go code:

```go
func main() {
    var data []int
    var f *os.File
    arguments := os.Args
    if len(arguments) < 3 {
        fmt.Printf("%s X Y input\n", filepath.Base(arguments[0]))
        os.Exit(0)
    }

    if len(arguments) == 3 {
        f = os.Stdin
    } else {
        filename := arguments[3]
        fTemp, err := os.Open(filename)
        if err != nil {
            fmt.Println(err)
            os.Exit(0)
        }
        f = fTemp
    }
    defer f.Close()

    x, _ = strconv.Atoi(arguments[1])
    y, _ = strconv.Atoi(arguments[2])
    fmt.Println("Image size:", x, y)
```

The fifth part of `plotData.go` is the following:

```go
    scanner := bufio.NewScanner(f)
    for scanner.Scan() {
        value, err := strconv.Atoi(scanner.Text())
        if err == nil {
            data = append(data, value)
        } else {
            fmt.Println("Error:", value)
        }
    }

    fmt.Println("Slice length:", len(data))
    if len(data)*2 > x {
        fmt.Println("Image size (x) too small!")
        os.Exit(-1)
    }

    maxValue := data[0]
    for _, temp := range data {
```

```
            if maxValue < temp {
                maxValue = temp
            }
    }

    if maxValue > y {
            fmt.Println("Image size (y) too small!")
            os.Exit(-1)
    }
    fmt.Println("maxValue:", maxValue)
    barHeighPerUnit := int(y / maxValue)
    fmt.Println("barHeighPerUnit:", barHeighPerUnit)
```

The last part of plotData.go is the following:

```
    PNGfile := arguments[1] + "x" + arguments[2] + ".png"
    OUTPUT, err := os.OpenFile(PNGfile, os.O_CREATE|os.O_WRONLY, 0644)
    if err != nil {
            fmt.Println(err)
            os.Exit(-1)
    }
    m = image.NewNRGBA(image.Rectangle{Min: image.Point{0, 0}, Max:
image.Point{x, y}})

    i := 0
    barWidth = int(x / len(data))
    fmt.Println("barWidth:", barWidth)
    for _, v := range data {
            c := getColor(v % 10)
            yy := v * barHeighPerUnit
            plotBar(barWidth*i, yy, c)
            fmt.Println("plotBar", barWidth*i, yy)
            i = i + 1
    }

    png.Encode(OUTPUT, m)
}
```

Although you can use plotData.go on its own, using the output of extractData.go as the input to plotData.go is as easy as executing the following command:

```
$ ./extractData.go 127.0.0.1 access.log{,.1} | awk '{print $2}' |
./plotData 6000 6500
Image size: 6000 6500
Slice length: 2
maxValue: 6333
barHeighPerUnit: 1
barWidth: 3000
```

```
plotBar 0 3129
plotBar 3000 6333
$ ls -l 6000x6500.png
-rw-r--r-- 1 mtsouk mtsouk 164915 Jun  5 18:25 6000x6500.png
```

The graphical output from the previous command can be an image like the one you can see in the following figure:

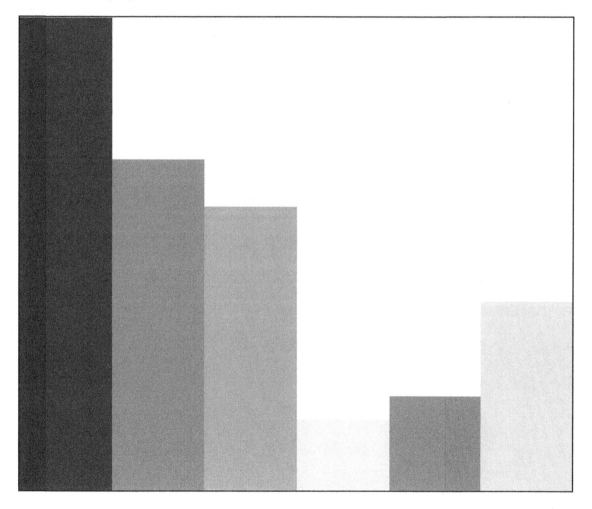

The output generated by the plotData.go utility

Unix sockets in Go

There exist two kinds of sockets: Unix sockets and network sockets. Network sockets will be explained in Chapter 12, *Network Programming*, whereas Unix sockets will be briefly explained in this section. However, as the presented Go functions also work with TCP/IP sockets, you will still have to wait tillChapter 12,*Network Programming*, in order to fully understand them as they will not be explained here. So, this section will just present the Go code of a Unix socket client, which is a program that uses a Unix socket, which is a special Unix file, to read and write data. The name of the program will be readUNIX.go and will be presented in three parts.

The first part is the following:

```
package main

import (
    "fmt"
    "io"
    "net"
    "strconv"
    "time"
)
```

The second part of readUNIX.go is the following:

```
func readSocket(r io.Reader) {
    buf := make([]byte, 1024)
    for {
        n, _ := r.Read(buf[:])
        fmt.Print("Read: ", string(buf[0:n]))
    }
}
```

The last part contains the following Go code:

```go
func main() {
    c, _ := net.Dial("unix", "/tmp/aSocket.sock")
    defer c.Close()

    go readSocket(c)
    n := 0
    for {
        message := []byte("Hi there: " + strconv.Itoa(n) + "\n")
        _, _ = c.Write(message)
        time.Sleep(5 * time.Second)
        n = n + 1
    }
}
```

The use of readUNIX.go requires the presence of another process that also reads and writes to the same socket file (/tmp/aSocket.sock).

The generated output depends on the implementation of the other part—in this case, that output was the following:

```
$ go run readUNIX.go
Read: Hi there: 0
Read: Hi there: 1
```

If the socket file cannot be found or if no program is watching it, you will get the following error message:

```
panic: runtime error: invalid memory address or nil pointer dereference
[signal SIGSEGV: segmentation violation code=0x1 addr=0x0 pc=0x10cfe77]
goroutine 1 [running]:
main.main()
        /Users/mtsouk/Desktop/goBook/ch/ch8/code/readUNIX.go:21 +0x67
exit status 2
```

RPC in Go

RPC stands for **Remote Procedure Call** and is a way of executing function calls to a remote server and getting the answer back in your clients. Once again, you will have to wait until Chapter 12, *Network Programming*, in order to learn how to develop an RPC server and an RPC client in Go.

Programming a Unix shell in Go

This section will briefly and naïvely present Go code that can be used as the foundation for the development of a Unix shell. Apart from the exit command, the only other command that the program can recognize is the version command that just prints the version of the program. All other user input will be echoed on the screen.

The Go code of UNIXshell.go will be presented in three parts. However, before that I will present to you the first version of the shell, which mainly contains comments in order to betterunderstand how I usually start the implementation of a relatively challenging program:

```
package main

import (
    "fmt"
)

func main() {

    // Present prompt

    // Read a line

    // Get the first word of the line

    // If it is a built-in shell command, execute the command

    // otherwise, echo the command

}
```

This is more or less the algorithm that I would use as a starting point—the good thing is that the comments briefly show how the program will operate. Keep in mind that the algorithm does not depend on the programming language. After that, it is easier to start implementing things because you know what you want to do.

So, the first part of the final version of the shell is the following:

```
package main

import (
    "bufio"
    "fmt"
    "os"
    "strings"
)

var VERSION string = "0.2"
```

The second part is the following:

```
func main() {
    scanner := bufio.NewScanner(os.Stdin)
    fmt.Print("> ")
    for scanner.Scan() {

        line := scanner.Text()
        words := strings.Split(line, " ")
        command := words[0]
```

Here, you just read the input from the user line by line and find out the first word of the input.

The last part of `UNIXshell.go` is the following:

```
        switch command {
        case "exit":
                fmt.Println("Exiting...")
                os.Exit(0)
        case "version":
                fmt.Println(VERSION)
        default:
                fmt.Println(line)
        }

        fmt.Print("> ")
    }
}
```

The aforementioned Go code checks the command that the user gave and acts accordingly.

Executing `UNIXshell.go` and interacting with it will generate the following output:

```
$ go run UNIXshell.go
> version
0.2
> ls -l
ls -l
> exit
Exiting...
```

Should you wish to learn more about creating your own Unix shell in Go, you can visit `https://github.com/elves/elvish`.

Yet another minor Go update

While I was writing this chapter, Go was updated—this is a minor update, which mainly fixes bugs:

```
$ date
Thu May 25 06:30:53 EEST 2017
$ go version
go version go1.8.3 darwin/amd64
```

Exercises

1. Put the plotting functionality of `plotIP.go` into a Go package and use that package to rewrite both `plotIP.go` and `plotData.go`.
2. Review the Go code of `ddGo.go` from Chapter 6, *File Input and Output*, in order to print information about its progress when receiving a `SIGINFO` signal.
3. Change the Go code of `cat.go` to add support for multiple input files.
4. Change the code of `plotData.go` in order to print gridlines to the generated image.
5. Change the code of `plotData.go` in order to leave a little space between the bars of the plot.
6. Try to make the `UNIXshell.go` program a little better by adding new features to it.

Summary

In this chapter, we talked about many interesting and handy topics, including signal handling and creating graphical images in Go. Additionally, we taught you how to add support for Unix pipes in your Go programs.

In the next chapter, we will talk about the most unique feature of Go, which is goroutines. You will learn what a goroutine is, how to create and synchronize them as well as how to create channels and pipelines. Have in mind that many people come to Go in order to learn a modern and safe programming language, but stay for its goroutines!

9
Goroutines – Basic Features

In the previous chapter, you learned about Unix signal handlingas well asadding support for pipesandcreating graphical images in Go.

The subject of this really important chapter is goroutines. Go uses goroutines and **channels** in order to program concurrent applications in its own way while providing support for traditional concurrency techniques. Everything in Go is executed using goroutines; when a program starts its execution, its single goroutine automatically calls the `main()` function in order to begin the actual execution of the program.

In this chapter, we will present the easy parts of goroutines using easy to follow code examples. However, in`Chapter 10`, *Goroutines - Advanced Features*, that is coming next, we will talk about more important and advanced techniques related to goroutines and channels; so, make sure that you fully understand this chapter before reading the next one.

Therefore, this chapter will tell you about the following:

- Creating goroutines
- Synchronizing goroutines
- About channels and how to use them
- Reading and writing to channels
- Creating and using pipelines
- Changing the Go code of the `wc.go` utility from `Chapter 6`,*File Input and Output,* in order to use goroutines in the new implementation
- Improving the goroutine version of `wc.go` even further

About goroutines

A **goroutine** is the minimum Go entity that can be executed concurrently. Note that the use of the word *minimum* is very important here because goroutines are not autonomous entities. Goroutines live in threads that live in Unix processes. Putting it simply, processes can be autonomous and exist on their own, whereas both goroutines and threads cannot. So, in order to create a goroutine, you will need to have a process with at least one thread. The good thing is that goroutines are lighter than threads, which are lighter than processes. Everything in Go is executed using goroutines, which makes perfect sense since Go is a concurrent programming language by design. As you have just learned, when a Go program starts its execution, its single goroutine calls the `main()` function, which starts the actual program execution.

You can define a new goroutine using the `go`keyword`followed by a function name or the full definition of an anonymous function. The `go` keyword starts the function argument to it in a new goroutine and allows the invoking function to continue on by itself.

However, as you will see, you cannot control or make any assumptions about the order your goroutines are going to get executed because this depends on the scheduler of the operating system as well as the load of the operating system.

Concurrency and parallelism

A very common misconception is that **concurrency** and **parallelism** refer to the same thing, which is far from true! Parallelism is the simultaneous execution of multiple things, whereas concurrency is a way of structuring your components so that they can be independently executed when possible.

Only when you build things concurrently you can safely execute them in parallel—when and if your operating system and your hardware permit it. The Erlang programming language did this a long time ago, long before CPUs had multiple cores and computers had lots of RAM.

In a valid concurrent design, adding concurrent entities makes the whole system run faster because more things can run in parallel. So, the desired parallelism comes from a better concurrent expression and implementation of the problem. The developer is responsible for taking concurrency into account during the design phase of a system and benefit from a potential parallel execution of the components of the system. So, the developer should not think about parallelism, but about breaking things into independent components that solve the initial problem when combined.

Even if you cannot run your functions in parallel on a Unix machine, a valid concurrent design will still improve the design and the maintainability of your programs. In other words, concurrency is better than parallelism!

The sync Go packages

The `sync` Go package contains functions that can help you synchronize goroutines; the most important functions of `sync` are `sync.Add`, `sync.Done` and `sync.Wait`. The synchronization of goroutines is a mandatory task for every programmer.

Note that the synchronization of goroutines has nothing to do with shared variables and shared state. Shared variables and shared state have to do with the method you want to use for performing concurrent interactions.

A simple example

In this subsection, we will present a simple program that creates two goroutines. The name of the sample program will be `aGoroutine.go` and will be presented in three parts; the first part is the following:

```
package main

import (
    "fmt"
    "time"
)

func namedFunction() {
    time.Sleep(10000 * time.Microsecond)
    fmt.Println("Printing from namedFunction!")
}
```

Apart from the expected `package` and `import` statements, you can see the implementation of a function named `namedFunction()` that sleeps for a while before printing a message on the screen.

The second part of `aGoroutine.go` contains the following Go code:

```
func main() {
    fmt.Println("Chapter 09 - Goroutines.")
    go namedFunction()
```

Here, you create a goroutine that executes the `namedFunction()` function. The last part of this naïve program is the following:

```
go func() {
        fmt.Println("An anonymous function!")
} ()

time.Sleep(10000 * time.Microsecond)
fmt.Println("Exiting...")
}
```

Here, you create another goroutine that executes an anonymous function that contains a single `fmt.Println()` statement.

As you can see, goroutines that run this way are totally isolated from each other and cannot exchange any kind of data, which is not always the operational style that is desired.

If you forget to call the `time.Sleep()` function in the `main()` function, or if `time.Sleep()` sleeps for a small amount of time, then `main()` will finish too early and the two goroutines will not have enough time to start and therefore finish their jobs; as a result, you will not see all the expected output on your screen!

Executing `aGoroutine.go` will generate the following output:

```
$ go run aGoroutine.go
Chapter 09 - Goroutines.
Printing from namedFunction!
Exiting...
```

Creating multiple goroutines

This subsection will show you how to create many goroutines and the problems that arise from having to handle more goroutines. The name of the program will be `moreGoroutines.go` and will be presented in three parts.

The first part of `moreGoroutines.go` is the following:

```
package main

import (
    "fmt"
    "time"
)
```

The second part of the program has the following Go code:

```go
func main() {
    fmt.Println("Chapter 09 - Goroutines.")

    for i := 0; i < 10; i++ {
        go func(x int) {
            time.Sleep(10)
            fmt.Printf("%d ", x)
        }(i)
    }
```

This time, the anonymous function takes a parameter named x, which has the value of the i variable. The for loop that uses the i variable creates ten goroutines, one by one.

The last part of the program is the following:

```go
    time.Sleep(10000)
    fmt.Println("Exiting...")
}
```

Once again, if you put a smaller value as the parameter to time.Sleep(), you will see different results when you execute the program.

Executing moreGoroutines.go will generate a somehow strange output:

```
$ go run moreGoroutines.go
Chapter 09 - Goroutines.
1 7 Exiting...
2 3
```

However, the big surprise comes when you execute moreGoroutines.go multiple times:

```
$ go run moreGoroutines.go
Chapter 09 - Goroutines.
Exiting...
$ go run moreGoroutines.go
Chapter 09 - Goroutines.
3 1 0 9 2 Exiting...
4 5 6 8 7
$ go run moreGoroutines.go
Chapter 09 - Goroutines.
2 0 1 8 7 3 6 5 Exiting...
4
```

As you can see, all previous outputs of the program are different from the first one! So, not only the output is not coordinated and there is not always enough time for all goroutines to get executed; you cannot be sure about the order the goroutines will get executed. However, although you cannot do anything about the latter problem because the order that goroutines get executed depends on various parameters that the developer cannot control, the next subsection will teach you how to synchronize goroutines and give them enough time to finish without having to call time.Sleep().

Waiting for goroutines to finish their jobs

This subsection will demonstrate to you the correct way to make a calling function that wait for its goroutines to finish their jobs. The name of the program will be waitGR.go and will be presented in four parts; the first part is the following:

```
package main

import (
    "fmt"
    "sync"
)
```

There is nothing special here apart from the absence of the time package and the addition of the sync package.

The second part has the following Go code:

```
func main() {
    fmt.Println("Waiting for Goroutines!")

    var waitGroup sync.WaitGroup
    waitGroup.Add(10)
```

Here, you create a new variable with a type of sync.WaitGroup, which waits for a group of goroutines to finish. The number of goroutines that belong to that group is defined by one or multiple calls to the sync.Add() function.

 Callingsync.Add() before the Go statement in order to prevent race conditionsis important.

Additionally, the `sync.Add(10)` call tells our program that we will wait for ten goroutines to finish.

The third part of the program is the following:

```
var i int64
for i = 0; i < 10; i++ {

    go func(x int64) {
        defer waitGroup.Done()
        fmt.Printf("%d ", x)
    }(i)
}
```

Here, you create the desired number of goroutines using a `for` loop, but you could have used multiple sequential Go statements. When each goroutine finishes its job, the `sync.Done()` function is executed—the use of the `defer` keyword right after the function definition tells the anonymous function to automatically call `sync.Done()` just before it finishes.

The last part of `waitGR.go` is the following:

```
    waitGroup.Wait()
    fmt.Println("\nExiting...")
}
```

The good thing here is that there is no need to call `time.Sleep()` because `sync.Wait()` does the necessary waiting for us.

Once again, it should be noted here that you should not make any assumptions about the order the goroutines will get executed in which is also verified by the following output:

```
$ go run waitGR.go
Waiting for Goroutines!
9 0 5 6 7 8 2 1 3 4
Exiting...
$ go run waitGR.go
Waiting for Goroutines!
9 0 5 6 7 8 3 1 2 4
Exiting...
$ go run waitGR.go
Waiting for Goroutines!
9 5 6 7 8 1 0 2 3 4
Exiting...
```

If you call `waitGroup.Add()` more times than needed, you will get the following error message when you execute `waitGR.go`:

```
Waiting for Goroutines!
fatal error: all goroutines are asleep - deadlock!
goroutine 1 [semacquire]:
sync.runtime_Semacquire(0xc42000e28c)
        /usr/local/Cellar/go/1.8.3/libexec/src/runtime/sema.go:47 +0x34
sync.(*WaitGroup).Wait(0xc42000e280)
        /usr/local/Cellar/go/1.8.3/libexec/src/sync/waitgroup.go:131 +0x7a
main.main()
        /Users/mtsouk/ch/ch9/code/waitGR.go:22 +0x13c
exit status 2
9 0 1 2 6 7 8 3 4 5
```

This happens because when you tell your program to wait for n+1 goroutines by calling `sync.Add(1)` n+1 times, your program cannot have only n goroutines (or less)! Putting it simply, this will make `sync.Wait()` to wait indefinitely for one or more goroutines to call `sync.Done()` without any luck, which is obviously a deadlock situation that prevents your program from finishing.

Creating a dynamic number of goroutines

This time, the number of goroutines that will be created will be given as a command-line argument—the name of the program will be `dynamicGR.go` and will be presented in four parts.

The first part of `dynamicGR.go` is the following:

```
package main

import (
    "fmt"
    "os"
    "path/filepath"
    "strconv"
    "sync"
)
```

The second part of `dynamicGR.go` contains the following Go code:

```
func main() {
    if len(os.Args) != 2 {
        fmt.Printf("usage: %s integer\n", filepath.Base(os.Args[0]))
        os.Exit(1)
```

```
        }

        numGR, _ := strconv.ParseInt(os.Args[1], 10, 64)
        fmt.Printf("Going to create %d goroutines.\n", numGR)
        var waitGroup sync.WaitGroup

        var i int64
        for i = 0; i < numGR; i++ {
                waitGroup.Add(1)
```

As you can see, the `waitGroup.Add(1)` statement is called just before you create a new goroutine.

The third part of the Go code of `dynamicGR.go` is the following:

```
        go func(x int64) {
                defer waitGroup.Done()
                fmt.Printf(" %d ", x)
        }(i)
        }
```

In the preceding part, each simplistic goroutine is created.

The last part of the program is the following:

```
        waitGroup.Wait()
        fmt.Println("\nExiting...")
    }
```

Here, you just tell the program to wait for all goroutines to finish using the `waitGroup.Wait()` statement.

The execution of `dynamicGR.go` requires an integer parameter, which is the number of goroutines you want to create:

```
$ go run dynamicGR.go 15
Going to create 15 goroutines.
 0  2  4  1  3  5  14  10  8  9  12  11  6  13  7
Exiting...
$ go run dynamicGR.go 15
Going to create 15 goroutines.
 5  3  14  4  10  6  7  11  8  9  12  2  13  1  0
Exiting...
$ go run dynamicGR.go 15
Going to create 15 goroutines.
 4  2  3  6  5  10  9  7  0  12  11  1  14  13  8
Exiting...
```

As you can imagine, the more goroutines you want to create, the more diverse outputs you will have because there is no way to control the order that the goroutines of a program are going to be executed.

About channels

A **channel**, putting it simply, is a communication mechanism that allows goroutines to exchange data. However, some rules exist here. First, each channel allows the exchange of a particular data type, which is also called the **element type** of the channel, and second, for a channel to operate properly, you will need to use some Go code to receive what is sent via the channel.

You should declare a new channel using the `chan` keyword and you can close a channel using the `close()` function. Additionally, as each channel has its own type, the developer should define it.

Last, a very important detail: when you are using a channel as a function parameter, you can specify its direction, that is, whether it will be used for writing or reading. In my opinion, if you know the purpose of a channel in advance, use this capability because it will make your program more robust as well as safer—otherwise, just do not define the purpose of the channel function parameter. As a result, if you declare that a channel function parameter will be used for reading only and you try to write to it, you will get an error message that will most likely save you from nasty bugs.

The error message you will get when you try to read from a write channel will be similar to the following:

```
# command-line-arguments
./writeChannel.go:13: invalid operation: <-c (receive from send-only type
chan<- int)
```

Writing to a channel

In this subsection, you will learn how to write to a channel. The presented program will be called `writeChannel.go` and you will see it in three parts.

The first part has the expected preamble:

```
package main

import (
    "fmt"
    "time"
)
```

As you can understand, the use of channels does not require any extra Go packages.

The second part of writeChannel.go is the following:

```
func writeChannel(c chan<- int, x int) {
    fmt.Println(x)
    c <- x
    close(c)
    fmt.Println(x)
}
```

Although the writeChannel() function writes to the channel, the data will be lost because currently nobody reads the channel in the program.

The last part of the program contains the following Go code:

```
func main() {
    c := make(chan int)
    go writeChannel(c, 10)
    time.Sleep(2 * time.Second)
}
```

Here, you can see the definition of a channel variable named c with the help of the chan keyword that is used for the int data.

Executing writeChannel.go will create the following output:

```
$ go run writeChannel.go
10
```

This is not what you expected to see! The cause of this unpredicted output is that the second fmt.Println(x) statement was not executed. The reason for this is pretty simple: the c <- x statement is blocking the execution of the rest of the writeChannel() function because nobody is reading from the c channel.

Reading from a channel

This subsection will improve the Go code of `writeChannel.go` by allowing you to read from a channel. The presented program will be called `readChannel.go` and be presented in four parts.

The first part is the following:

```
package main

import (
    "fmt"
    "time"
)
```

The second part of `readChannel.go` has the following Go code:

```
func writeChannel(c chan<- int, x int) {
    fmt.Println(x)
    c <- x
    close(c)
    fmt.Println(x)
}
```

Once again, note that if nobody collects the data written to a channel, the function that sent it will stall while waiting for someone to read its data. However, in Chapter 10, *Goroutines - Advanced Features*, you will see a very pretty solution to this problem.

The third part has the following Go code:

```
func main() {
    c := make(chan int)
    go writeChannel(c, 10)
    time.Sleep(2 * time.Second)
    fmt.Println("Read:", <-c)
    time.Sleep(2 * time.Second)
```

Here, the `<-c` statement in the `fmt.Println()` function is used for reading a single value from the channel—the same statement can be used for storing the value of a channel into a variable. However, if you do not store the value you read from a channel, it will be lost.

The last part of readChannel.go is the following:

```
_, ok := <-c
if ok {
        fmt.Println("Channel is open!")
} else {
        fmt.Println("Channel is closed!")
}
}
```

Here, you see a technique that allows you to find out whether the channel that you want to read from is closed or not. However, if the channel was open, the presented Go code will discard the read value of the channel because of the use of the _ character in the assignment.

Executing readChannel.go will create the following output:

```
$ go run readChannel.go
10
Read: 10
10
Channel is closed!
$ go run readChannel.go
10
10
Read: 10
Channel is closed!
```

Explaining h1s.go

In Chapter 8, *Processes and Signals*, you saw how Go handles Unix signals using many examples including h1s.go. However, now that you understand more about goroutines and channels, it is time to explain the Go code of h1s.go a little more.

As you already know thath1s.go uses channels and goroutines, it should be clear now that the anonymous function that is executed as a goroutine reads from the sigs channel using an infinite for loop. This means that each time there is a signal that interests us, the goroutine will read it from the sigs channel and handle it.

Pipelines

Go programs rarely use a single channel. One very common technique that uses multiple channels is called a **pipeline**. So, a pipeline is a method for connecting goroutines so that the output of a goroutine becomes the input of another with the help of channels. The benefits of using pipelines are as follows:

- One of the benefits you get from using pipelines is that there is a constant flow in your program because nobody waits for everything to be completed in order to start the execution of goroutines and channels of the program
- Additionally, you are using less variables and therefore less memory space because you do not have to save everything
- Last, the use of pipelines simplifies the design of the program and improves its maintainability

The code of `pipelines.go`, which works with a pipeline of integers, will be presented in five parts; the first part is the following:

```
package main

import (
    "fmt"
    "os"
    "path/filepath"
    "strconv"
)
```

The second part contains the following Go code:

```
func genNumbers(min, max int64, out chan<- int64) {

    var i int64
    for i = min; i <= max; i++ {
        out <- i
    }
    close(out)
}
```

Here, you define a function that takes three arguments: two integers and one output channel. The output channel will be used for writing data that will be read in another function—this is how a pipeline is created.

The third part of the program is the following:

```
func findSquares(out chan<- int64, in <-chan int64) {
    for x := range in {
            out <- x * x
    }
    close(out)
}
```

This time, the function takes two arguments that are both channels. However, out is an output channel, whereas in is an input channel used for reading data.

The fourth part contains the definition of another function:

```
func calcSum(in <-chan int64) {
    var sum int64
    sum = 0
    for x2 := range in {
            sum = sum + x2
    }
    fmt.Printf("The sum of squares is %d\n", sum)
}
```

The last function of pipelines.go takes just one argument, which is a channel used for reading data.

The last part of pipelines.go is the implementation of the main() function:

```
func main() {
    if len(os.Args) != 3 {
            fmt.Printf("usage: %s n1 n2\n", filepath.Base(os.Args[0]))
            os.Exit(1)
    }
    n1, _ := strconv.ParseInt(os.Args[1], 10, 64)
    n2, _ := strconv.ParseInt(os.Args[2], 10, 64)

    if n1 > n2 {
            fmt.Printf("%d should be smaller than %d\n", n1, n2)
            os.Exit(10)
    }

    naturals := make(chan int64)
    squares := make(chan int64)
    go genNumbers(n1, n2, naturals)
    go findSquares(squares, naturals)
    calcSum(squares)
}
```

Here, the `main()` function firstly reads its two command-line arguments and creates the necessary channel variables (`naturals` and `squares`). Then, it calls the functions of the pipeline—note that the last function of the channel is not being executed as a goroutine.

The following figure shows a graphical representation of the pipeline used in `pipelines.go` in order to the way this particular pipeline works:

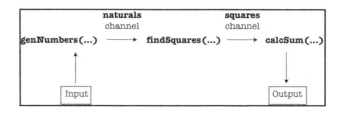

A graphical representation of the pipeline structure used in pipelines.go

Running `pipelines.go` generates the following output:

```
$ go run pipelines.go
usage: pipelines n1 n2
exit status 1
$ go run pipelines.go 3 2
3 should be smaller than 2
exit status 10
$ go run pipelines.go 3 20
The sum of squares is 2865
$ go run pipelines.go 1 20
The sum of squares is 2870
$ go run pipelines.go 20 20
The sum of squares is 400
```

A better version of wc.go

As we talked about in Chapter 6, *File Input and Output*, in this chapter, you will learn how to create a version of `wc.go` that uses goroutines. The name of the new utility will be `dWC.go` and will be presented in four parts. Note that the current version of `dWC.go` considers each command-line argument as a file.

The first part of the utility is the following:

```
package main

import (
```

```
    "bufio"
    "fmt"
    "io"
    "os"
    "path/filepath"
    "regexp"
    "sync"
)
```

The second part has the following Go code:

```go
func count(filename string) {
    var err error
    var numberOfLines int = 0
    var numberOfCharacters int = 0
    var numberOfWords int = 0

    f, err := os.Open(filename)
    if err != nil {
        fmt.Printf("%s\n", err)
        return
    }
    defer f.Close()

    r := bufio.NewReader(f)
    for {
        line, err := r.ReadString('\n')

        if err == io.EOF {
            break
        } else if err != nil {
            fmt.Printf("error reading file %s\n", err)
        }
        numberOfLines++
        r := regexp.MustCompile("[^\\s]+")
        for range r.FindAllString(line, -1) {
            numberOfWords++
        }
        numberOfCharacters += len(line)
    }

    fmt.Printf("\t%d\t", numberOfLines)
    fmt.Printf("%d\t", numberOfWords)
    fmt.Printf("%d\t", numberOfCharacters)
    fmt.Printf("%s\n", filename)
}
```

The count () function does all the processing without returning any information to the main () function—it just prints the lines, words, and characters of its input file and exits. Although the current implementation of the count () function does the desired job, it is not the correct way to design a program because there is no way to control its output of the program.

The third part of the utility is the following:

```
func main() {
    if len(os.Args) == 1 {
        fmt.Printf("usage: %s <file1> [<file2> [... <fileN]]\n",
            filepath.Base(os.Args[0]))
        os.Exit(1)
    }
```

The last part of dWC.go is the following:

```
    var waitGroup sync.WaitGroup
    for _, filename := range os.Args[1:] {
        waitGroup.Add(1)
        go func(filename string) {
            count(filename)
            defer waitGroup.Done()
        }(filename)
    }
    waitGroup.Wait()
}
```

As you can see, each input file is being processed by a different goroutine. As expected, you cannot make any assumptions about the order the input files will be processed.

Executing dWC.go will generate the following output:

```
$ go run dWC.go /tmp/swtag.log /tmp/swtag.log doesnotExist
open doesnotExist: no such file or directory
        48     275    3571   /tmp/swtag.log
        48     275    3571   /tmp/swtag.log
```

Here, you can see that although the doesnotExist filename is the last command-line argument, it is the first one in the output of dWC.go!

Although dWC.go uses goroutines, there is no cleverness in it because goroutines run without communicating with each other and without performing any other tasks. Additionally, the output might get scrambled because there is no guarantee that the fmt.Printf() statements of the count () function will not get interrupted.

As a result, the forthcoming section as well as some of the techniques that will be presented in Chapter 10, *Goroutines - Advanced Features*, will improve dWC.go.

Calculating totals

The current version of dWC.go cannot calculate totals, which can be easily solved by processing the output of dWC.go with awk:

```
$ go run dWC.go /tmp/swtag.log /tmp/swtag.log | awk '{sum1+=$1; sum2+=$2;
sum3+=$3} END {print "\t", sum1, "\t", sum2, "\t", sum3}'
         96    550    7142
```

Still, this is far from being perfect and elegant!

The main reason that the current version of dWC.go cannot calculate totals is that its goroutines have no way of communicating with each other. This can be easily solved with the help of channels and pipelines. The new version of dWC.go will be called dWCtotal.go and will be presented in five parts.

The first part of dWCtotal.go is the following:

```go
package main

import (
    "bufio"
    "fmt"
    "io"
    "os"
    "path/filepath"
    "regexp"
)

type File struct {
    Filename   string
    Lines      int
    Words      int
    Characters int
    Error      error
}
```

Here, a new struct type is defined. The new structure is called File and has four fields and an additional field for keeping error messages. This is the correct way for a pipeline to circulate multiple values. One might argue that a better name for the File structure would have been Counts, Results, FileCounts, or FileResults.

The second part of the program is the following:

```go
func process(files []string, out chan<- File) {
    for _, filename := range files {
        var fileToProcess File
        fileToProcess.Filename = filename
        fileToProcess.Lines = 0
        fileToProcess.Words = 0
        fileToProcess.Characters = 0
        out <- fileToProcess
    }
    close(out)
}
```

A better name of the process() function would have been beginProcess() or processResults(). You can try to make that change on your own throughout the dWCtotal.go program.

The third part of dWCtotal.go has the following Go code:

```go
func count(in <-chan File, out chan<- File) {
    for y := range in {
        filename := y.Filename
        f, err := os.Open(filename)
        if err != nil {
            y.Error = err
            out <- y
            continue
        }
        defer f.Close()
        r := bufio.NewReader(f)
        for {
            line, err := r.ReadString('\n')
            if err == io.EOF {
                break
            } else if err != nil {
                fmt.Printf("error reading file %s", err)
                y.Error = err
                out <- y
                continue
            }
            y.Lines = y.Lines + 1
            r := regexp.MustCompile("[^\\s]+")
            for range r.FindAllString(line, -1) {
                y.Words = y.Words + 1
            }
            y.Characters = y.Characters + len(line)
        }
```

```
            out <- y
    }
    close(out)
}
```

Although the `count()` function still calculates the counts, it does not print them. It just sends the counts of lines, words, and characters as well as the filename to another channel using a `struct` variable of the `File`type.

There exists one very important detail here, which is the last statement of the `count()` function—in order to properly end a pipeline, you should close all involved channels, starting from the first one. Otherwise, the execution of the program will fail with an error message similar to the following one:

fatal error: all goroutines are asleep – deadlock!

However, as far as closing the channels of a pipeline is concerned, you should also be careful about closing channels too early, especially when there are splits in a pipeline.

The fourth part of the program contains the following Go code:

```
func calculate(in <-chan File) {
    var totalWords int = 0
    var totalLines int = 0
    var totalChars int = 0
    for x := range in {
            totalWords = totalWords + x.Words
            totalLines = totalLines + x.Lines
            totalChars = totalChars + x.Characters
            if x.Error == nil {
                    fmt.Printf("\t%d\t", x.Lines)
                    fmt.Printf("%d\t", x.Words)
                    fmt.Printf("%d\t", x.Characters)
                    fmt.Printf("%s\n", x.Filename)
            }
    }

    fmt.Printf("\t%d\t", totalLines)
    fmt.Printf("%d\t", totalWords)
    fmt.Printf("%d\ttotal\n", totalChars)
}
```

There is nothing special here—the `calculate()` function does the dirty job of printing the output of the program.

The last part of `dWCtotal.go` is the following:

```
func main() {
    if len(os.Args) == 1 {
        fmt.Printf("usage: %s <file1> [<file2> [... <fileN]]\n",
            filepath.Base(os.Args[0]))
        os.Exit(1)
    }

    files := make(chan File)
    values := make(chan File)

    go process(os.Args[1:], files)
    go count(files, values)
    calculate(values)
}
```

Since the `files` channel is only used for passing around filenames, it could have been a `string` channel instead of a `File` channel. However, this way the code is more consistent.

Now `dWCtotal.go` automatically generates totals even if it has to process just one file:

```
$ go run dWCtotal.go /tmp/swtag.log
        48     275    3571   /tmp/swtag.log
        48     275    3571   total
$ go run dWCtotal.go /tmp/swtag.log /tmp/swtag.log doesNotExist
        48     275    3571   /tmp/swtag.log
        48     275    3571   /tmp/swtag.log
        96     550    7142   total
```

Note that both dWCtotal.go and dWC.go implement the same core functionality, which is counting the words, characters, and lines of a file—it is the way the information is handled that is different because dWCtotal.go uses a pipeline and not isolated goroutines.

Chapter 10, *Goroutines - Advanced Features*, will use other techniques to implement the functionality of dWCtotal.go.

Doing some benchmarking

In this section, we will compare the performance of wc.go from Chapter 6, *File Input and Output*, with the performance of wc(1), dWC.go and dWCtotal.go. In order for the results to be more accurate, all three utilities will process relatively big files:

```
$ wc /tmp/*.data
  712804 3564024 9979897 /tmp/connections.data
  285316  855948 4400685 /tmp/diskSpace.data
  712523 1425046 8916670 /tmp/memory.data
 1425500 2851000 5702000 /tmp/pageFaults.data
  285658  840622 4313833 /tmp/uptime.data
 3421801 9536640 33313085 total
```

So, the time(1) utility will measure the following commands:

```
$ time wc /tmp/*.data /tmp/*.data
$ time wc /tmp/uptime.data /tmp/pageFaults.data
$ time ./dWC /tmp/*.data /tmp/*.data
$ time ./dWC /tmp/uptime.data /tmp/pageFaults.data
$ time ./dWCtotal /tmp/*.data /tmp/*.data
$ time ./dWCtotal /tmp/uptime.data /tmp/pageFaults.data
$ time ./wc /tmp/uptime.data /tmp/pageFaults.data
$ time ./wc /tmp/*.data /tmp/*.data
```

The following figure shows a graphical representation of the real field from the output of the time(1) utility when used to measure the aforementioned commands:

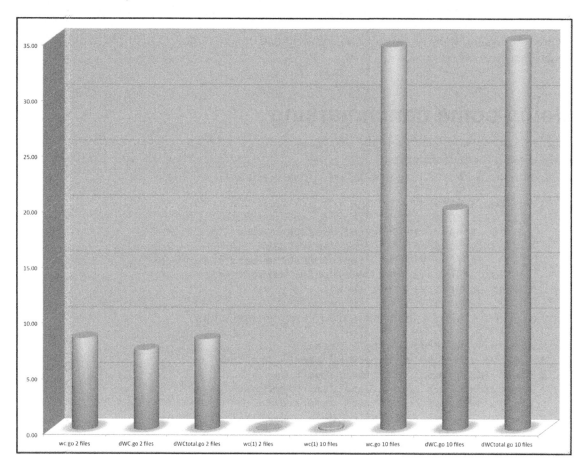

Plotting the real field of the time(1) utility

The original wc(1) utility is by far the fastest of all. Additionally, dWC.go is faster than both dWCtotal.go and wc.go. Apart from dWC.go, the remaining two Go versions have the same performance.

Exercises

1. Create a pipeline that reads text files, finds the number of occurrences of a given word, and calculates the total number of occurrences of the word in all files.
2. Try to make `dWCtotal.go` faster.
3. Create a simple Go program that plays ping pong using channels. You should define the total number of pings and pongs using a command-line argument.

Summary

In this chapter, we talked about creating and synchronizing goroutines as well as about creating and using pipelines and channels to allow goroutines to communicate with each other. Additionally, we developed two versions of the `wc(1)` utility that use goroutines to process their input files.

Make sure that you fully understand the concepts of this chapter before continuing with the next chapter because in the next chapter, we will talk about more advanced features related to goroutines and channels including shared memory, buffered channels, the `select` keyword, the `GOMAXPROCS` environment variable, and signal channels.

10
Goroutines - Advanced Features

This is the second chapter of this book that deals with goroutines—the most important feature of the Go programming language—as well as channels that greatly improve what goroutines can do, and we will continue this from where we stopped it in Chapter 9, *Goroutines - Basic Features*.

Thus, you will learn how to use various types of channels, including buffered channels, signal channels, nil channels, and channels of channels! Additionally, you will learn how you can utilize shared memory and mutexes with goroutines as well as how to time out a program when it is taking too long to finish.

Specifically, this chapter will discuss the following topics:

- Buffered channels
- The `select` keyword
- Signal channels
- Nil channels
- Channel of channels
- Timing out a program and avoiding waiting forever for it to end
- Shared memory and goroutines
- Using `sync.Mutex` in order to guard shared data
- Using `sync.RWMutex` in order to protect your shared data
- Changing the code of `dWC.go` from `Chapter 9`, *Goroutines - Basic Features*, in order to add support for buffered channels and mutexes to it

The Go scheduler

In the previous chapter, we said that the kernel scheduler is responsible for the order your goroutines will be executed in, which is not completely accurate. The kernel scheduler is responsible for the execution of the threads your programs have. The Go runtime has its own scheduler that is responsible for the execution of the goroutines using a technique known as **m:n scheduling**, where *m* goroutines are executed using *n* operating system threads using multiplexing. As the Go scheduler has to deal with the goroutines of a single program, its operation is much cheaper and faster than the operation of the kernel scheduler.

The sync Go package

Once again, we will use functions and data types from the `sync` package in this chapter. Particularly, you will learn about the usefulness of the `sync.Mutex` and `sync.RWMutex` types and the functions supporting them.

The select keyword

A `select` statement in Go is like a `switch` statement for channels and allows a goroutine to wait on multiple communication operations. Therefore, the main advantage you get from using the `select` keyword is that the same function can deal with multiple channels using a single `select` statement! Additionally, you can have nonblocking operations on channels.

The name of the program that will be used for illustrating the `select` keyword will be `useSelect.go` and will be presented in five parts. The `useSelect.go` program allows you to generate the number of random you want, which is defined in the first command-line argument, up to a certain limit, which is the second command-line argument.

The first part of useSelect.go is the following:

```
package main

import (
    "fmt"
    "math/rand"
    "os"
    "path/filepath"
    "strconv"
    "time"
)
```

The second part of useSelect.go is the following:

```
func createNumber(max int, randomNumberChannel chan<- int, finishedChannel
chan bool) {
    for {
        select {
        case randomNumberChannel <- rand.Intn(max):
        case x := <-finishedChannel:
            if x {
                close(finishedChannel)
                close(randomNumberChannel)
                return
            }
        }
    }
}
```

Here, you can see how the select keyword allows you to listen to and coordinate two channels (randomNumberChannel and finishedChannel) at the same time. The select statement waits for a channel to unblock and then executes on that.

The for loop of the createNumber() function will not end on this own. Therefore, createNumber() will keep generating random numbers for as long as the randomNumberChannel branch of the select statement is used. The createNumber() function will exit when it gets the Boolean value true in the finishedChannel channel.

A better name for the finishedChannel channel would have been done or even noMoreData.

The third part of the program contains the following Go code:

```go
func main() {
    rand.Seed(time.Now().Unix())
    randomNumberChannel := make(chan int)
    finishedChannel := make(chan bool)

    if len(os.Args) != 3 {
        fmt.Printf("usage: %s count max\n", filepath.Base(os.Args[0]))
        os.Exit(1)
    }

    n1, _ := strconv.ParseInt(os.Args[1], 10, 64)
    count := int(n1)
    n2, _ := strconv.ParseInt(os.Args[2], 10, 64)
    max := int(n2)

    fmt.Printf("Going to create %d random numbers.\n", count)
```

There is nothing special here—you just read the command-line arguments before starting the desired goroutine.

The fourth part of useSelect.go is where you will start the desired goroutine and create a for loop in order to generate the desired number of random numbers:

```go
    go createNumber(max, randomNumberChannel, finishedChannel)
    for i := 0; i < count; i++ {
        fmt.Printf("%d ", <-randomNumberChannel)
    }

    finishedChannel <- false
    fmt.Println()
    _, ok := <-randomNumberChannel
    if ok {
        fmt.Println("Channel is open!")
    } else {
        fmt.Println("Channel is closed!")
    }
```

Here, you also send a message to finishedChannel and check whether the randomNumberChannel channel is open or closed after sending the message to finishedChannel. As you sent false to finishedChannel, the finishedChannel channel will remain open. Note that a message sent to a closed channel panics, whereas a message received from a closed channel returns the zero value immediately.

Note that once you close a channel, you cannot write to this channel. However, you can still read from that channel!

The last part of useSelect.gohas the following Go code:

```
finishedChannel <- true
_, ok = <-randomNumberChannel
if ok {
        fmt.Println("Channel is open!")
} else {
        fmt.Println("Channel is closed!")
}
}
```

Here, you sent the true value to finishedChannel, so your channels will close and the createNumber() goroutine will exit.

Running useSelect.go will create the following output:

```
$ go run useSelect.go 2 100
Going to create 2 random numbers.
19 74
Channel is open!
Channel is closed!
```

As you will see in the bufChannels.go program that explains buffered channels, the select statement can also save you from overflowing a buffered channel.

Signal channels

A **signal channel** is a channel that is used just for signaling. Signal channels will be illustrated using the signalChannel.go program with a rather unusual example that will be presented in five parts. The program executes four goroutines—when the first one is finished, it sends a signal to a signal channel by closing it, which will unblock the second goroutine. When the second goroutine finishes its job, it closes another channel that unblocks the remaining two goroutines. Note that signal channels are not the same as channels that carry theos.Signal values.

The first part of the program is the following:

```
package main

import (
    "fmt"
    "time"
)

func A(a, b chan struct{}) {
    <-a
    fmt.Println("A!")
    time.Sleep(time.Second)
    close(b)
}
```

The A() functionis blocked by the channel defined in the a parameter. This means that until this channel is closed, theA() functioncannot continue its execution. The last statement of the function closes the channel that is stored in thebvariable, which will be used for unblocking other goroutines.

The second part of the program is the implementation of the B() function:

```
func B(b, c chan struct{}) {
    <-b
    fmt.Println("B!")
    close(c)
}
```

Similarly, the B() functionis blocked by the channel stored in the b argument, which means that until the bchannelis closed, the B() functionwill be waiting in its first statement.

The third part of signalChannel.go is the following:

```
func C(a chan struct{}) {
    <-a
    fmt.Println("C!")
}
```

Once again, the C() functionis blocked by the channel stored in its a argument.

The fourth part of the program is the following:

```
func main() {
    x := make(chan struct{})
    y := make(chan struct{})
    z := make(chan struct{})
```

> Defining a signal channel as an empty `struct` with no fieldsis a very common practicebecause empty structures take no memory space. In such a case, you could have used a `bool` channel instead.

The last part of `signalChannel.go`has the following Go code:

```
    go A(x, y)
    go C(z)
    go B(y, z)
    go C(z)

    close(x)
    time.Sleep(2 * time.Second)
}
```

Here, you start four goroutines. However, until you close the `a`channel,all of them will be blocked! Additionally, `A()` will finish first and unblock `B()` that will unblock the two `C()` goroutines. So, this technique allows you to define the order of execution of your goroutines.

If you execute `signalChannel.go`, you will get the following output:

```
$ go run signalChannel.go
A!
B!
C!
C!
```

As you can see, the goroutines are being executed in the desired order despite the `A()` functiontaking more time to execute than the others due to the `time.Sleep()` function call.

Buffered channels

Buffered channels allow the Go scheduler to put jobs in the queue quickly in order to be able to serve more requests. Moreover, you can use buffered channels as **semaphores** in order to limit throughput. The technique works as follows: incoming requests are forwarded to a channel, which processes one request at a time. When the channel is done, it sends a message to the original caller saying that it is ready to process a new request. So, the capacity of the buffer of the channel restricts the number of simultaneous requests it can keep and process—this can be easily implemented using a `for` loop with a call to `time.Sleep()` at its end.

Buffered channels will be illustrated in `bufChannels.go`, which will be presented in four parts.

The first part of the program is the following:

```
package main

import (
    "fmt"
)
```

The preamble proves that you do not need any extra packages for supporting buffered channels in your Go program.

The second part of the program has the following Go code:

```
func main() {
    numbers := make(chan int, 5)
```

Here, you create a new channel named `numbers` with 5 places, which is denoted by the last parameter of the `make` statement. This means that you can write five integers to that channel without having to read any one of them in order to make space for the others. However, you cannot put six integers on a channel with fiveinteger places!

The third part of bufChannels.go is the following:

```
counter := 10
for i := 0; i < counter; i++ {
        select {
        case numbers <- i:
        default:
                fmt.Println("Not enough space for", i)
        }
}
```

Here, you try to put 10 integers to a buffered channel with 5 places. However, the use of the select statement allows you to know whether you have enough space for storing all the integers or not and act accordingly!

The last part of bufChannels.go is the following:

```
for i := 0; i < counter*2; i++ {
        select {
        case num := <-numbers:
                fmt.Println(num)
        default:
                fmt.Println("Nothing more to be done!")
                break
        }
    }
}
```

Here, you also use a select statement while trying to read 20 integers from a channel. However, as soon as reading from the channel fails, the for loop exits using a break statement. This happens because when there is nothing left to read from the numbers channel, the num := <-numbers statement will block, which makes the case statement to go to the default branch.

As you can see from the code, there is no goroutine in bufChannels.go, which means that buffered channels can work on their own.

Executing bufChannels.go will generate the following output:

```
$ go run bufChannels.go
Not enough space for 5
Not enough space for 6
Not enough space for 7
Not enough space for 8
Not enough space for 9
0
1
```

```
2
3
4
Nothing more to be done!
Nothing more to be done!
Nothing more to be done!
Nothing more to be done!
Nothing more to be done!
Nothing more to be done!
Nothing more to be done!
Nothing more to be done!
Nothing more to be done!
Nothing more to be done!
Nothing more to be done!
Nothing more to be done!
Nothing more to be done!
Nothing more to be done!
Nothing more to be done!
Nothing more to be done!
```

About timeouts

Can you imagine waiting forever for something to perform an action? Neither can I! So, in this section you will learn how to implement **timeouts** in Go with the help of the `select` statement.

The program with the sample code will be named `timeOuts.go` and will be presented in four parts; the first part is the following:

```
package main

import (
    "fmt"
    "time"
)
```

The second part of `timeOuts.go` is the following:

```
func main() {
    c1 := make(chan string)
    go func() {
        time.Sleep(time.Second * 3)
        c1 <- "c1 OK"
    }()
```

The `time.Sleep()` statement in the goroutine is used for simulating the time it will take for the goroutine to do its real job.

The third part of `timeOuts.go` has the following code:

```
select {
case res := <-c1:
        fmt.Println(res)
case <-time.After(time.Second * 1):
        fmt.Println("timeout c1")
}
```

This time the use of `time.After()` is required for declaring the time you want to wait before timing out. The wonderful thing here is that if the time of `time.After()` expires without the `select` statement having received any data from the `c1` channel, the case branch of `time.After()` will get executed.

The last part of the program will have the following Go code:

```
c2 := make(chan string)
go func() {
        time.Sleep(time.Second * 3)
        c2 <- "c2 OK"
}()

select {
case res := <-c2:
        fmt.Println(res)
case <-time.After(time.Second * 4):
        fmt.Println("timeout c2")
}
}
```

In the previous code, you see an operation that does not time out because it is completed within the desired time, which means that the first branch of the `select` block will get executed instead of the second one that signifies the timeout.

The execution of `timeOuts.go` will generate the following output:

```
$ go run timeOuts.go
timeout c1
c2 OK
```

An alternative way to implement timeouts

The technique of this subsection will let you not wait for any stubborn goroutines to finish their jobs. Therefore, this subsection will show you how to time out goroutines with the help of the timeoutWait.go program that will be presented in four parts. Despite the code differences between timeoutWait.go and timeOuts.go, the general idea is exactly the same.

The first part of timeoutWait.go contains the expected preamble:

```
package main

import (
    "fmt"
    "sync"
    "time"
)
```

The second part of timeoutWait.go is the following:

```
func timeout(w *sync.WaitGroup, t time.Duration) bool {
    temp := make(chan int)
    go func() {
        defer close(temp)
        w.Wait()
    }()

    select {
    case <-temp:
        return false
    case <-time.After(t):
        return true
    }
}
```

Here, you declare a function that does the entire job. The core of the function is the select block that works the same way as in timeOuts.go. The anonymous function of timeout() will successfully end when the w.Wait() statement returns, which will happen when the appropriate number of sync.Done() calls have been executed, which means that all goroutines will be finished. In this case, the first case of the select statement will be executed.

Note that the `temp` channel is needed in the `select` block and nowhere else. Additionally, the element type of the `temp` channel could have been anything, including `bool`.

The third part of `timeOuts.go` has the following code:

```go
func main() {
    var w sync.WaitGroup
    w.Add(1)

    t := 2 * time.Second
    fmt.Printf("Timeout period is %s\n", t)

    if timeout(&w, t) {
        fmt.Println("Timed out!")
    } else {
        fmt.Println("OK!")
    }
```

The last fragment of the program has the following Go code:

```go
    w.Done()
    if timeout(&w, t) {
        fmt.Println("Timed out!")
    } else {
        fmt.Println("OK!")
    }
}
```

After the anticipated `w.Done()` call has been executed, the `timeout()` function will return `true`, which will prevent the timeout from happening.

As mentioned at the beginning of this subsection, `timeoutWait.go` actually prevents your program from having to wait indefinitely for one or more goroutines to end.

Executing `timeoutWait.go` will create the following output:

```
$ go run timeoutWait.go
Timeout period is 2s
Timed out!
OK!
```

Channels of channels

In this section, we will talk about creating and using a channel of channels. Two possible reasons to use such a channel are as follows:

- For acknowledging that an operation finished its job
- For creating many worker processes that will be controlled by the same channel variable

The name of the naïve program that will be developed in this section is cOfC.go and will be presented in four parts.

The first part of the program is the following:

```
package main

import (
    "fmt"
)

var numbers = []int{0, -1, 2, 3, -4, 5, 6, -7, 8, 9, 10}
```

The second part of the program is the following:

```
func f1(cc chan chan int, finished chan struct{}) {
    c := make(chan int)
    cc <- c
    defer close(c)

    total := 0
    i := 0
    for {
            select {
            case c <- numbers[i]:
                    i = i + 1
                    i = i % len(numbers)
                    total = total + 1
            case <-finished:
                    c <- total
                    return
            }
    }
}
```

The f1() function returns integer numbers that belong to the numbers variable. When it is about to end, it also returns the number of integers it has sent back to the caller function using the c <- total statement.

As you cannot use a channel of channelsdirectly, you should first read from it (cc <- c) and get a channel that you can actually use. The handy thing here is that although you can close thecchannel, the channel of channels (cc) will be still up and running.

The third part of cOfC.go is the following:

```
func main() {
    c1 := make(chan chan int)
    f := make(chan struct{})

    go f1(c1, f)
    data := <-c1
```

In this Go code, you can see that you can declare a channel of channels using the chan keyword two consecutive times.

The last part of cOfC.go has the following Go code:

```
    i := 0
    for integer := range data {
            fmt.Printf("%d ", integer)
            i = i + 1
            if i == 100 {
                    close(f)
            }
    }
    fmt.Println()
}
```

Here, you limit the number of integers that will be created by closing the f channel when you have the number of integers you want.

Executing cOfC.go will generate the following output:

```
$ go run cOfC.go
0 -1 2 3 -4 5 6 -7 8 9 10 0 -1 2 3 -4 5 6 -7 8 9 10 0 -1 2 3 -4 5 6 -7 8 9
10 0 -1 2 3 -4 5 6 -7 8 9 10 0 -1 2 3 -4 5 6 -7 8 9 10 0 -1 2 3 -4 5 6 -7 8
9 10 0 -1 2 3 -4 5 6 -7 8 9 10 0 -1 2 3 -4 5 6 -7 8 9 10 0 -1 2 3 -4 5 6 -7
8 9 10 0 100
```

A channel of channels is an advanced Go feature that you probably will not need to use in your system software. However, it is good to know that it exists.

Nil channels

This section will talk about **nil channels**, which are a special sort of channel that will always block. The name of the program will be `nilChannel.go` and will be presented in four parts.

The first part of the program contains the expected preamble:

```
package main

import (
    "fmt"
    "math/rand"
    "time"
)
```

The second portion contains the implementation of the `addIntegers()` function:

```
func addIntegers(c chan int) {
    sum := 0
    t  := time.NewTimer(time.Second)

    for {
            select {
            case input := <-c:
                    sum = sum + input
            case <-t.C:
                    c = nil
                    fmt.Println(sum)
            }
    }
}
```

The `addIntegers()` function stops after the time defined in the `time.NewTimer()` function passes and will go to the relevant branch of the `case` statement. There, it makes `c` a nil channel, which means that the channel will stop receiving new data and that the function will just wait there.

The third part of `nilChannel.go` is the following:

```
func sendIntegers(c chan int) {
    for {
            c <- rand.Intn(100)
    }
}
```

Here, the `sendIntegers()` function keeps generating random numbers and sends them to the c channel as long as the c channel is open. However, here you also have a goroutine that is never cleaned up.

The last part of the program has the following Go code:

```
func main() {
    c := make(chan int)
    go addIntegers(c)
    go sendIntegers(c)
    time.Sleep(2 * time.Second)
}
```

Executing `nilChannel.go` will generate the following output:

```
$ go run nilChannel.go
162674704
$ go run nilChannel.go
165021841
```

Shared memory

Shared memory is the traditional way that threads use for communicating with each other. Go comes with built-in synchronization features that allow a single goroutine to own a shared piece of data. This means that other goroutines must send messages to this single goroutine that owns the shared data, which prevents the corruption of the data! Such a goroutine is called a **monitor goroutine**. In Go terminology, this is *sharing by communicating instead of communicating by sharing*.

This technique will be illustrated in the `sharedMem.go` program, which will be presented in five parts. The first part of `sharedMem.go` has the following Go code:

```
package main

import (
    "fmt"
    "math/rand"
    "sync"
    "time"
)
```

The second part is the following:

```
var readValue = make(chan int)
var writeValue = make(chan int)

func SetValue(newValue int) {
    writeValue <- newValue
}

func ReadValue() int {
    return <-readValue
}
```

The `ReadValue()` function is used for reading the shared variable, whereas the `SetValue()` function is used for setting the value of the shared variable. Also, the two channels used in the program need to be global variables in order to avoid passing them as arguments to all the functions of the program. Note that these global variables are usually wrapped up in a Go library or a `struct` with methods.

The third part of `sharedMem.go` is the following:

```
func monitor() {
    var value int
    for {
        select {
        case newValue := <-writeValue:
            value = newValue
            fmt.Printf("%d ", value)
        case readValue <- value:
        }
    }
}
```

The logic of `sharedMem.go` can be found in the implementation of the `monitor()` function. When you have a read request, the `ReadValue()` function attempts to read from the `readValue` channel. Then, the `monitor()` function returns the current value that is kept in the `value` parameter. Similarly, when you want to change the stored value, you call `SetValue()`, which writes to the `writeValue` channel that is also handled by the `select` statement. Once again, the `select` block plays a key role because it orchestrates the operations of the `monitor()` function.

The fourth portion of the program has the following Go code:

```
func main() {
    rand.Seed(time.Now().Unix())
    go monitor()
    var waitGroup sync.WaitGroup

    for r := 0; r < 20; r++ {
        waitGroup.Add(1)
        go func() {
            defer waitGroup.Done()
            SetValue(rand.Intn(100))
        }()
    }
```

The last part of the program is the following:

```
    waitGroup.Wait()
    fmt.Printf("\nLast value: %d\n", ReadValue())
}
```

Executing `sharedMem.go` will generate the following output:

```
$ go run sharedMem.go
33 45 67 93 33 37 23 85 87 23 58 61 9 57 20 61 73 99 42 99
Last value: 99
$ go run sharedMem.go
71 66 58 83 55 30 61 73 94 19 63 97 12 87 59 38 48 81 98 49
Last value: 49
```

If you want to share more values, you can define a new structure that will hold the desired variables with the data types you prefer.

Using sync.Mutex

Mutex is an abbreviation for **mutual exclusion**; the `Mutex` variables are mainly used for thread synchronization and for protecting shared data when multiple writes can occur at the same time. A mutex works like a buffered channel of capacity 1 that allows at most one goroutine to access a shared variable at a time. This means that there is no way for two or more goroutines to try to update that variable simultaneously. Although this is a perfectly valid technique, the general Go community prefers to use the `monitor` goroutine technique presented in the previous section.

In order to use `sync.Mutex`, you will have to declare a `sync.Mutex` variable first. You can lock that variable using the `Lock` method and release it using the `Unlock` method. The `sync.Lock()` method gives you exclusive access over the shared variable for a region of code that finishes when you call the `Unlock()` method and is called a **critical section**.

Each critical section of a program cannot be executed without locking it first using `sync.Lock()`. However, if a lock has already been taken, everybody should wait for its release first. Although multiple functions might wait to get a lock, only one of them will get it when it will be released.

You should try to make critical sections as small as possible; in other words, do not delay releasing a lock because other goroutines might want to use it. Additionally, forgetting to unlock `Mutex` will most likely result in a deadlock.

The name of the Go program with the code for illustrating the use of `sync.Mutex` will be `mutexSimple.go` and will be presented in five chunks.

The first part of `mutexSimple.go` contains the expected preamble:

```
package main

import (
    "fmt"
    "os"
    "path/filepath"
    "strconv"
    "sync"
)
```

The second part of the program is the following:

```
var aMutex sync.Mutex
var sharedVariable string = ""

func addDot() {
    aMutex.Lock()
    sharedVariable = sharedVariable + "."
    aMutex.Unlock()
}
```

Note that a critical section is not always obvious and you should be very careful when specifying it. Also note that a critical section cannot be embedded in another critical section when both critical sections use the same Mutex variable! Putting it simply, avoid, at almost all costs, spreading mutexes across functions because that makes really hard to see whether you are embedding or not!

Here, addDot() adds a dot character at the end of the sharedVariable string. However, as the string should be altered simultaneously by multiple goroutines, you use a sync.Mutex variable to protect it. As the critical section contains just one command, the waiting period for getting access to the mutex will be fairly small, if not instantaneous. However, in a real-world situation, the waiting period might be much longer, especially on software such as database servers where many things happen simultaneously by thousands of processes—you can simulate that by adding a call to time.Sleep() in the critical section.

Note that it is the responsibility of the developer to associate a mutex with one or more shared variables!

The third code segment of mutexSimple.go is the implementation of another function that uses the mutex:

```
func read() string {
    aMutex.Lock()
    a := sharedVariable
    aMutex.Unlock()
    return a
}
```

Although locking the shared variable while reading it is not absolutely necessary, this kind of locking prevents the shared variable from changing while you are reading it. This might look like a small issue here but imagine reading the balance of your bank account instead!

The fourth part is where you define the number of goroutines that you will start:

```
func main() {
    if len(os.Args) != 2 {
        fmt.Printf("usage: %s n\n", filepath.Base(os.Args[0]))
        os.Exit(1)
    }

    numGR, _ := strconv.ParseInt(os.Args[1], 10, 64)
    var waitGroup sync.WaitGroup
```

The final part of `mutexSimple.go` contains the following Go code:

```
    var i int64
    for i = 0; i < numGR; i++ {
        waitGroup.Add(1)
        go func() {
            defer waitGroup.Done()
            addDot()
        }()
    }
    waitGroup.Wait()
    fmt.Printf("-> %s\n", read())
    fmt.Printf("Length: %d\n", len(read()))
}
```

Here, you start the desired number of goroutines. Each goroutine calls the `addDot()` function that accesses the shared variable—and you wait for them to finish before reading the value of the shared variable using the `read()` function.

The output you will get from executing `mutexSimple.go` will be similar to the following:

```
$ go run mutexSimple.go 20
-> ....................
Length: 20
$ go run mutexSimple.go 30
-> ..............................
Length: 30
```

Using sync.RWMutex

Go offers another type of mutex, called `sync.RWMutex`, that allows multiple readers to hold the lock but only a single writer - `sync.RWMutex` is an extension of `sync.Mutex` that adds two methods named `sync.RLock` and `sync.RUnlock`, which are used for locking and unlocking for reading purposes. Locking and unlocking a `sync.RWMutex` for exclusive writing should be done with `Lock()` and `Unlock()`, respectively.

This means that either one writer can hold the lock or multiple readers—not both! You will most likely use such a mutex when most of the goroutines want to read a variable and you do not want goroutines to wait in order to get an exclusive lock.

In order to demystify `sync.RWMutex` a little, you should discover that the `sync.RWMutex` type is a Go structure currently defined as follows:

```
type RWMutex struct {
    w           Mutex
    writerSem   uint32
    readerSem   uint32
    readerCount int32
    readerWait  int32
}
```

So, there is nothing to be afraid of here! Now, it is time to see a Go program that uses `sync.RWMutex`. The program will be named `mutexRW.go` and will be presented in five parts.

The first part of `mutexRW.go` contains with the expected preamble as well as the definition of a global variable and a new `struct` type:

```
package main

import (
    "fmt"
    "sync"
    "time"
)

var Password = secret{counter: 1, password: "myPassword"}

type secret struct {
    sync.RWMutex
    counter  int
    password string
}
```

The `secret` structure embeds `sync.RWMutex` and therefore it can call all the methods of `sync.RWMutex`.

The second part of `mutexRW.go` has the following Go code:

```
func Change(c *secret, pass string) {
    c.Lock()
    fmt.Println("LChange")
    time.Sleep(20 * time.Second)
    c.counter = c.counter + 1
    c.password = pass
    c.Unlock()
}
```

This function makes changes to one of its arguments, which means that it requires an exclusive lock, hence the use of the `Lock()` and `Unlock()` functions.

The third part of the sample code is the following:

```
func Show(c *secret) string {
    fmt.Println("LShow")
    time.Sleep(time.Second)


    c.RLock()
    defer c.RUnlock()
    return c.password
}

func Counts(c secret) int {
    c.RLock()
    defer c.RUnlock()
    return c.counter
}
```

Here, you can see the definition of two functions that use an `sync.RWMutex` for reading. This means that multiple instances of them can get the `sync.RWMutex` lock.

The fourth portion of the program is the following:

```
func main() {
    fmt.Println("Pass:", Show(&Password))
    for i := 0; i < 5; i++ {
        go func() {
                fmt.Println("Go Pass:", Show(&Password))
            }()
    }
```

Here, you start fivegoroutines in order to make things more interesting and random.

The last part of mutexRW.go is the following:

```
go func() {
        Change(&Password, "123456")
}()

fmt.Println("Pass:", Show(&Password))
time.Sleep(time.Second)
fmt.Println("Counter:", Counts(Password))
}
```

> Although shared memory and the use of a mutex are still a valid approach to concurrent programming, using goroutines and channels is a more modern way that follows the Go philosophy. Therefore, if you can solve a problem using channels and pipelines, you should prefer that way instead of using shared variables.

Executing mutexRW.go will generate the following output:

```
$ go run mutexRW.go
LShow
Pass: myPassword
LShow
LShow
LShow
LShow
LShow
LShow
LChange
Go Pass: 123456
Go Pass: 123456
Pass: 123456
Go Pass: 123456
Go Pass: 123456
Go Pass: 123456
Counter: 2
```

If the implementation of Change() was using a RLock() call as well as a RUnlock() call, which would have been totally wrong, then the output of the program would have been the following:

```
$ go run mutexRW.go
LShow
Pass: myPassword
LShow
```

```
        LShow
        LShow
        LShow
        LShow
        LShow
        LChange
        Go Pass: myPassword
        Pass: myPassword
        Go Pass: myPassword
        Go Pass: myPassword
        Go Pass: myPassword
        Go Pass: myPassword
        Counter: 1
```

Put simply, you should be fully aware of the locking mechanism you are using and the way it works. In this case, it is the timing that is deciding what `Counts()` will return—the timing depends on the `time.Sleep()` call of the `Change()` function that emulates the processing that will happen in a real function. The problem is that the use of `RLock()` and `RUnlock()` in `Change()` allows multiple goroutines to read the shared variable and therefore get the wrong output from the `Counts()` function.

The dWC.go utility revisited

In this section, we will change the implementation of the `dWC.go` utility developed in the previous chapter.

The first version of the program will use a buffered channel whereas the second version of the program will use shared memory for keeping the counts for each file you process.

Using a buffered channel

The name of this implementation will be `WCbuffered.go` and will be presented in five parts.

The first part of the utility is the following:

```
package main

import (
    "bufio"
    "fmt"
    "io"
    "os"
```

```
    "path/filepath"
    "regexp"
)

type File struct {
    Filename    string
    Lines       int
    Words       int
    Characters  int
    Error       error
}
```

The `File` structure will keep the counts for each input file. The second chunk of `WCbuffered.go` has the following Go code:

```
func monitor(values <-chan File, count int) {
    var totalWords int = 0
    var totalLines int = 0
    var totalChars int = 0
    for i := 0; i < count; i++ {
        x := <-values
        totalWords = totalWords + x.Words
        totalLines = totalLines + x.Lines
        totalChars = totalChars + x.Characters
        if x.Error == nil {
            fmt.Printf("\t%d\t", x.Lines)
            fmt.Printf("%d\t", x.Words)
            fmt.Printf("%d\t", x.Characters)
            fmt.Printf("%s\n", x.Filename)
        } else {
            fmt.Printf("\t%s\n", x.Error)
        }
    }
    fmt.Printf("\t%d\t", totalLines)
    fmt.Printf("%d\t", totalWords)
    fmt.Printf("%d\ttotal\n", totalChars)
}
```

The `monitor()` function collects all the information and prints it. The `for` loop inside `monitor()` makes sure that it will collect the right amount of data.

The third part of the program contains the implementation of the `count()` function:

```
func count(filename string, out chan<- File) {
    var err error
    var nLines int = 0
    var nChars int = 0
    var nWords int = 0
```

```
    f, err := os.Open(filename)
    defer f.Close()
    if err != nil {
            newValue := File{
Filename: filename,
Lines: 0,
Characters: 0,
Words: 0,
Error: err }
            out <- newValue
            return
    }

    r := bufio.NewReader(f)
    for {
            line, err := r.ReadString('\n')

            if err == io.EOF {
                    break
            } else if err != nil {
                    fmt.Printf("error reading file %s\n", err)
            }
            nLines++
            r := regexp.MustCompile("[^\\s]+")
            for range r.FindAllString(line, -1) {
                    nWords++
            }
            nChars += len(line)
    }
    newValue := File {
Filename: filename,
Lines: nLines,
Characters: nChars,
Words: nWords,
Error: nil }

    out <- newValue


}
```

When the `count ()` function is done, it sends the information to the buffered channel, so there is nothing special here.

The fourth portion of `WCbuffered.go` is the following:

```go
func main() {
    if len(os.Args) == 1 {
        fmt.Printf("usage: %s <file1> [<file2> [... <fileN]]\n",
            filepath.Base(os.Args[0]))
        os.Exit(1)
    }

    values := make(chan File, len(os.Args[1:]))
```

Here, you create a buffered channel named `values` with as many places as the number of files you will process.

The last portion of the utility is the following:

```go
    for _, filename := range os.Args[1:] {
        go func(filename string) {
            count(filename, values)
        }(filename)
    }
    monitor(values, len(os.Args[1:]))
}
```

Using shared memory

The good thing with shared memory and mutexes is that, in theory, they usually take a very small amount of the code, which means that the rest of the code can work concurrently without any other delays. However, only after you have implemented something can you see what really happens!

The name of this implementation will be `WCshared.go` and will be presented in five parts—the first part of the utility is the following:

```go
package main

import (
    "bufio"
    "fmt"
    "io"
    "os"
    "path/filepath"
    "regexp"
    "sync"
)
```

```
type File struct {
    Filename   string
    Lines      int
    Words      int
    Characters int
    Error      error
}

var aM sync.Mutex
var values = make([]File, 0)
```

The `values` slice will be the shared variable of the program whereas the name of the mutex variable will be `aM`.

The second chunk of `WCshared.go` has the following Go code:

```
func count(filename string) {
    var err error
    var nLines int = 0
    var nChars int = 0
    var nWords int = 0

    f, err := os.Open(filename)
    defer f.Close()
    if err != nil {
        newValue := File{Filename: filename, Lines: 0, Characters: 0,
Words: 0, Error: err}
        aM.Lock()
        values = append(values, newValue)
        aM.Unlock()
        return
    }

    r := bufio.NewReader(f)
    for {
        line, err := r.ReadString('\n')

        if err == io.EOF {
            break
        } else if err != nil {
            fmt.Printf("error reading file %s\n", err)
        }
        nLines++
        r := regexp.MustCompile("[^\\s]+")
        for range r.FindAllString(line, -1) {
            nWords++
        }
        nChars += len(line)
```

```
    }

    newValue := File{Filename: filename, Lines: nLines, Characters: nChars,
Words: nWords, Error: nil}
    aM.Lock()
    values = append(values, newValue)
    aM.Unlock()
}
```

So, just before the `count()` function exits, it adds an element to the values slice using a critical section.

The third part of `WCshared.go` is the following:

```
func main() {
    if len(os.Args) == 1 {
        fmt.Printf("usage: %s <file1> [<file2> [... <fileN]]\n",
            filepath.Base(os.Args[0]))
        os.Exit(1)
    }
```

Here, you just deal with the command-line arguments of the utility.

The fourth part of `WCshared.go` contains the following Go code:

```
    var waitGroup sync.WaitGroup
    for _, filename := range os.Args[1:] {
        waitGroup.Add(1)
        go func(filename string) {
            defer waitGroup.Done()
            count(filename)
        }(filename)
    }

    waitGroup.Wait()
```

Here, you just start the desired number of goroutines and wait for them to finish their jobs.

The last code slice of the utility is the following:

```
var totalWords int = 0
var totalLines int = 0
var totalChars int = 0
for _, x := range values {
        totalWords = totalWords + x.Words
        totalLines = totalLines + x.Lines
        totalChars = totalChars + x.Characters
        if x.Error == nil {
                fmt.Printf("\t%d\t", x.Lines)
                fmt.Printf("%d\t", x.Words)
                fmt.Printf("%d\t", x.Characters)
                fmt.Printf("%s\n", x.Filename)
        }
}
fmt.Printf("\t%d\t", totalLines)
fmt.Printf("%d\t", totalWords)
fmt.Printf("%d\ttotal\n", totalChars)
}
```

When all goroutines are done, it is time to process the contents of the shared variable, calculate totals, and print the desired output. Note that in this case, there is no shared variable of any kind and therefore there is no need for a mutex—you just wait to gather all results and print them.

More benchmarking

This section will measure the performance of WCbuffered.go and WCshared.go using the handy time(1) utility. However, this time, instead of presenting a graph, I will give you the actual output of the time(1) utility:

```
$ time go run WCshared.go /tmp/*.data /tmp/*.data
real    0m31.836s
user    0m31.659s
sys     0m0.165s
$ time go run WCbuffered.go /tmp/*.data /tmp/*.data
real    0m31.823s
user    0m31.656s
sys     0m0.171s
```

As you can see, both utilities performed equally well, or equally badly if you prefer! However, apart from the speed of a program, what also matters is the clarity of its design and how easy it is to make code changes to it! Additionally, the presented way also times the compile times of both utilities, which might make the results less accurate.

The reason that both programs can easily generate totals is that they both have a control point. For the WCshared.go utility, the control point is the shared variable, whereas for WCbuffered.go, the control point is the buffered channel that collects the desired information inside the monitor() function.

Detecting race conditions

If you use the -race flag when running or building a Go program, you will turn on the Go **race detector**, which makes the compiler create a modified version of the typical executable file. This modified version can record the accesses to shared variables as well as all synchronization events that take place, including calls to sync.Mutex, sync.WaitGroup, and so on. After doing some analysis of the events, the race detector prints a report that can help you identify potential problems so that you can correct them.

In order to showcase the operation of the race detector, we will use the code of the rd.go program, which will be presented in four parts. For this particular program, the **data race** will happen because two or more goroutines access the same variable concurrently and at least one of them changes the value of the variable in some way.

 Note that the main() program is also a goroutine in Go!

The first part of the program is the following:

```
package main

import (
    "fmt"
    "os"
    "path/filepath"
    "strconv"
    "sync"
)
```

Nothing special here, so if there is a problem with the program, it is not in the preamble.

The second part of `rd.go` is the following:

```
func main() {
    arguments := os.Args
    if len(arguments) != 2 {
        fmt.Printf("usage: %s number\n", filepath.Base(arguments[0]))
        os.Exit(1)
    }
    numGR, _ := strconv.ParseInt(os.Args[1], 10, 64)
    var waitGroup sync.WaitGroup
    var i int64
```

Once again, there is no problem in this particular code.

The third segment of `rd.go` has the following Go code:

```
    for i = 0; i < numGR; i++ {
        waitGroup.Add(1)
        go func() {
            defer waitGroup.Done()
            fmt.Printf("%d ", i)
        }()
    }
```

This code is very suspicious because you try to print the value of a variable that keeps changing all the time because of the `for` loop.

The last part of `rd.go` is the following:

```
    waitGroup.Wait()
    fmt.Println("\nExiting...")
}
```

There is nothing special in the last chunk of code.

Enabling the Go race detector for `rd.go` will generate the following output:

```
$ go run -race rd.go 10
==================
WARNING: DATA RACE
Read at 0x00c420074168 by goroutine 6:
  main.main.func1()
      /Users/mtsouk/Desktop/goBook/ch/ch10/code/rd.go:25 +0x6c
Previous write at 0x00c420074168 by main goroutine:
  main.main()
      /Users/mtsouk/Desktop/goBook/ch/ch10/code/rd.go:21 +0x30c
Goroutine 6 (running) created at:
  main.main()
```

```
        /Users/mtsouk/Desktop/goBook/ch/ch10/code/rd.go:26 +0x2e2
==================
==================
WARNING: DATA RACE
Read at 0x00c420074168 by goroutine 7:
 main.main.func1()
        /Users/mtsouk/Desktop/goBook/ch/ch10/code/rd.go:25 +0x6c
Previous write at 0x00c420074168 by main goroutine:
 main.main()
        /Users/mtsouk/Desktop/goBook/ch/ch10/code/rd.go:21 +0x30c
Goroutine 7 (running) created at:
  main.main()
        /Users/mtsouk/Desktop/goBook/ch/ch10/code/rd.go:26 +0x2e2
==================
2 3 4 4 5 6 7 8 9 10
Exiting...
Found 2 data race(s)
exit status 66
```

So, the race detector found two data races. The first one happens when number 1 was not printed at all and the second when number 4 was printed two times. Additionally, number 0 was not printed despite being the initial value of i. Last, you should not get number 10 in the output but you did get it because the last value of i is indeed 10. Note that the main.main.func1() notation found in the preceding output means that Go talks about an anonymous function.

Put simply, what the previous two messages tell you is that there is something wrong with the i variable because it keeps changing while the goroutines of the program try to read it. Additionally, you cannot deterministically tell what will happen first.

Running the same program without the race detector will generate the following output:

```
$ go run rd.go 10
10 10 10 10 10 10 10 10 10 10
Exiting...
```

The problem with rd.go can be found in the anonymous function. As the anonymous function takes no arguments, it uses the current value of i, which cannot be determined with any certainty as it depends on the operating system and the Go scheduler—this is where the race situation happens! So, have in mind that one of the easiest places to have a race condition is inside a goroutine spawned from an anonymous function! As a result, if you have to solve such as situation, start by converting the anonymous function into regular functions with defined arguments!

Programs that use the race detector are slower and need more RAM than the same programs without the race detector. Last, if the race detector has nothing to report, it will generate no output.

About GOMAXPROCS

The GOMAXPROCS environment variable (and Go function) allows you to limit the number of operating system threads that can execute user-level Go code simultaneously.

 Starting with Go version 1.5, the default value of GOMAXPROCS should be the number of cores available on your Unix system.

Although using a GOMAXPROCS value that is smaller than the number of the cores a Unix machine has might affect the performance of a program, specifying a GOMAXPROCS value that is bigger than the number of the available cores will not make your program run faster!

The code of goMaxProcs.go allows you to determine the value of the GOMAXPROCS - it will be presented in two parts.

The first part is the following:

```
package main

import (
    "fmt"
    "runtime"
)


func getGOMAXPROCS() int {
    return runtime.GOMAXPROCS(0)
}
```

The second part is the following:

```
func main() {
    fmt.Printf("GOMAXPROCS: %d\n", getGOMAXPROCS())
}
```

Executing `goMaxProcs.go` on an Intel i7 machine with hyper threading support and the latest Go version gives the following output:

```
$ go run goMaxProcs.go
GOMAXPROCS: 8
```

However, if you execute `goMaxProcs.go` on a Debian Linux machine that runs an older Go version and has an older processor, it will generate the following output:

```
$ go version
go version go1.3.3 linux/amd64
$ go run goMaxProcs.go
GOMAXPROCS: 1
```

The way to change the value of GOMAXPROCS on the fly is as follows:

```
$ export GOMAXPROCS=80; go run goMaxProcs.go
GOMAXPROCS: 80
```

However, putting a value bigger than 256 will not work:

```
$ export GOMAXPROCS=800; go run goMaxProcs.go
GOMAXPROCS: 256
```

Last, have in mind that if you are running a concurrent program such asdWC.go using a single core, the concurrent version of the program might not be faster than the version of the program without goroutines! In some situations, this happens because the use of goroutines as well as the various calls to thesync.Add, sync.Wait, and sync.Done functions slows down the performance of a program. This can be verified by the following output:

```
$ export GOMAXPROCS=8; time go run dWC.go /tmp/*.data
real    0m10.826s
user    0m31.542s
sys     0m5.043s
$ export GOMAXPROCS=1; time go run dWC.go /tmp/*.data
real    0m15.362s
user    0m15.253s
sys     0m0.103s
$ time go run wc.go /tmp/*.data
real    0m15.158sexit
user    0m15.023s
sys     0m0.120s
```

Exercises

1. Read carefully the documentation page of the `sync` package that can be found at `https://golang.org/pkg/sync/`.
2. Try to implement `dWC.go` using a different shared memory technique than the one used in this chapter.
3. Implement a `struct` data type that holds your account balance and make functions that read the amount of money you have and make changes to the money. Create an implementation that uses `sync.RWMutex` and another one that uses `sync.Mutex`.
4. What would happen to `mutexRW.go` if you used `Lock()` and `Unlock()` everywhere instead of `RLock()` and `RUnlock()`?
5. Try to implement `traversc.go` from `Chapter 5`, *Files and Directories* using goroutines.
6. Try to create an implementation of `improvedFind.go` from `Chapter 5`, *Files and Directories* using goroutines.

Summary

This chapter talked about some advanced Go features related to goroutines, channels, and concurrent programming. However, the moral of this chapter is that channels can do many things and can be used in many situations, which means that the developer must be able to choose the appropriate technique to implement a task based on their experience.

The subject of the next chapter will be web development in Go and it will contain very interesting material, including sending and receiving JSON data, developing web servers and web clients, as well as talking to a MongoDB database from your Go code.

Writing Web Applications in Go

In the previous chapter, we discussed many advanced topics related to goroutines and channels as well as shared memory and mutexes.

The main subject of this chapter is the development of web applications in Go. However, this chapter will also talk about how to interact with two popular databases in your Go programs. The Go standard library provides packages that can help you develop web applications using higher level functions, which means that you can do complex things such as reading web pages by just calling a couple of Go functions with the right arguments. Although this kind of programming hides the complexity behind a request and offers less control over the details, it allows you to develop difficult applications using fewer lines of code, which also results in having fewer bugs in your programs.

However, as this book is about systems programming, this chapter will not go into too much depth—you might consider the presented information as a good starting point for anyone who wants to learn about web development in Go.

More specifically, this chapter will talk about the following topics:

- Creating a Go utility for MySQL database administrators
- Administering a MongoDB database
- Using the Go MongoDB driver to talk to a MongoDB database
- Creating a web server in Go
- Creating a web client in Go
- The `http.ServeMux` type
- Dealing with JSON data in Go
- The `net/http` package
- The `html/template` Go standard package
- Developing a command-line utility that searches web pages for a given keyword

What is a web application?

A web application is a client-server software application where the client part runs on a web browser.Web applications include webmail, instant messaging services, and online stores.

About the net/http Go package

The hero of this chapter will be the `net/http` package that can help you write web applications in Go. However, if you are interested in dealing with TCP/IP connections at a lower level, then you should go to `Chapter 12`, *Network Programming*, which talks about developing TCP/IP applications using lower level function calls.

The `net/http` package offers a built-in web server as well as a built-in web client that are both pretty powerful. The `http.Get()` method can be used for making HTTP and HTTPS requests, whereas the `http.ListenAndServe()` function can be used for creating naïve web servers by specifying the IP address and the TCP port the server will listen to, as well as the functions that will handle incoming requests.

Another very convenient package is `html/template`, which is part of the Go standard library and allows you to generate an HTML output using Go HTML template files.

Developing web clients

In this section, you will learn how to develop web clients in Go and how to time out a web connection that takes too long to finish.

Fetching a single URL

In this subsection, you will learn how to read a single web page with the help of the `http.Get()` function, which is going to be demonstrated in the `getURL.go` program. The utility will be presented in four parts; the first part of the program is the expected preamble:

```
package main

import (
    "fmt"
    "io"
    "net/http"
    "os"
```

```
    "path/filepath"
)
```

Although there is nothing new here, you might find impressive the fact that you will use Go packages that are related to file input and output operations even though you are reading data from the internet. The explanation for this is pretty simple: Go has a uniform interface for reading and writing data regardless of the medium it is in.

The second part of `getURL.go` has the following Go code:

```
func main() {
    if len(os.Args) != 2 {
        fmt.Printf("Usage: %s URL\n", filepath.Base(os.Args[0]))
        os.Exit(1)
    }

    URL :=os.Args[1]
    data, err := http.Get(URL)
```

The URL you want to fetch is given as a command-line argument to the program. Additionally, you can see the call to `http.Get()`, which does all the dirty work! What `http.Get()` returns is a `Response` variable, which in reality is a Go structure with various properties and methods.

The third part is the following:

```
    if err != nil {
        fmt.Println(err)
        os.Exit(100)
    } else {
```

If there is an error after calling `http.Get()`, this is the place to check for it.

The fourth part contains the following Go code:

```
        defer data.Body.Close()
        _, err := io.Copy(os.Stdout, data.Body)
        if err != nil {
            fmt.Println(err)
            os.Exit(100)
        }
    }
}
```

As you can see, the data of URL is written in standard output using os.Stdout, which is the preferred way for printing data on the screen. Additionally, the data is saved in the Body property of the return value of the http.Get() call. However, not all HTTP requests are simple. If the response streams a video or something similar, it would make sense to be able to read it one piece at a time instead of getting all of it in a single data piece. You can do that with io.Reader and the Body part of the response.

Executing getURL.go will generate the following raw results, which is what a web browser would have gotten and rendered:

```
$ go run getURL.go http://www.mtsoukalos.eu/ | head
<!DOCTYPE html PUBLIC "-//W3C//DTD XHTML+RDFa 1.0//EN"
   "http://www.w3.org/MarkUp/DTD/xhtml-rdfa-1.dtd">
<htmlxmlns="http://www.w3.org/1999/xhtml" xml:lang="en" version="XHTML+RDFa
1.0" dir="ltr"
xmlns:content=http://purl.org/rss/1.0/modules/content/
. . .
</script>
</body>
</html>
```

Generally speaking, although getURL.go does the desired job, the way it works is not so sophisticated because it gives you no flexibility or a way to be creative.

Setting a timeout

In this subsection, you will learn how to set a timeout for a http.Get() request. For reasons of simplicity, it will be based on the Go code of getURL.go. The name of the program will be timeoutHTTP.go and will be presented in five parts.

The first part of the program is the following:

```
package main

import (
    "fmt"
    "io"
    "net"
    "net/http"
    "os"
    "path/filepath"
    "time"
)

var timeout = time.Duration(time.Second)
```

Here, you declare the desired timeout period, which is 1 second, as a global parameter.

The second part of `timeoutHTTP.go` has the following Go code:

```
func Timeout(network, host string) (net.Conn, error) {
    conn, err := net.DialTimeout(network, host, timeout)
    if err != nil {
        return nil, err
    }
    conn.SetDeadline(time.Now().Add(timeout))
    return conn, nil
}
```

Here, you define two types of timeouts, the first one is defined with `net.DialTimeout()` and is for the time it will take your client to connect to the server. The second one is the read/write timeout, which has to do with the time you want to wait to get a response from the web server after connecting to it—this is defined with the call to the `conn.SetDeadline()` function.

The third part of the presented program is the following:

```
func main() {
    if len(os.Args) != 2 {
        fmt.Printf("Usage: %s URL\n", filepath.Base(os.Args[0]))
        os.Exit(1)
    }

    URL :=os.Args[1]
```

The fourth portion of the program is the following:

```
    t := http.Transport{
        Dial: Timeout,
    }

    client := http.Client{
        Transport: &t,
    }
    data, err := client.Get(URL)
```

Here, you define the desired parameters of the connection using an `http.Transport` variable.

The last part of the program contains the following Go code:

```
    if err != nil {
        fmt.Println(err)
```

```
                os.Exit(100)
        } else {
                deferdata.Body.Close()
                _, err := io.Copy(os.Stdout, data.Body)
                if err != nil {
                        fmt.Println(err)
                        os.Exit(100)
                }
        }
}
```

This part of the program is all about error handling!

Executing `timeoutHTTP.go` will generate the following output in case of a timeout:

```
$ go run timeoutHTTP.go http://localhost:8001
Get http://localhost:8001: read tcp [::1]:58018->[::1]:8001: i/o timeout
exit status 100
```

The simplest way to deliberately create a timeout during a web connection is to call the `time.Sleep()` function in the handler function of a web server.

Developing better web clients

Although `getURL.go` does the required job pretty quickly and without writing too much Go code, it is in a way not adaptable or informative. It just prints a bunch of raw HTML code without any other information and without the capability of dividing the HTML code into its logical parts. Therefore, `getURL.go` needs to be improved!

The name of the new utility will be `webClient.go` and will be presented to you in five segments of Go code.

The first part of the utility is the following:

```
package main

import (
    "fmt"
    "net/http"
    "net/http/httputil"
    "net/url"
    "os"
    "path/filepath"
    "strings"
)
```

The second part of the Go code from `webClient.go` is the following:

```
func main() {
    if len(os.Args) != 2 {
        fmt.Printf("Usage: %s URL\n", filepath.Base(os.Args[0]))
        os.Exit(1)
    }

    URL, err :=url.Parse(os.Args[1])
    if err != nil {
        fmt.Println("Parse:", err)
        os.Exit(100)
    }
```

The only new thing here is the use of the `url.Parse()` function that creates a URL structure from a URL that is given as a string to it.

The third part of `webClient.go` has the following Go code:

```
    c := &http.Client{}

    request, err := http.NewRequest("GET", URL.String(), nil)
    if err != nil {
        fmt.Println(err)
        os.Exit(100)
    }

    httpData, err := c.Do(request)
    if err != nil {
        fmt.Println(err)
        os.Exit(100)
    }
```

In this Go code, you first create an `http.Client` variable. Then, you construct a GET HTTP request using `http.NewRequest()`. Last, you send the HTTP request using the `Do()` function, which returns the actual response data saved in the `httpData` variable.

The fourth code part of the utility is the following:

```
    fmt.Println("Status code:", httpData.Status)
    header, _ := httputil.DumpResponse(httpData, false)
    fmt.Print(string(header))

    contentType := httpData.Header.Get("Content-Type")
    characterSet := strings.SplitAfter(contentType, "charset=")
    fmt.Println("Character Set:", characterSet[1])

    if httpData.ContentLength == -1 {
```

```
        fmt.Println("ContentLength in unknown!")
    } else {
        fmt.Println("ContentLength:", httpData.ContentLength)
    }
```

Here, you find the status code of the HTTP request using the `Status` property. Then, you do a little digging into the `Header` part of the response in order to find the character set of the response. Last, you check the value of the `ContentLength` property, which equals -1 for dynamic pages—this means that you do not know the page size in advance.

The last part of the program has the following Go code:

```
    length := 0
    var buffer [1024]byte


    r := httpData.Body
    for {
        n, err := r.Read(buffer[0:])
        if err != nil {
            fmt.Println(err)
            break
        }
        length = length + n
    }
    fmt.Println("Response data length:", length)
}
```

Here, you find the length of the response by reading from the `Body` reader and counting its data. If you want to print the contents of the response, this is the right place to do it.

Executing `webClient.go` will create the following output:

```
$ go run webClient.go invalid
Get invalid: unsupported protocol scheme ""
exit status 100
$ go run webClient.go https://www.mtsoukalos.eu/
Get https://www.mtsoukalos.eu/: dial tcp 109.74.193.253:443: getsockopt:
connection refused
exit status 100
$ go run webClient.go http://www.mtsoukalos.eu/
Status code: 200 OK
HTTP/1.1 200 OK
Accept-Ranges: bytes
Age: 0
Cache-Control: no-cache, must-revalidate
Connection: keep-alive
```

```
Content-Language: en
Content-Type: text/html; charset=utf-8
Date: Mon, 10 Jul 2017 07:29:48 GMT
Expires: Sun, 19 Nov 1978 05:00:00 GMT
Server: Apache/2.4.10 (Debian) PHP/5.6.30-0+deb8u1 mod_wsgi/4.3.0
Python/2.7.9
Vary: Accept-Encoding
Via: 1.1 varnish-v4
X-Content-Type-Options: nosniff
X-Frame-Options: SAMEORIGIN
X-Generator: Drupal 7 (http://drupal.org)
X-Powered-By: PHP/5.6.30-0+deb8u1
X-Varnish: 6922264
Character Set: utf-8
ContentLength in unknown!
EOF
Response data length: 50176
```

A small web server

Enough with the web clients—in this section, you will learn how to develop web servers in Go!

The Go code for the implementation of a naïve web server can be found in `webServer.go`, and this will be presented in four parts; the first part is the following:

```
package main

import (
    "fmt"
    "net/http"
    "os"
)
```

The second part is where things start to get tricky and strange:

```
func myHandler(w http.ResponseWriter, r *http.Request) {
    fmt.Fprintf(w, "Serving: %s\n", r.URL.Path)
    fmt.Printf("Served: %s\n", r.Host)
}
```

This is a kind of function that handles HTTP requests—the function takes two arguments, a `http.ResponseWriter` variable and a pointer to an `http.Request` variable. The first argument will be used for constructing the HTTP response, whereas the `http.Request` variable holds the details of the HTTP request that was received by the server, including the requested URL and the IP address of the client.

The third part of `webServer.go` has the following Go code:

```
func main() {
    PORT := ":8001"
    arguments := os.Args
    if len(arguments) == 1 {
        fmt.Println("Using default port number: ", PORT)
    } else {
        PORT = ":" + arguments[1]
    }
```

Here, you just deal with the port number of the web server—the default port number is `8001`, unless there is a command-line argument.

The last chunk of Go code for `webServer.go` is the following:

```
    http.HandleFunc("/", myHandler)
    err := http.ListenAndServe(PORT, nil)
    if err != nil {
        fmt.Println(err)
        os.Exit(10)
    }
}
```

The `http.HandleFunc()` call defines the name of the handler function (`myHandler`) as well as the URLs that it will support—you can call `http.HandleFunc()` multiple times. The current handler supports /URL, which in Go matches all URLs!

After you are done with the `http.HandleFunc()` calls, you are ready to call `http.ListenAndServe()` and start waiting for incoming connections! If you do not specify an IP address in the `http.ListenAndServe()` function call, then the web server will listen to all configured network interfaces of the machine.

Executing `webServer.go` will generate no output, unless you try to fetch some data from it—in this case, it will print logging information on your Terminal, which will show the server name (`localhost`) and port number (`8001`) of the request, as shown here:

```
$ go run webServer.go
Using default port number:   :8001

Served: localhost:8001
Served: localhost:8001
Served: localhost:8001
```

The following screenshot shows three outputs of `webServer.go` on a web browser:

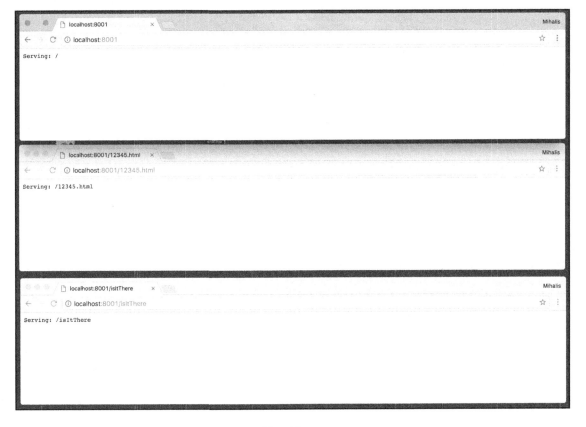

Using webServer.go

However, if you use a command-line utility such as wget (1) or getURL.go instead of a web browser, you will get the following output when you try to connect to the Go web server:

```
$ go run getURL.go http://localhost:8001/
Serving: /
```

 The biggest advantage you get from custom made web servers is security because they are really difficult to hack when developed with security as well as easier customizationin mind.

The next subsection will show how to create web servers using http.ServeMux.

The http.ServeMux type

In this subsection, you will learn how to use the http.ServeMux type in order to improve the way your Go web server will operate. Putting it simply, http.ServeMux is a HTTP request router.

Using http.ServeMux

The web server implementation of this section will support multiple paths with the help of http.ServeMux, which will be illustrated in the serveMux.go program that will be displayed in four parts.

The first part of the program is the following:

```
package main

import (
    "fmt"
    "net/http"
    "time"
)
```

The second part of `serveMux.go` has the following Go code:

```go
func about(w http.ResponseWriter, r *http.Request) {
    fmt.Fprintf(w, "This is the /about page at %s\n", r.URL.Path)
    fmt.Printf("Served: %s\n", r.Host)
}

func cv(w http.ResponseWriter, r *http.Request) {
    fmt.Fprintf(w, "This is the /CV page at %s\n", r.URL.Path)
    fmt.Printf("Served: %s\n", r.Host)
}

func timeHandler(w http.ResponseWriter, r *http.Request) {
    currentTime := time.Now().Format(time.RFC1123)
    title := currentTime
    Body := "The current time is:"
    fmt.Fprintf(w, "<h1 align=\"center\">%s</h1><h2
align=\"center\">%s</h2>", Body, title)
    fmt.Printf("Served: %s for %s\n", r.URL.Path, r.Host)
}
```

Here, you have the implementation of three HTTP handler functions. The first two display a static page, whereas the third one displays the current time, which is a dynamic text.

The third part of the program is the following:

```go
func home(w http.ResponseWriter, r *http.Request) {
    ifr.URL.Path == "/" {
        fmt.Fprintf(w, "Welcome to my home page!\n")
    } else {
        fmt.Fprintf(w, "Unknown page: %s from %s\n", r.URL.Path, r.Host)
    }
    fmt.Printf("Served: %s for %s\n", r.URL.Path, r.Host)
}
```

The `home()` handler function will have to make sure that it is actually serving /Path, because /Path catches everything!

The last part of `serveMux.go` contains the following Go code:

```go
func main() {
    m := http.NewServeMux()
    m.HandleFunc("/about", about)
    m.HandleFunc("/CV", cv)
    m.HandleFunc("/time", timeHandler)
    m.HandleFunc("/", home)

    http.ListenAndServe(":8001", m)
}
```

Here, you define the paths that your web server will support. Note that paths are case sensitive and that the last path in the preceding code catches everything. This means that if you put `m.HandleFunc("/", home)` first, you will not be able to match anything else. Putting it simply, the order of the `m.HandleFunc()` statements matters. Also, note that if you want to support both `/about` and `/about/`, you should have both `m.HandleFunc("/about", about)` and `m.HandleFunc("/about/", about)`.

Running `serveMux.go` will generate the following output:

```
$ go run serveMux.go
Served: / for localhost:8001
Served: /123 for localhost:8001
Served: localhost:8001
Served: /cv for localhost:8001
```

The following screenshot shows the various kinds of outputs generated by `serveMux.go` on a web browser—note that the browser output is not related to the preceding output from the `go run serveMux.go` command:

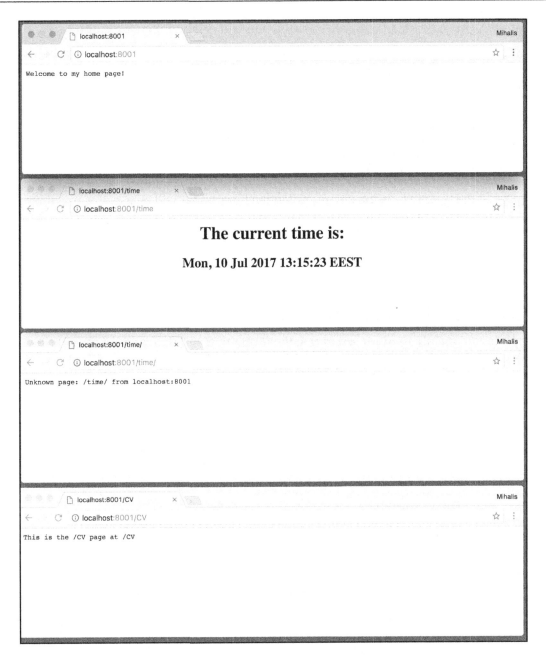

Using serveMux.go

If you use `wget (1)` instead of a web browser, you will get the following output:

```
$ wget -qO- http://localhost:8001/CV
This is the /CV page at /CV
$ wget -qO- http://localhost:8001/cv
Unknown page: /cv from localhost:8001
$ wget -qO- http://localhost:8001/time
<h1 align="center">The current time is:</h1><h2 align="center">Mon, 10 Jul
2017 13:13:27 EEST</h2>
$ wget -qO- http://localhost:8001/time/
Unknown page: /time/ from localhost:8001
```

So, `http.HandleFunc()` is the default call in the library that will be used for first time implementations, whereas the `HandleFunc()` function of `http.NewServeMux()` is for everything else. Putting it simply, it is better to use the `http.NewServeMux()` version instead of the default one except in the simplest of cases.

The html/template package

Templates are mainly used for separating the formatting and data parts of the output. Note that a Go template can be either a file or string—the general idea is to use strings for smaller templates and files for bigger ones.

In this section, we will talk about the `html/template` package by showing an example, which can be found in the `template.go` file and will be presented in six parts. The general idea behind `template.go` is that you are reading a text file with records that you want to present in HTML format. Given that the name of the package is `html/template`, a better name for the program would have been `genHTML.go` or `genTemplate.go`.

There is also the `text/template` package, which is more useful for creating plain text output. However, you cannot import both `text/template` and `html/template` on the same Go program without taking some extra steps to disambiguate them because the two packages have the same package name (`template`). The key distinction between the two packages is that `html/template` does sanitization of the data input for HTML injection, which means that it is more secure.

The first part of the source file is the following:

```
package main

import (
    "bufio"
    "fmt"
    "html/template"
    "net/http"
    "os"
    "strings"
)

type Entry struct {
    WebSite string
    WebName string
    Quality string
}


var filename string
```

The definition of the structure is really important because this is how your data is going to be passed to the `template` file.

The second part of `template.go` has the following Go code:

```
func dynamicContent(w http.ResponseWriter, r *http.Request) {
    var Data []Entry
    var f *os.File
    if filename == "" {
        f = os.Stdin
    } else {
        fileHandler, err := os.Open(filename)
        if err != nil {
            fmt.Printf("error opening %s: %s", filename, err)
            os.Exit(1)
        }
        f = fileHandler
    }
    defer f.Close()
    scanner := bufio.NewScanner(f)
    myT := template.Must(template.ParseGlob("template.gohtml"))
```

The `template.ParseGlob()` function is used for reading the external template file, which can have any file extension you want. Using the `.gohtml` extension might make your life simpler when you are looking for Go template files in your projects.

Although I personally prefer the `.gohtml` extension for Go template files, `.tpl` is a pretty common extension that is widely used. You can choose whichever you like.

The third chunk of code from `template.go` is the following:

```
    for scanner.Scan() {

        parts := strings.Fields(scanner.Text())
        if len(parts) == 3 {
            temp := Entry{WebSite: parts[0], WebName: parts[1], Quality:
parts[2]}
            Data = append(Data, temp)
        }
    }

    fmt.Println("Serving", r.Host, "for", r.URL.Path)
    myT.ExecutcTemplate(w, "template.gohtml", Data)
}
```

The third parameter to the `ExecuteTemplate()` function is the data you want to process. In this case, you pass a slice of records to it.

The fourth part of the program is the following:

```
func staticPage(w http.ResponseWriter, r *http.Request) {
    fmt.Println("Serving", r.Host, "for", r.URL.Path)
    myT := template.Must(template.ParseGlob("static.gohtml"))
    myT.ExecuteTemplate(w, "static.gohtml", nil)
}
```

This function displays a static HTML page, which we are just going to pass through the template engine with the `nil` data, which is signified by the third argument of the `ExecuteTemplate()` function. If you have the same function handling different pieces of data, you may end up with cases where there is nothing to render, but keep it there for common code structure.

The fifth part of `template.go` contains the following Go code:

```
func main() {
    arguments := os.Args

    if len(arguments) == 1 {
        filename = ""
    } else {
        filename = arguments[1]
    }
```

The last chunk of Go code from `template.go` is where you define the supported paths and start the web server using port number 8001:

```
http.HandleFunc("/static", staticPage)
http.HandleFunc("/dynamic", dynamicContent)
http.ListenAndServe(":8001", nil)
}
```

The contents of the `template.gohtml` file are as follows:

```
<!doctype html>
<htmllang="en">
<head>
    <meta charset="UTF-8">
    <title>Using Go HTML Templates</title>
    <style>
        html {
                font-size: 16px;
        }
        table, th, td {
        border: 3px solid gray;
        }
    </style>
</head>
<body>

<h2 alight="center">Presenting Dynamic content!</h2>

<table>
    <thead>
        <tr>
                <th>Web Site</th>
                <th>Quality</th>
        </tr>
    </thead>
    <tbody>
{{ range . }}
<tr>
    <td><a href="{{ .WebSite }}">{{ .WebName }}</a></td>
    <td> {{ .Quality }} </td>
</tr>
{{ end }}
    </tbody>
</table>

</body>
</html>
```

The dot (.) character represents the current data being processed—to put it simply, the dot (.) character is a variable. The `{{ range . }}` statement is equivalent to a `for` loop that visits all the elements of the input slice, which are structures in this case. You can access the fields of each structure as `.WebSite`, `.WebName`, and `.Quality`.

The contents of the `static.gohtml` file are the following:

```
<!doctype html>
<htmllang="en">
<head>
    <meta charset="UTF-8">
    <title>A Static HTML Template</title>
</head>
<body>

<H1>Hello there!</H1>

</body>
</html>
```

If you execute `template.go`, you will get the following output on the screen:

```
$ go run template.go /tmp/sites.html
Serving localhost:8001 for /dynamic
Serving localhost:8001 for /static
```

The following screenshot shows the two outputs of `template.go` as displayed on a web browser. The `sites.html` file has three columns, which are the URL, the name and the quality and can have multiple lines. The good thing here is that if you change the contents of the `/tmp/sites.html` file and reload the web page, you will see the updated contents!

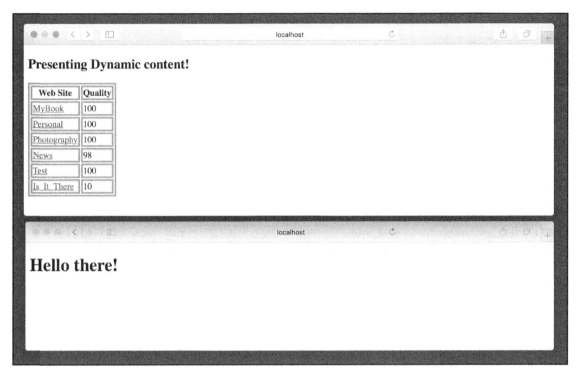

Using template.go

About JSON

JSON stands for JavaScript Object Notation. This is a text-based format designed as an easy and light way to pass information between JavaScript systems.

A simple JSON document has the following format:

```
{ "name":"Mihalis",


"surname":"Tsoukalos",
"country":"Greece" }
```

The preceding JSON document has three fields named `name`, `surname`, and `country`. Each field has a single value.

However, JSON documents can have more complex structures with multiple depth levels.

Before seeing some code, I think that it would be very useful to talk about the `encoding/json` Go package first. The `encoding/json` package offers the `Encode()` and `Decode()` functions that allow the conversion of a Go object into a JSON document and vice versa. Additionally, the `encoding/json` package offers the `Marshal()` and `Unmarshal()` functions that work similarly to `Encode()` and `Decode()` and are based on the `Encode()` and `Decode()` methods.

The main difference between `Marshal()`–`Unmarshal()` and `Encode()`–`Decode()` is that the former functions work on single objects, whereas the latter functions can work on multiple objects as well as streams of bytes.

Last, the `encoding/json` Go package includes two interfaces named `Marshaler` and `Unmarshaler`—each one of them requires the implementation of a single method, named `MarshalJSON()` and `UnmarshalJSON()`, respectively. These two interfaces allow you to perform custom JSON **Marshalling** and **Unmarshalling** in Go. Unfortunately, those two interfaces will not be covered in this book.

Saving JSON data

This subsection will teach you how to convert regular data into JSON format in order to send it over a network connection. The Go code of this subsection will be saved as `writeJSON.go` and will be presented in four parts.

The first chunk of Go code is the expected preamble of the program as well as the definition of two new `struct` types named `Record` and `Telephone`, respectively:

```go
package main

import (
    "encoding/json"
    "fmt"
    "os"
)

type Record struct {
    Name     string
    Surname  string
    Tel      []Telephone
```

```
}

type Telephone struct {
    Mobile bool
    Number string
}
```

 Note that only the members of a structure that begin with an uppercase letter will be in the JSON output because members that begin with a lowercase letter are considered private—in this case, all members of `Record` and `Telephone` structures are public and will get exported.

The second part is the definition of a function named `saveToJSON()`:

```
funcsaveToJSON(filename string, key interface{}) {
    out, err := os.Create(filename)
    if err != nil {
        fmt.Println(err)
        return
    }

    encodeJSON := json.NewEncoder(out)
    err = encodeJSON.Encode(key)
    if err != nil {
        fmt.Println(err)
        return
    }

    out.Close()
}
```

The `saveToJSON()` function does all the work for us as it creates a JSON encoder variable named `encodeJSON`, which is associated with a filename, which is where the data is going to be saved. Then, the call to `Encode()` saves the data of the record to the associated filename and we are done! As you will see in the next section, a similar process will help you read a JSON file and convert it into a Go variable.

The third part of the program has the following Go code:

```
func main() {
    arguments := os.Args
    if len(arguments) == 1 {
        fmt.Println("Please provide a filename!")
        os.Exit(100)
    }

    filename := arguments[1]
```

There is nothing special here—you just get the first command-line argument of the program.

The last part of the utility is the following:

```
myRecord := Record{
      Name:    "Mihalis",
      Surname: "Tsoukalos",
      Tel: []Telephone{Telephone{Mobile: true, Number: "1234-567"},
            Telephone{Mobile: true, Number: "1234-abcd"},
            Telephone{Mobile: false, Number: "abcc-567"},
      }}

   saveToJSON(filename, myRecord)
}
```

Here, we do two things. The first is defining a new `Record` variable and filling it with data. The second is the call to `saveToJSON()` for saving the `myRecord` variable in the JSON format to the selected file.

Executing `writeJSON.go` will generate the following output:

```
$ go run writeJSON.go /tmp/SavedFile
```

After that, the contents of `/tmp/SavedFile` will be the following:

```
$ cat /tmp/SavedFile
{"Name":"Mihalis","Surname":"Tsoukalos","Tel":[{"Mobile":true,"Number":"123
4-567"},{"Mobile":true,"Number":"1234-
abcd"},{"Mobile":false,"Number":"abcc-567"}]}
```

Sending JSON data over a network requires the use of the net Go standard package that will be discussed in the next chapter.

Parsing JSON data

This subsection will illustrate how to read a JSON record and convert it into one Go variable that you can use in your own programs. The name of the presented program will be `readJSON.go` and will be shown to you in four parts.

The first part of the utility is identical to the first part of the writeJSON.go utility:

```
package main

import (
    "encoding/json"
    "fmt"
    "os"
)

type Record struct {
    Name     string
    Surname  string
    Tel      []Telephone
}

type Telephone struct {
    Mobile bool
    Number string
}
```

The second part of the Go code is the following:

```
funcloadFromJSON(filename string, key interface{}) error {
    in, err := os.Open(filename)
    if err != nil {
            return err
    }

    decodeJSON := json.NewDecoder(in)
    err = decodeJSON.Decode(key)
    if err != nil {
            return err
    }
    in.Close()
    return nil
}
```

Here, you define a new function named loadFromJSON() that is used for decoding a JSON file according to a data structure that is given as the second argument to it. You first call the json.NewDecoder() function to create a new JSON decode variable that is associated with a file, and then you call the Decode() function for actually decoding the contents of the file.

The third part of `readJSON.go` has the following Go code:

```
func main() {
    arguments := os.Args
    iflen(arguments) == 1 {
        fmt.Println("Please provide a filename!")
        os.Exit(100)
    }

    filename := arguments[1]
```

The last part of the program is the following:

```
    var myRecord Record
    err := loadFromJSON(filename, &myRecord)
    if err == nil {
        fmt.Println(myRecord)
    } else {
        fmt.Println(err)
    }
}
```

If you run `readJSON.go`, you will get the following output:

```
$ go run readJSON.go /tmp/SavedFile
{Mihalis Tsoukalos [{true 1234-567} {true 1234-abcd} {false abcc-567}]}
```

Reading your JSON data from a network will be discussed in the next chapter, as JSON records do not differ from any other kind of data transferred over a network.

Using Marshal() and Unmarshal()

In this subsection, you will see how to use `Marshal()` and `Unmarshal()` in order to implement the functionality of `readJSON.go` and `writeJSON.go`. The Go code that illustrates the `Marshal()` and `Unmarshal()` functions can be found in `marUnmar.go`, and this will be presented in four parts.

The first part of `marUnmar.go` is the expected preamble:

```
package main

import (
    "encoding/json"
    "fmt"
    "os"
)
```

```
type Record struct {
    Name    string
    Surname string
    Tel     []Telephone
}

type Telephone struct {
    Mobile bool
    Number string
}
```

The second part of the program contains the following Go code:

```
func main() {
    myRecord := Record{
        Name:    "Mihalis",
        Surname: "Tsoukalos",
        Tel: []Telephone{Telephone{Mobile: true, Number: "1234-567"},
            Telephone{Mobile: true, Number: "1234-abcd"},
            Telephone{Mobile: false, Number: "abcc-567"},
        }}
```

This is the same record that is used in the `writeJSON.go` program. Therefore, so far there is nothing special.

The third part of `marUnmar.go` is where the marshalling happens:

```
    rec, err := json.Marshal(&myRecord)
    if err != nil {
        fmt.Println(err)
        os.Exit(100)
    }
    fmt.Println(string(rec))
```

Note that `json.Marshal()` requires a pointer for passing data to it even if the value is a map, array, or slice.

The last part of the program contains the following Go code that performs the unmarshalling operation:

```
    var unRec Record
    err1 := json.Unmarshal(rec, &unRec)
    if err1 != nil {
        fmt.Println(err1)
        os.Exit(100)
    }
    fmt.Println(unRec)
}
```

As you can see from the code, json.Unmarshal() requires the use of a pointer for saving the data even if the value is a map, array, or slice.

Executing marUnmar.go will create the following output:

```
$ go run marUnmar.go
{"Name":"Mihalis","Surname":"Tsoukalos","Tel":[{"Mobile":true,"Number":"123
4-567"},{"Mobile":true,"Number":"1234-
abcd"},{"Mobile":false,"Number":"abcc-567"}]}
{Mihalis Tsoukalos [{true 1234-567} {true 1234-abcd} {false abcc-567}]}
```

As you can see, the Marshal() and Unmarshal() functions cannot help you store your data into a file—you will need to implement that on your own.

Using MongoDB

A relational database is a structured collection of data that is strictly organized into tables. The dominant language for querying databases is SQL. NoSQL databases, such as **MongoDB**, do not use SQL, but various other query languages and do not have a strict structure in their tables, which are called **collections** in the NoSQL terminology.

You can categorize NoSQL databases according to their data model as Document, Key-Value, Graph, and Column-family. MongoDB is the most popular document-oriented NoSQL database that is appropriate for use in web applications.

Document databases were not made for dealing with Microsoft Word documents, but for storing semistructured data.

Basic MongoDB administration

If you want to use MongoDB on your Go applications, it would be very practical to know how to perform some basic administrative tasks on a MongoDB database.

Most of the tasks presented in this section will be performed from the Mongo shell, which starts by executing the `mongo` command. If no MongoDB instance is running on your Unix machine, you will get the following output:

```
$ mongo
MongoDB shell version v3.4.5
connecting to: mongodb://127.0.0.1:27017
2017-07-06T19:37:38.291+0300 W NETWORK  [thread1] Failed to connect to
127.0.0.1:27017, in(checking socket for error after poll), reason:
Connection refused
2017-07-06T19:37:38.291+0300 E QUERY    [thread1] Error: couldn't connect
to server 127.0.0.1:27017, connection attempt failed :
connect@src/mongo/shell/mongo.js:237:13
@(connect):1:6
exception: connect failed
```

The previous output tells us two things:

- The default TCP port number for the MongoDB server process is `27017`
- The mongo executable tries to connect to the `127.0.0.1` IP address, which is the IP address of the local machine

In order to execute the following commands, you should start a MongoDB server instance on your local machine. Once the MongoDB server process is up and running, executing `mongo` will create the following output:

```
$ mongo
MongoDB shell version: 2.4.10
connecting to: test
>
```

The following commands will show you how to create a new MongoDB database and a new MongoDB collection, and how to insert some documents in to that collection:

```
>use go;
switched to db go
>db.someData.insert({x:0, y:1})
>db.someData.insert({x:1, y:2})
>db.someData.insert({x:2, y:3})
>db.someData.count()
3
```

Once you try to insert a document into a collection using `db.someData.insert()`, the collection (`someData`) will be automatically created if it does not already exist. The last command counts the number of records stored into the `someData` collection of the current database.

MongoDB will not inform you about any typographical errors you might have. Putting it simply, if you mistype the name of a database or a collection, MongoDB will create a totally new database or a new collection while you are trying to find out what went wrong! Additionally, if you put more, less, or different fields on a document and try to save it, MongoDB will not complain!

You can find the records of a collection using the `find()` function:

```
>db.someData.find()
{ "_id" : ObjectId("595e84cd63883cb3fe7f42f3"), "x" : 0, "y" : 1 }
{ "_id" : ObjectId("595e84d263883cb3fe7f42f4"), "x" : 1, "y" : 2 }
{ "_id" : ObjectId("595e84d663883cb3fe7f42f5"), "x" : 2, "y" : 3 }
```

You can find the list of databases on a running MongoDB instance as follows:

```
>show databases;
LXF    0.203125GB
go     0.0625GB
local 0.078125GB
```

Similarly, you can find the names of the collections stored in the current MongoDB database as follows:

```
>db.getCollectionNames()
[ "someData", "system.indexes" ]
```

You can delete all the records of a MongoDB collection as follows:

```
>db.someData.remove()
>show collections
someData
system.indexes
```

Last, you can delete an entire collection, including its records, as follows:

```
>db.someData.drop()
true
>show collections
system.indexes
```

The preceding information will get you going for now, but if you want to learn more about MongoDB, you should visit the documentation site of MongoDB at `https://docs.mongodb.com/`.

Using the MongoDB Go driver

In order to use MongoDB in your Go programs, you should first have the MongoDB Go driver installed on your Unix machine. The name of the MongoDB Go driver is `mgo` and you can learn more information about the MongoDB Go driver by visiting `https://github.com/go-mgo/mgo`, `https://labix.org/mgo`, and `https://docs.mongodb.com/ecosystem/drivers/go/`.

As the driver is not part of the standard Go library, you should first download the required packages using the following two commands:

```
$ go get labix.org/v2/mgo
$ go get labix.org/v2/mgo/bson
```

After that, you will be free to use it in your own Go utilities. If you try to execute the program without having the two packages on your Unix system, you will get an error message similar to the following:

```
$ go run testMongo.go
testMongo.go:5:2: cannot find package "labix.org/v2/mgo" in any of:
        /usr/local/Cellar/go/1.8.3/libexec/src/labix.org/v2/mgo (from
$GOROOT)
        /Users/mtsouk/go/src/labix.org/v2/mgo (from $GOPATH)
testMongo.go:6:2: cannot find package "labix.org/v2/mgo/bson" in any of:
        /usr/local/Cellar/go/1.8.3/libexec/src/labix.org/v2/mgo/bson (from
$GOROOT)
        /Users/mtsouk/go/src/labix.org/v2/mgo/bson (from $GOPATH)
```

Note that you might need to install Bazaar on your Unix system in order to execute the two `go get` commands. You can get more information about the Bazaar version control system at `https://bazaar.canonical.com/`.

So, you should first try to run a simple Go program that connects to a MongoDB database, creates a new database and a new collection, and adds new documents to it in order to make sure that everything works as expected—the name of the program will be `testMongo.go` and will be presented in four parts.

The first part of the program is the following:

```
package main

import (
    "fmt"
    "labix.org/v2/mgo"
    "labix.org/v2/mgo/bson"
    "os"
    "time"
)

type Record struct {
    Xvalueint
    Yvalueint
}
```

Here, you see the use of the Go MongoDB driver in the import block. Additionally, you see the definition of a new Go structure named `Record` that will hold the data of each MongoDB document.

The second part of `testMongo.go` has the following Go code:

```
func main() {
    mongoDBDialInfo := &mgo.DialInfo{
        Addrs:   []string{"127.0.0.1:27017"},
        Timeout: 20 * time.Second,
    }

    session, err := mgo.DialWithInfo(mongoDBDialInfo)
    if err != nil {
        fmt.Printf("DialWithInfo: %s\n", err)
        os.Exit(100)
    }
    session.SetMode(mgo.Monotonic, true)

    collection := session.DB("goDriver").C("someData")
```

Now the `collection` variable will be used for dealing with the `someData` collection of the `goDriver` database—a better name for the database would have been `myDB`. Note that there was not a `goDriver` database in the MongoDB instance before running the Go program; this also means that neither the `someData` collection was there.

The third part of the program is the following:

```
err = collection.Insert(&Record{1, 0})
if err != nil {
        fmt.Println(err)
        os.Exit(100)
}

err = collection.Insert(&Record{-1, 0})
if err != nil {
        fmt.Println(err)
        os.Exit(100)
}
```

Here, you insert two documents to the MongoDB database using the `Insert()` function.

The last portion of `testMongo.go` contains the following Go code:

```
var recs []Record
err = collection.Find(bson.M{"yvalue": 0}).All(&recs)
if err != nil {
        fmt.Println(err)
        os.Exit(100)
}

for x, y := range recs {
        fmt.Println(x, y)
}
fmt.Println("Found:", len(recs), "results!")
}
```

As you do not know the number of documents that you will get from the `Find()` query, you should use a slice of records for storing them.

Additionally, note that you should put the `yvalue` field in lowercase in the `Find()` function because MongoDB will automatically convert the fields of the `Record` structure in lowercase when you are storing them!

Now, execute `testMongo.go`, as shown here:

```
$ go run testMongo.go
0 {1 0}
1 {-1 0}
Found: 2 results!
```

Note that if you execute `testMongo.go` multiple times, you will find the same documents inserted multiple times into the `someData` collection. However, MongoDB will not have any problems differentiating between all these documents because the key of each document is the `_id` field, which is automatically inserted by MongoDB each time you insert a new document to a collection.

After that, connect to your MongoDB instance using the `MongoDB` shell command to make sure that everything worked as expected:

```
$ mongo
MongoDB shell version v3.4.5
connecting to: mongodb://127.0.0.1:27017
MongoDB server version: 3.4.5
>use goDriver
switched to db goDriver
>show collections
someData
>db.someData.find()
{ "_id" : ObjectId("595f88593fb7048f4846e555"), "xvalue" : 1, "yvalue" : 0
}
{ "_id" : ObjectId("595f88593fb7048f4846e557"), "xvalue" : -1, "yvalue" : 0
}
>
```

Here, it is important to understand that MongoDB documents are presented in JSON format, which you already know how to handle in Go.

Also, note that the Go MongoDB driver has many more capabilities than the ones presented here. Unfortunately, talking more about it is beyond the scope of this book, but you can learn more by visiting `https://github.com/go-mgo/mgo`, `https://labix.org/mgo`, and `https://docs.mongodb.com/ecosystem/drivers/go/`.

Creating a Go application that displays MongoDB data

The name of the utility will be `showMongo.go` and it will be presented in three parts. The utility will connect to a MongoDB instance, read a collection, and display the documents of the collection as a web page. Note that `showMongo.go` is based on the Go code of `template.go`.

The first part of the web application is the following:

```
package main

import (
    "fmt"
    "html/template"
    "labix.org/v2/mgo"
    "net/http"
    "os"
    "time"
)

var DatabaseName string
var collectionName string

type Document struct {
    P1 int
    P2 int
    P3 int
    P4 int
    P5 int
}
```

You should know in advance the structure of the MongoDB documents that you will retrieve because the field names are hard coded in the `struct` type and need to match.

The second part of the program is the following:

```
func content(w http.ResponseWriter, r *http.Request) {
    var Data []Document
    myT := template.Must(template.ParseGlob("mongoDB.gohtml"))

    mongoDBDialInfo := &mgo.DialInfo{
        Addrs:   []string{"127.0.0.1:27017"},
        Timeout: 20 * time.Second,
    }

    session, err := mgo.DialWithInfo(mongoDBDialInfo)
    if err != nil {
        fmt.Printf("DialWithInfo: %s\n", err)
        return
    }
    session.SetMode(mgo.Monotonic, true)
    c := session.DB(DatabaseName).C(collectionName)
```

```
err = c.Find(nil).All(&Data)
if err != nil {
    fmt.Println(err)
    return
}

fmt.Println("Found:", len(Data), "results!")
myT.ExecuteTemplate(w, "mongoDB.gohtml", Data)
}
```

As before, you connect to MongoDB using `mgo.DialWithInfo()` with the parameters that were defined in the `mgo.DialInfo` structure.

The last part of the web application is the following:

```
func main() {
    arguments := os.Args

    iflen(arguments) <= 2 {
        fmt.Println("Please provide a Database and a Collection!")
        os.Exit(100)
    } else {
        DatabaseName = arguments[1]
        collectionName = arguments[2]
    }

    http.HandleFunc("/", content)
    http.ListenAndServe(":8001", nil)
}
```

The contents of `MongoDB.gohtml` are similar to the contents of `template.gohtml` and will not be presented here. You can refer to *The html/template package* section for the contents of `template.gohtml`.

The execution of `showMongo.go` will not display the actual data on the screen—you will need to use a web browser for that:

```
$ go run showMongo.go goDriver Numbers
Found: 0 results!
Found: 10 results!
Found: 14 results!
```

The good thing is that if the data of the collections is changed, you will not need to recompile your Go code in order to see the changes—you will just need to reload the web page.

The following screenshot shows the output of `showMongo.go` as displayed on a web browser:

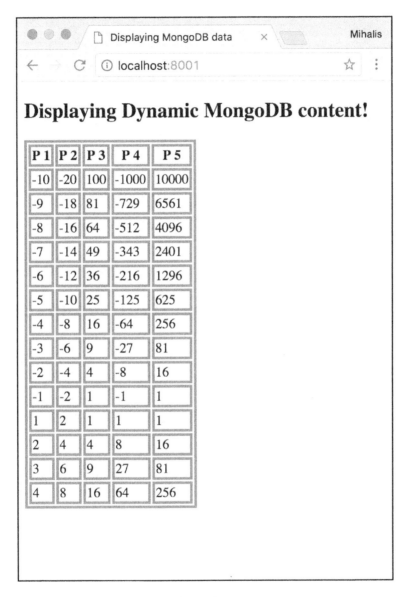

Using showMongo.go

Note that the Numbers collection contains the following documents:

```
>db.Numbers.findOne()


{


        "_id" : ObjectId("596530aeaab5252f5c1ab100"),
        "p1" : -10,
        "p2" : -20,
        "p3" : 100,
        "p4" : -1000,
        "p5" : 10000
}
```

> Have in mind that extra data in the MongoDB structure that does not have corresponding fields in the Go structure is ignored.

Creating an application that displays MySQL data

In this subsection, we will present a Go utility that executes a query on a MySQL table. The name of the new command-line utility will be showMySQL.go and will be presented in five parts.

> Note that showMySQL.go will use the database/sql package that provides a generic SQL interface to relational databases for querying the MySQL database.

The presented utility requires two parameters—a username with administrative privileges and its password.

The first part of showMySQL.go is the following:

```
package main

import (
    "database/sql"
    "fmt"
    _ "github.com/go-sql-driver/mysql"
    "os"
    "text/template"
)
```

There is a small change here, as showMySQL.go uses text/template instead of html/template. Note that the drivers that conform to the database/sql interface are never really referenced directly in your code, but they still need to be initialized and imported. The _ character in front of "github.com/go-sql-driver/mysql" does this by telling Go to ignore the fact that the "github.com/go-sql-driver/mysql" package is not actually used in the code.

You will also need to download the MySQL Go driver:

$ go get github.com/go-sql-driver/mysql

The second part of the utility has the following Go code:

```
func main() {
    var username string
    var password string

    arguments := os.Args
    if len(arguments) == 3 {
        username = arguments[1]
        password = arguments[2]
    } else {
        fmt.Println("programName Username Password!")
        os.Exit(100)
    }
```

The third chunk of Go code from showMySQL.go is the following:

```
    connectString := username + ":" + password +
"@unix(/tmp/mysql.sock)/information_schema"
    db, err := sql.Open("mysql", connectString)

    rows, err := db.Query("SELECT DISTINCT(TABLE_SCHEMA) FROM TABLES;")
    if err != nil {
          fmt.Println(err)
          os.Exit(100)
    }
```

Here, you manually construct the connection string to MySQL. For reasons of security, a default MySQL installation works with a socket (/tmp/mysql.sock) instead of a network connection. The name of the database that will be used is the last part of the connection string (information_schema).

You will most likely have to adjust these parameters for your own database.

The fourth part of showMySQL.go is the following:

```
    var DATABASES []string
    for rows.Next() {
          var databaseName string
          err := rows.Scan(&databaseName)
          if err != nil {
                fmt.Println(err)
                os.Exit(100)
          }
          DATABASES = append(DATABASES, databaseName)
    }
    db.Close()
```

The Next() function iterates over all the records returned from the select query and returns them one by one with the help of the for loop.

The last part of the program is the following:

```
t := template.Must(template.New("t1").Parse(`
{{range $k := .}} {{ printf "\tDatabase Name: %s" $k}}
{{end}}
`))
t.Execute(os.Stdout, DATABASES)
fmt.Println()
}
```

This time, instead of presenting the data as a web page, you will receive it as plain text. Additionally, as the text template is small, it is defined in line with the help of the t variable.

> Is the use of the template necessary here? Of course not! But it is good to learn how to define Go templates without using an external template file.

Therefore, the output of showMySQL.go will be similar to the following:

```
$ go run showMySQL.go root 12345
    Database Name: information_schema
    Database Name: mysql
    Database Name: performance_schema
    Database Name: sys
```

The preceding output shows information about the available databases for the current MySQL instance, which is a great way to get information about a MySQL database without having to connect using the MySQL client.

A handy command-line utility

In this section, we will develop a handy command-line utility that reads a number of web pages, which can be found in a text file or read from standard input, and returns the number of times a given keyword was found in these web pages. In order to be faster, the utility will use goroutines to get the desired data and a monitoring process to gather the data and present it on the screen. The name of the utility will be findKeyword.go and will be presented in five parts.

The first part of the utility is the following:

```
package main

import (
    "bufio"
    "fmt"
    "net/http"
    "net/url"
    "os"
    "regexp"
)

type Data struct {
    URL     string
    Keyword string
    Times   int
    Error   error
}
```

The `Data struct` type will be used for passing information between channels.

The second part of `findKeyword.go` has the following Go code:

```
func monitor(values <-chan Data, count int) {
    fori := 0; i< count;  i++ {
        x := <-values
        if x.Error == nil {
            fmt.Printf("\t%s\t", x.Keyword)
            fmt.Printf("\t%d\t in\t%s\n", x.Times, x.URL)
        } else {
            fmt.Printf("\t%s\n", x.Error)
        }
    }
}
```

The `monitor()` function is where all the information is collected and printed on the screen.

The third part is the following:

```
func processPage(myUrl, keyword string, out chan<- Data) {
    var err error
    times := 0

    URL, err :=url.Parse(myUrl)
    if err != nil {
        out<- Data{URL: myUrl, Keyword: keyword, Times: 0, Error: err}
        return
```

```
    }

    c := &http.Client{}
    request, err := http.NewRequest("GET", URL.String(), nil)
    if err != nil {
            out<- Data{URL: myUrl, Keyword: keyword, Times: 0, Error: err}
            return
    }

    httpData, err := c.Do(request)
    if err != nil {
            out<- Data{URL: myUrl, Keyword: keyword, Times: 0, Error: err}
            return
    }

    bodyHTML := ""


    var buffer [1024]byte
    reader := httpData.Body
    for {
            n, err := reader.Read(buffer[0:])
            if err != nil {
                    break
            }
            bodyHTML = bodyHTML + string(buffer[0:n])
    }

    regExpr := keyword


    r := regexp.MustCompile(regExpr)
    matches := r.FindAllString(bodyHTML, -1)
    times = times + len(matches)

    newValue := Data{URL: myUrl, Keyword: keyword, Times: times, Error: nil}
    out<- newValue
}
```

Here, you can see the implementation of the processPage() function that is executed in a goroutine. If the Error field of the Data structure is not nil, then there was an error somewhere.

The reason for using the bodyHTML variable to save the entire contents of a URL is for not having a keyword split between two consecutive calls to reader.Read(). After that, a regular expression (r) is used for searching the bodyHTML variable for the desired keyword.

The fourth part contains the following Go code:

```
func main() {
    filename := ""
    var f *os.File
    var keyword string

    arguments := os.Args
    iflen(arguments) == 1 {
        fmt.Println("Not enough arguments!")
        os.Exit(-1)
    }

    iflen(arguments) == 2 {
        f = os.Stdin
        keyword = arguments[1]
    } else {
        keyword = arguments[1]
        filename = arguments[2]
        fileHandler, err := os.Open(filename)
        if err != nil {
            fmt.Printf("error opening %s: %s", filename, err)
            os.Exit(1)
        }
        f = fileHandler
    }

    deferf.Close()
```

As you can see, `findKeyword.go` expects its input from a text file or from standard input, which is the common Unix practice—this technique was first illustrated back in Chapter 8, *Processes and Signals*, in the *Reading from standard input* section.

The last chunk of Go code for `findKeyword.go` is the following:

```
    values := make(chan Data, len(os.Args[1:]))

    scanner := bufio.NewScanner(f)
    count := 0
    forscanner.Scan() {
        count = count + 1
        gofunc(URL string) {
            processPage(URL, keyword, values)
        }(scanner.Text())
    }

    monitor(values, count)
}
```

There is nothing special here—you just start the desired goroutines and the `monitor()` function to take care of them.

Executing `findKeyword.go` will create the following output:

```
$ go run findKeyword.go Tsoukalos /tmp/sites.html
  Get http://really.doesnotexist.com: dial tcp: lookup
really.doesnotexist.com: no such host
  Tsoukalos        8       in      http://www.highiso.net/
  Tsoukalos        4       in      http://www.mtsoukalos.eu/
  Tsoukalos        3       in
https://www.packtpub.com/networking-and-servers/go-systems-programming
  Tsoukalos        0       in      http://cnn.com/
  Tsoukalos        0       in      http://doesnotexist.com
```

The funny thing here is that the `doesnotexist.com` domain does actually exist!

Exercises

1. Download and install MongoDB on your Unix machine.
2. Visit the documentation page of the `net/http` Go standard package at `https://golang.org/pkg/net/http/`.
3. Visit the documentation page of the `html/template` Go standard package at `https://golang.org/pkg/html/template/`.
4. Change the Go code of `getURL.go` in order to make it able to fetch multiple web pages.
5. Read the documentation of the `encoding/json` package that can be found at `https://golang.org/pkg/encoding/json/`.
6. Visit the MongoDB site at `https://www.mongodb.org/`.
7. Learn how to use `text/template` by developing your own example.
8. Change the Go code of `findKeyword.go` in order to be able to search multiple keywords.

Summary

In this chapter, we talked about web development in Go including parsing, marshalling and unmarshalling JSON data, interacting with a MongoDB database; reading data from a MySQL database; creating web servers in Go; creating web clients in Go; and using the `http.ServeMux` type.

In the next chapter, we will talk about network programming in Go, which includes creating TCP and UDP clients and servers using low level commands. We will also teach you how to develop an RCP client and an RCP server in Go. If you love developing TCP/IP applications, then the last chapter of this book is for you!

12
Network Programming

In the previous chapter, we talked about developing web applications, talking to databases, and dealing with JSON data in Go.

The topic of this chapter is the development of Go applications that work over TCP/IP networks. In addition, you will learn how to create TCP and UDP clients and servers. The central Go package of this chapter will be the net package—most of its functions are quite low level and require a good knowledge of TCP/IP and its family of protocols.

However, have in mind that network programming is a huge theme that cannot be covered in a single chapter. This chapter will give you the foundational directions for how to create TCP/IP applications in Go.

More analytically, this chapter will talk about the following topics:

- How TCP/IP operates
- The net Go standard package
- Developing TCP clients and servers
- Programing UDP clients and servers
- Developing an RPC client
- Implementing an RPC server
- The Wireshark and tshark(1) network traffic analyzers
- Unix sockets
- Performing DNS lookups from Go programs

About network programming

Network programming is the development of applications that can operate over computer networks using TCP/IP, which is the dominant networking protocol. Therefore, without knowing the way TCP/IP and its protocols work, you cannot create network applications and develop TCP/IP servers.

The best two advices that I can give to developers of network applications, are to know the theory behind the task they want to perform and to know that networks fail all the time for several reasons. The nastiest types of network failures have to do with malfunctioning or misconfigured DNS servers, because such problems are challenging to find and difficult to correct.

About TCP/IP

TCP/IP is a family of protocols that help the internet to operate. Its name comes from its two most well-known protocols: **TCP** and **IP**.

Every device that uses TCP/IP must have an IP address, which should be unique at least to its local network. It also needs a **network mask**(used for dividing big IP networks into smaller networks) that is related to its current network, one or more **DNS servers**(used for translating an IP address to a human-memorable format and vice versa) and, if you want to communicate with devices beyond your local network, the IP address of a device that will act as the **default gateway**(a network device that TCP/IP sends a network packet to when it cannot find where else to send it).

Each TCP/IP service, which in reality is a Unix process, listens to a port number that is unique to each machine. Note that port numbers 0-1023 are restricted and can only be used by the root user, so it is better to avoid using them and choose something else, provided that it is not already in use by a different process.

About TCP

TCP stands for Transmission Control Protocol. TCP software transmits data between machines using segments, which are called TCP **packets**. The main characteristic of TCP is that it is a reliable protocol, which means that it attempts to make sure that a packet was delivered. If there is no proof of a packet delivery, TCP resends that particular packet. Among other things, a TCP packet can be used for establishing connections, transferring data, sending acknowledgments, and closing connections.

When a TCP connection is established between two machines, a full duplex virtual circuit, similar to the telephone call, is created between these two machines. The two machines constantly communicate to make sure that data are sent and received correctly. If the connection fails for some reason, the two machines try to find the problem and report to the relevant application.

TCP assigns a sequence number to each transmitted packet and expects a positive acknowledgment (ACK) from the receiving TCP stack. If the ACK is not received within a timeout interval, the data is retransmitted as the original packet is considered undelivered. The receiving TCP stack uses the sequence numbers to rearrange the segments when they arrive out of order, which also eliminates duplicate segments.

The TCP header of each packet includes **source port and destination port** fields. These two fields plus the source and destination IP addresses are combined to uniquely identify each TCP connection. The TCP header also includes a 6-bit flags field that is used to relay control information between TCP peers. The possible flags include SYN, FIN, RESET, PUSH, URG, and ACK. The SYN and ACK flags are used for the initial TCP 3-way handshake. The RESET flag signifies that the receiver wants to abort the connection.

The TCP handshake!

When a connection is initiated, the client sends a TCP SYN packet to the server. The TCP header also includes a sequence number field that has an arbitrary value in the SYN packet. The server sends back a TCP [SYN, ACK] packet, which includes the sequence number of the opposite direction and an acknowledgment of the previous sequence number. Finally, in order to truly establish the TCP connection, the client sends a TCP ACK packet in order to acknowledge the sequence number of the server.

> Although all these actions take place automatically, it is good to know what is happening behind the scenes!

About UDP and IP

IP stands for **Internet Protocol**. The main characteristic of IP is that it is not a reliable protocol by nature. IP encapsulates the data that travels in a TCP/IP network because it is responsible for delivering packets from the source host to the destination host according to the IP addresses. IP has to find an addressing method to effectively send the packet to its destination. Although there exist dedicated devices called routers that perform IP routing, every TCP/IP device has to perform some basic routing.

UDP (short for**User Datagram Protocol**) is based on IP, which means that it is also unreliable. Generally speaking, UDP is simpler than TCP mainly because UDP is not reliable by design. As a result, UDP messages can be lost, duplicated, or arrive out of order. Furthermore, packets can arrive faster than the recipient can process them. So, UDP is used when speed is more important than reliability! An example for this is live video and audio applications where catching up is way more important than buffering and not losing any data.

So, when you do not need too many network packets to transfer the desired information, using a protocol that is based on IP might be more efficient than using TCP, even if you have to retransmit a network packet, because there is no traffic overhead from the TCP handshake.

About Wireshark and tshark

Wireshark is a graphical application for analyzing network traffic of almost any kind. Nevertheless, there are times that you need something lighter that you can execute remotely without a graphical user interface. In such situations, you can use `tshark`, which is the command-line version of Wireshark.

In order to help you find the network data you really want, Wireshark and `tshark` have support for capture filters and display filters.

Capture filters are the filters that are applied during network data capturing; therefore, they make Wireshark discard network traffic that does not match the filter. Display filters are the filters that are applied after packet capturing; therefore, they just hide some network traffic without deleting it—you can always disable a display filter and get your hidden data back. Generally speaking, display filters are considered more useful and versatile than capture filters because, normally, you do not know in advance what you will capture or want to examine. Nevertheless, applying filters at capture time can save you time and disk space and that is the main reason for using them.

The following screenshot shows the traffic of a TCP handshake in more detail as captured by Wireshark. The client IP address is `10.0.2.15` and the destination IP address is `80.244.178.150`. Additionally, a simple display filter (`tcp && !http`) makes Wireshark display fewer packets and makes the output less cluttered and therefore easier to read:

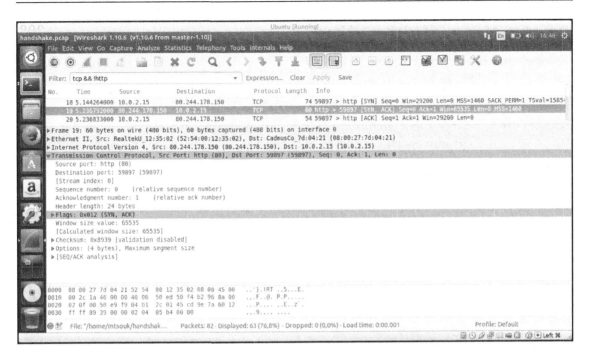

The TCP handshake!

The same information can be seen in text format using `tshark(1)`:

```
$ tshark -r handshake.pcap -Y '(tcp.flags.syn==1 ) || (tcp.flags == 0x0010
&& tcp.seq==1 && tcp.ack==1)'
      18    5.144264    10.0.2.15 → 80.244.178.150 TCP 74 59897 → 80 [SYN]
Seq=0 Win=29200 Len=0 MSS=1460 SACK_PERM=1 TSval=1585402 TSecr=0 WS=128
      19    5.236792 80.244.178.150 → 10.0.2.15     TCP 60 80 → 59897 [SYN,
ACK] Seq=0 Ack=1 Win=65535 Len=0 MSS=1460
      20    5.236833    10.0.2.15 → 80.244.178.150 TCP 54 59897 → 80 [ACK]
Seq=1 Ack=1 Win=29200 Len=0
```

The `-r` parameter followed by an existing filename allows you to replay a previously captured data file on your screen, whereas a more complex display filter, which is defined after the `-Y` parameter, does the rest of the job!

You can learn more about Wireshark at `https://www.wireshark.org/` and by looking at its documentation at `https://www.wireshark.org/docs/`.

About the netcat utility

There are times that you will need to test a TCP/IP client or a TCP/IP server—the netcat(1) utility can help you with that by playing the role of the client or server in a TCP or UDP application.

You can use netcat(1) as a client for a TCP service that runs on a machine with the 192.168.1.123 IP address and listens to port number 1234, as follows:

```
$ netcat 192.168.1.123 1234
```

Similarly, you can use netcat(1) as a client for a UDP service that runs on a Unix machine named amachine.com and listens to port number 2345, as shown here:

```
$ netcat -vv -u amachine.com 2345
```

The -1 option tells netcat(1) to listen for incoming connections, which makes netcat(1) to act as a TCP or UDP server. If you try to use netcat(1) as a server with a port that is already in use, you will get the following output:

```
$ netcat -vv -l localhost -p 80
Can't grab 0.0.0.0:80 with bind : Permission denied
```

The net Go standard package

The most useful Go package for creating TCP/IP applications is the net Go standard package. The net.Dial() function is used for connecting to a network as a client, and the net.Listen() function is used for accepting connections as a server. The first parameter of both functions is the network type, but this is where the similarities end.

For the net.Dial() function, the network type can be one of tcp, tcp4 (IPv4-only), tcp6 (IPv6-only), udp, udp4 (IPv4-only), udp6 (IPv6-only), ip, ip4 (IPv4-only), ip6 (IPv6-only), Unix, Unixgram, or Unixpacket. For the net.Listen() function, the first parameter can be one of tcp, tcp4, tcp6, Unix, or Unixpacket.

The return value of the net.Dial() function is of the net.Conn interface type, which implements the io.Reader and io.Writer interfaces! This means that you already know how to access the variables of the net.Conn interface!

So, although the way you create a network connection is different from the way you create a text file, their access methods are the same because the `net.Conn` interface implements the `io.Reader` and `io.Writer` interfaces. Therefore, as network connections are treated as files, you might need to review `Chapter 6`, *File Input and Output*, at this moment.

Unix sockets revisited

Back in `Chapter 8`, *Processes and Signals*, we talked a little about Unix sockets and presented a small Go program that was acting as a Unix socket client. This section will also create a Unix socket server to make things even clearer. However, the Go code of the Unix socket client will be also explained here in more detail and will be enriched with error handling code.

A Unix socket server

The Unix socket server will act as an Echo server, which means that it will sendthe received messageback to the client. The name of the program will be `socketServer.go` and it will be presented to you in four parts.

The first part of `socketServer.go` is the following:

```
package main

import (
    "fmt"
    "net"
    "os"
)
```

The second part of the Unix socket server is the following:

```
func echoServer(c net.Conn) {
    for {
        buf := make([]byte, 1024)
        nr, err := c.Read(buf)
        if err != nil {
            return
        }

        data := buf[0:nr]
        fmt.Printf("->: %v\n", string(data))
        _, err = c.Write(data)
        if err != nil {
```

```
                fmt.Println(err)
        }
    }
}
```

This is where the function that serves incoming connections is implemented.

The third portion of the program has the following Go code:

```
func main() {
    arguments := os.Args
    if len(arguments) == 1 {
        fmt.Println("Please provide a socket file.")
        os.Exit(100)
    }
    socketFile := arguments[1]

    l, err := net.Listen("unix", socketFile)
    if err != nil {
        fmt.Println(err)
os.Exit(100)
    }
```

Here, you can see the use of the `net.Listen()` function with the `unix` argument for creating the desired socket file.

Finally, the last part contains the following Go code:

```
    for {
        fd, err := l.Accept()
        if err != nil {
            fmt.Println(err)
            os.Exit(100)
        }
        go echoServer(fd)
    }
}
```

As you can see, each connection is first handled by the `Accept()` function and served by its own goroutine.

When `socketServer.go` serves a client, it generates the following output:

```
$ go run socketServer.go /tmp/aSocket
->: Hello Server!
```

If you cannot create the desired socket file, for instance, if it already exists, you will get an error message similar to the following:

```
$ go run socketServer.go /tmp/aSocket
listen unix /tmp/aSocket: bind: address already in use
exit status 100
```

A Unix socket client

The name of the Unix socket client program is `socketClient.go` and will be presented in four parts.

The first part of the utility contains the expected preamble:

```go
package main

import (
    "fmt"
    "io"
    "log"
    "net"
    "os"
    "time"
)
```

There is nothing special here, just the required Go packages. The second portion contains the definition of a Go function:

```go
func readSocket(r io.Reader) {

    buf := make([]byte, 1024)
    for {
        n, err := r.Read(buf[:])
        if err != nil {
            fmt.Println(err)
            return
        }
        fmt.Println("-> ", string(buf[0:n]))
    }
}
```

The `readSocket()` function reads the data from a socket file using `Read()`. Note that, although `socketClient.go` just reads from the socket file, the socket is bisectional, which means that you can also write to it.

The third part has the following Go code:

```go
func main() {
    arguments := os.Args
    if len(arguments) == 1 {
        fmt.Println("Please provide a socket file.")
        os.Exit(100)
    }
    socketFile := arguments[1]

    c, err := net.Dial("unix", socketFile)
    if err != nil {
        fmt.Println(err)
        os.Exit(100)
    }
    defer c.Close()
```

The `net.Dial()` function with the right first argument allows you to connect to the socket file before you try to read from it.

The last part of `socketClient.go` is the following:

```go
    go readSocket(c)
    for {
        _, err := c.Write([]byte("Hello Server!"))
        if err != nil {
            fmt.Println(err)
            os.Exit(100)
        }
        time.Sleep(1 * time.Second)
    }
}
```

In order to use `socketClient.go`, you must have another program dealing with the Unix socket file, which, in this case will be `socketServer.go`. So, if `socketServer.go` is already running, you will get the following output from `socketClient.go`:

```
$ go run socketClient.go /tmp/aSocket
->: Hello Server!
```

If you do not have enough Unix file permissions to read the desired socket file, then `socketClient.go` will fail with the following error message:

```
$ go run socketClient.go /tmp/aSocket
dial unix /tmp/aSocket: connect: permission denied
exit status 100
```

Similarly, if the socket file you want to read does not exist, `socketClient.go` will fail with the following error message:

```
$ go run socketClient.go /tmp/aSocket
dial unix /tmp/aSocket: connect: no such file or directory
exit status 100
```

Performing DNS lookups

There exist many types of DNS lookups, but two of them are the most popular. In the first type, you want to go from an IP address to a domain name and in the second type you want to go from a domain name to an IP address.

The following output shows an example of the first type of DNS lookup:

```
$ host 109.74.193.253
253.193.74.109.in-addr.arpa domain name pointer
li140-253.members.linode.com.
```

The following output shows three examples of the second type of DNS lookup:

```
$ host www.mtsoukalos.eu
www.mtsoukalos.eu has address 109.74.193.253
$ host www.highiso.net
www.highiso.net has address 109.74.193.253
$ host -t a cnn.com
cnn.com has address 151.101.1.67
cnn.com has address 151.101.129.67
cnn.com has address 151.101.65.67
cnn.com has address 151.101.193.67
```

As you just saw in the aforementioned examples, an IP address can serve many hosts and a host name can have many IP addresses.

The Go standard library provides the `net.LookupHost()` and `net.LookupAddr()` functions that can answer DNS queries for you. However, none of them allow you to define the DNS server you want to query. While using standard Go libraries is ideal, there exist external Go libraries that allow you to choose the DNS server you desire, which is mainly required when troubleshooting DNS configurations.

Using an IP address as input

The name of the Go utility that will return the hostname of an IP address will be `lookIP.go` and will be presented in three parts.

The first part is the following:

```
package main

import (
    "fmt"
    "net"
    "os"
)
```

The second part has the following Go code:

```
func main() {
    arguments := os.Args
    if len(arguments) == 1 {
        fmt.Println("Please provide an IP address!")
        os.Exit(100)
    }

    IP := arguments[1]
    addr := net.ParseIP(IP)
    if addr == nil {
        fmt.Println("Not a valid IP address!")
        os.Exit(100)
    }
}
```

The `net.ParseIP()` function allows you to verify the validity of the given IP address and is pretty handy for catching illegal IP addresses such as `288.8.8.8` and `8.288.8.8`.

The last part of the utility is the following:

```
hosts, err := net.LookupAddr(IP)
if err != nil {
        fmt.Println(err)
        os.Exit(100)
}

for _, hostname := range hosts {
        fmt.Println(hostname)
}
}
```

As you can see, the net.LookupAddr() function returns a string slice with the list of names that match the given IP address.

Executing lookIP.go will generate the following output:

```
$ go run lookIP.go 288.8.8.8
Not a valid IP address!
exit status 100
$ go run lookIP.go 8.8.8.8
google-public-dns-a.google.com.
```

You can validate the output of dnsLookup.go using host(1) or dig(1):

```
$ host 8.8.8.8
8.8.8.8.in-addr.arpa domain name pointer google-public-dns-a.google.com.
```

Using a host name as input

The name of this DNS utility will be lookHost.go and will be presented in three parts. The first part of the lookHost.go utility is the following:

```
package main

import (
    "fmt"
    "net"
    "os"
)
```

The second part of the program has the following Go code:

```
func main() {
    arguments := os.Args
    if len(arguments) == 1 {
        fmt.Println("Please provide an argument!")
        os.Exit(100)
    }

    hostname := arguments[1]
    IPs, err := net.LookupHost(hostname)
```

Similarly, the net.LookupHost() function also returns a string slice with the desired information.

The third part of the program has the following code, which is for error checking and printing the output of net.LookupHost():

```
    if err != nil {
        fmt.Println(err)
        os.Exit(100)
    }

    for _, IP := range IPs {
        fmt.Println(IP)
    }
}
```

Executing lookHost.go will generate the following output:

```
$ go run lookHost.go www.google
lookup www.google: no such host
exit status 100
$ go run lookHost.go www.google.com
2a00:1450:4001:81f::2004
172.217.16.164
```

The first line of the output is the IPv6 address, whereas the second output line is the IPv4 address of www.google.com.

You can verify the operation of lookHost.go by comparing its output with the output of the host(1) utility:

```
$ host www.google.com
www.google.com has address 172.217.16.164
www.google.com has IPv6 address 2a00:1450:4001:81a::2004
```

Getting NS records for a domain

This subsection will present an additional kind of DNS lookup that returns the domain name servers for a given domain. This is very handy for troubleshooting DNS-related problems and finding out the status of a domain. The presented program will be named `lookNS.go` and will be presented in three parts.

The first part of the utility is the following:

```
package main

import (
    "fmt"
    "net"
    "os"
)
```

The second part has the following Go code:

```
func main() {
    arguments := os.Args
    if len(arguments) == 1 {
        fmt.Println("Please provide a domain!")
        os.Exit(100)
    }

    domain := arguments[1]

    NSs, err := net.LookupNS(domain)
```

The `net.LookupNS()` function does all the work for us by returning a slice of `NS` elements.

The last part of the code is mainly for printing the results:

```
    if err != nil {
        fmt.Println(err)
        os.Exit(100)
    }

    for _, NS := range NSs {
        fmt.Println(NS.Host)
    }
}
```

Executing `lookNS.go` will generate the following output:

```
$ go run lookNS.go mtsoukalos.eu
ns5.linode.com.
ns2.linode.com.
ns3.linode.com.
ns1.linode.com.
ns4.linode.com.
```

The reason that the following query will fail is that `www.mtsoukalos.eu` is not a domain but a single host, which means that it has no `NS` records associated with it:

```
$ go run lookNS.go www.mtsoukalos.eu
lookup www.mtsoukalos.eu on 8.8.8.8:53: no such host
exit status 100
```

You can use the `host(1)` utility to verify the previous output:

```
$ host -t ns mtsoukalos.eu
mtsoukalos.eu name server ns5.linode.com.
mtsoukalos.eu name server ns4.linode.com.
mtsoukalos.eu name server ns3.linode.com.
mtsoukalos.eu name server ns1.linode.com.
mtsoukalos.eu name server ns2.linode.com.
$ host -t ns www.mtsoukalos.eu
www.mtsoukalos.eu has no NS record
```

Developing a simple TCP server

This section will develop a TCP server that implements the **Echo** service. The Echo service is usually implemented using the UDP protocol due to its simplicity, but it can also be implemented with TCP. The Echo service usually uses port number 7, but our implementation will use other port numbers:

```
$ grep echo /etc/services
echo        7/tcp
echo        7/udp
```

The `TCPserver.go` file will hold the Go code of this section and will be presented in six parts. For reasons of simplicity, each connection is handled inside the `main()` function without calling a separate function. However, this is not the recommended practice.

The first part contains the expected preamble:

```
package main

import (
    "bufio"
    "fmt"
    "net"
    "os"
    "strings"
)
```

The second part of the TCP server is the following:

```
func main() {
    arguments := os.Args
    if len(arguments) == 1 {
        fmt.Println("Please provide port number")
        os.Exit(100)
    }
```

The third part of TCPserver.go contains the following Go code:

```
    PORT := ":" + arguments[1]
    l, err := net.Listen("tcp", PORT)
    if err != nil {
        fmt.Println(err)
        os.Exit(100)
    }
    defer l.Close()
```

What is important to remember here is that net.Listen() returns a Listener variable, which is a generic network listener for stream-oriented protocols. Additionally, the Listen() function can support more formats—check the documentation of the net package to find more information about that.

The fourth part of the TCP server has the following Go code:

```
    c, err := l.Accept()
    if err != nil {
        fmt.Println(err)
        os.Exit(100)
    }
```

Only after a successful call to Accept(), the TCP server can start interacting with TCP clients. Nonetheless, the current version of TCPserver.go has a very serious shortcoming: it can only serve a single TCP client, the first one that will connect to it.

The fifth portion of the `TCPserver.go` code is the following:

```
for {
        netData, err := bufio.NewReader(c).ReadString('\n')
        if err != nil {
                fmt.Println(err)
                os.Exit(100)
        }
```

Here, you read data from your client using `bufio.NewReader().ReadString()`. The aforementioned call allows you to read your input line by line. Additionally, the `for` loop allows you to keep reading data from the TCP client for as long as you wish.

The last part of the Echo TCP server is the following:

```
        fmt.Print("-> ", string(netData))
        c.Write([]byte(netData))
        if strings.TrimSpace(string(netData)) == "STOP" {
                fmt.Println("Exiting TCP server!")
                return
        }
    }
}
```

The current version of `TCPserver.go` stops when it receives the `STOP` string as input. Although TCP servers do not usually terminate in that style, this is a pretty handy way to terminate a TCP server process that will only serve a single client!

Next, we will test `TCPserver.go` with `netcat(1)`:

```
$ go run TCPserver.go 1234
-> Hi!
-> STOP
Exiting TCP server!
```

The `netcat(1)` part is the following:

```
$ nc localhost 1234


Hi!
Hi!
STOP
STOP
```

Here, the first and third lines are our input, whereas the second and fourth lines are the responses from the Echo server.

If you try to use an improper port number, `TCPserver.go` will generate the following error message and exit:

```
$ go run TCPserver.go 123456
listen tcp: address 123456: invalid port
exit status 100
```

Developing a simple TCP client

In this section, we will develop a TCP client named `TCPclient.go`. The port number the client will try to connect to as well as the server address will be given as command-line arguments to the program. The Go code of the TCP client will be presented in five parts; the first part is the following:

```
package main

import (
    "bufio"
    "fmt"
    "net"
    "os"
    "strings"
)
```

The second part of `TCPclient.go` is the following:

```
func main() {
    arguments := os.Args
    if len(arguments) == 1 {
        fmt.Println("Please provide host:port.")
        os.Exit(100)
    }
}
```

The third part of `TCPclient.go` has the following Go code:

```
CONNECT := arguments[1]
c, err := net.Dial("tcp", CONNECT)
if err != nil {
    fmt.Println(err)
    os.Exit(100)
}
```

Once again, you use the `net.Dial()` function to try to connect to the desired port of the desired TCP server.

The fourth part of the TCP client is the following:

```
for {
        reader := bufio.NewReader(os.Stdin)
        fmt.Print(">> ")
        text, _ := reader.ReadString('\n')
        fmt.Fprintf(c, text+"\n")
```

Here, you read data from the user that you will send to the TCP server using `fmt.Fprintf()`.

The last part of `TCPclient.go` is the following:

```
        message, _ := bufio.NewReader(c).ReadString('\n')
        fmt.Print("->: " + message)
        if strings.TrimSpace(string(text)) == "STOP" {
                fmt.Println("TCP client exiting...")
                return
        }
    }
}
```

In this part, you get data from the TCP server using `bufio.NewReader().ReadString()`. The reason for using the `strings.TrimSpace()` function is to remove any spaces and newline characters from the variable you want to compare with the static string (`STOP`).

So, now it is time to verify that `TCPclient.go` works as expected using it to connect to `TCPserver.go`:

```
$ go run TCPclient.go localhost:1024
>> 123
->: 123
>> Hello server!
->: Hello server!
>> STOP
->: STOP
TCP client exiting...
```

If no process listens to the specified TCP port at the specified host, then you will get an error message similar to the following:

```
$ go run TCPclient.go localhost:1024
dial tcp [::1]:1024: getsockopt: connection refused
exit status 100
```

Using other functions for the TCP server

In this subsection, we will develop the functionality of `TCPserver.go` using some slightly different functions. The name of the new TCP server will be `TCPs.go` and will be presented in four parts.

The first part of `TCPs.go` is the following:

```
package main

import (
    "fmt"
    "net"
    "os"
)
```

The second part of the TCP server is the following:

```
func main() {
    arguments := os.Args
    if len(arguments) == 1 {
        fmt.Println("Please provide a port number!")
        os.Exit(100)
    }

    SERVER := "localhost" + ":" + arguments[1]
```

So far, there are no differences from the code of `TCPserver.go`.

The differences start in the third part of `TCPs.go`, which is the following:

```
    s, err := net.ResolveTCPAddr("tcp", SERVER)
    if err != nil {
        fmt.Println(err)
        os.Exit(100)
    }

    l, err := net.ListenTCP("tcp", s)
    if err != nil {
        fmt.Println(err)
        os.Exit(100)
    }
```

Here, you use the net.ResolveTCPAddr() and net.ListenTCP() functions. Is this version better than TCPserver.go? Not really. But the Go code might look a little clearer and this is a big advantage for some people. Additionally, net.ListenTCP() returns a TCPListener value that when used with net.AcceptTCP() instead of net.Accept() will return TCPConn, which offers more methods that allow you to change more socket options.

The last part of TCPs.go has the following Go code:

```
buffer := make([]byte, 1024)

for {
        conn, err := l.Accept()
        n, err := conn.Read(buffer)
        if err != nil {
                fmt.Println(err)
                os.Exit(100)
        }

        fmt.Print("> ", string(buffer[0:n]))


        _, err = conn.Write(buffer)

        conn.Close()
        if err != nil {
                fmt.Println(err)
                os.Exit(100)
        }
    }
}
```

There is nothing special here. You still use Accept() to get and process client requests. However, this version uses Read() to get the client data all at once, which is great when you do not have to process lots of input.

The operation of TCPs.go is the same with the operation of TCPserver.go, so it will not be shown here.

If you try to create a TCP server using an invalid port number, TCPs.go will generate an informative error message, as shown here:

```
$ go run TCPs.go 123456
address 123456: invalid port
exit status 100
```

Using alternative functions for the TCP client

Once again, we will implement `TCPclient.go` using some slightly different functions that are provided by the `net` Go standard package. The name of the new version will be `TCPc.go` and will be shown in four code segments.

The first part is the following:

```
package main

import (
    "fmt"
    "net"
    "os"
)
```

The second code segment of the program is the following:

```
func main() {
    arguments := os.Args
    if len(arguments) == 1 {
        fmt.Println("Please provide a server:port string!")
        os.Exit(100)
    }

    CONNECT := arguments[1]
    myMessage := "Hello from TCP client!\n"
```

This time, we will send a static message to the TCP server.

The third part of `TCPc.go` is the following:

```
    tcpAddr, err := net.ResolveTCPAddr("tcp", CONNECT)
    if err != nil {
        fmt.Println(err)
        os.Exit(100)
    }

    conn, err := net.DialTCP("tcp", nil, tcpAddr)
    if err != nil {
        fmt.Println(err)
        os.Exit(100)
    }
```

In this part, you see the use of `net.ResolveTCPAddr()` and `net.DialTCP()`, which is where the differences between `TCPc.go` and `TCPclient.go` exist.

The last part of the TCP client is the following:

```
_, err = conn.Write([]byte(myMessage))
if err != nil {
        fmt.Println(err)
        os.Exit(100)
}

fmt.Print("-> ", myMessage)
buffer := make([]byte, 1024)


n, err := conn.Read(buffer)
if err != nil {
        fmt.Println(err)
        os.Exit(100)
}

fmt.Print(">> ", string(buffer[0:n]))
conn.Close()
}
```

You might ask if you can use `TCPc.go` with `TCPserver.go` or `TCPs.go` with `TCPclient.go`. The answer is a definitive *yes* because the implementation and the function names have nothing to do with the actual TCP/IP operations that take place.

Developing a simple UDP server

This section will also develop an Echo server. However, this time the Echo server will use the UDP protocol. The name of the program will be `UDPserver.go` and will be presented to you in five parts.

The first part contains the expected preamble:

```
package main

import (
    "fmt"
    "net"
    "os"
    "strings"
)
```

The second part is the following:

```
func main() {
    arguments := os.Args
    if len(arguments) == 1 {
        fmt.Println("Please provide a port number!")
        os.Exit(100)
    }
    PORT := ":" + arguments[1]
```

The third part of UDPserver.go is the following:

```
s, err := net.ResolveUDPAddr("udp", PORT)
if err != nil {
    fmt.Println(err)
    os.Exit(100)
}

connection, err := net.ListenUDP("udp", s)
if err != nil {
    fmt.Println(err)
    os.Exit(100)
}
```

The UDP approach is similar to the TCP approach—you just call functions with different names.

The fourth part of the program has the following Go code:

```
defer connection.Close()
buffer := make([]byte, 1024)

for {
    n, addr, err := connection.ReadFromUDP(buffer)
    fmt.Print("-> ", string(buffer[0:n]))
    data := []byte(buffer[0:n])
    _, err = connection.WriteToUDP(data, addr)
    if err != nil {
        fmt.Println(err)
        os.Exit(100)
    }
}
```

In the UDP case, you use ReadFromUDP() to read from a UDP connection and WriteToUDP() to write to an UDP connection. Additionally, the UDP connection does not need to call a function similar to net.Accept().

The last part of the UDP server is the following:

```
        if strings.TrimSpace(string(data)) == "STOP" {
                fmt.Println("Exiting UDP server!")
                return
        }
    }
}
```

Once again, we will test UDPserver.go with netcat(1):

```
$ go run UDPserver.go 1234
-> Hi!
-> Hello!
-> STOP
Exiting UDP server!
```

Developing a simple UDP client

In this section, we will develop a UDP client, which we will name UDPclient.go and present in five parts.

As you will see, the code differences between the Go code of UDPclient.go and TCPc.go are basically the differences in the names of the functions used—the general idea is exactly the same.

The first part of the UDP client is the following:

```
package main

import (
    "fmt"
    "net"
    "os"
)
```

The second part of the utility contains the following Go code:

```
func main() {
    arguments := os.Args
    if len(arguments) == 1 {
        fmt.Println("Please provide a host:port string")
        os.Exit(100)
    }
    CONNECT := arguments[1]
```

The third part of `UDPclient.go` has the following Go code:

```
s, err := net.ResolveUDPAddr("udp", CONNECT)
c, err := net.DialUDP("udp", nil, s)

if err != nil {
        fmt.Println(err)
        os.Exit(100)
}

fmt.Printf("The UDP server is %s\n", c.RemoteAddr().String())
defer c.Close()
```

Nothing special here—just the use of `net.ResolveUDPAddr()` and `net.DialUDP()` to connect to the UDP server.

The fourth part of the UDP client is the following:

```
data := []byte("Hello UDP Echo server!\n")
_, err = c.Write(data)

if err != nil {
        fmt.Println(err)
        os.Exit(100)
}
```

This time, you send your data to the UDP server using `Write()`, although you will read from the UDP server using `ReadFromUDP()`.

The last part of `UDPclient.go` is the following:

```
buffer := make([]byte, 1024)
n, _, err := c.ReadFromUDP(buffer)
fmt.Print("Reply: ", string(buffer[:n]))
}
```

As we have `UDPserver.go` and we know that it works, we can test the operation of `UDPclient.go` using `UDPserver.go`:

```
$ go run UDPclient.go localhost:1234
The UDP server is 127.0.0.1:1234
Reply: Hello UDP Echo server!
```

If you execute `UDPclient.go` without a UDP server listening to the desired port, you will get the following output, which does not clearly state that it could not connect to an UDP server—it just shows an empty reply:

```
$ go run UDPclient.go localhost:1024
The UDP server is 127.0.0.1:1024
Reply:
```

A concurrent TCP server

In this section, you will learn how to develop a concurrent TCP server—each client connection will be assigned to a new goroutine that will serve the client request. Note that although TCP clients initially connect to the same port, they are served using a different port number than the main port number of the server—this is automatically handled by TCP and is the way TCP works.

Although creating a concurrent UDP server is also a possibility, it might not be absolutely necessary due to the way UDP works. However, if you have a really busy UDP service, then you might consider developing a concurrent UDP server.

The name of the program will be `concTCP.go` and will be presented in five parts. The good thing is that once you define a function to handle incoming connections, all you need is to execute that function as a goroutine, and the rest will be handled by Go!

The first part of `concTCP.go` is the following:

```go
package main

import (
    "bufio"
    "fmt"
    "net"
    "os"
    "strings"
    "time"
)
```

The second part of the concurrent TCP server is the following:

```
func handleConnection(c net.Conn) {
    for {
            netData, err := bufio.NewReader(c).ReadString('\n')
            if err != nil {
                    fmt.Println(err)
                    os.Exit(100)
            }

            fmt.Print("-> ", string(netData))
            c.Write([]byte(netData))
            if strings.TrimSpace(string(netData)) == "STOP" {
                    break
            }
    }
    time.Sleep(3 * time.Second)
    c.Close()
}
```

Here is the implementation of the function that handles each TCP request. The time delay at the end of it is used for giving you the necessary time to connect with another TCP client and prove that concTCP.go can serve multiple TCP clients.

The third part of the program contains the following Go code:

```
func main() {
    arguments := os.Args
    if len(arguments) == 1 {
            fmt.Println("Please provide a port number!")
            os.Exit(100)
    }

    PORT := ":" + arguments[1]
```

The fourth part of concTCP.go has the following Go code:

```
    l, err := net.Listen("tcp", PORT)
    if err != nil {
            fmt.Println(err)
            os.Exit(100)
    }
    defer l.Close()
```

So far, there is nothing special in the main() function because although concTCP.go will handle multiple requests, it only needs a single call to net.Listen().

The last chunk of Go code is the following:

```
for {
        c, err := l.Accept()
        if err != nil {
                fmt.Println(err)
                os.Exit(100)
        }
        go handleConnection(c)
    }
}
```

All the differences in the way `concTCP.go` processes its requests can be found in the last lines of Go code. Each time the program accepts a new network request using `Accept()`, a new goroutine gets started and `concTCP.go` is immediately ready to accept more requests. Note that in order to terminate `concTCP.go`, you will have to press *Ctrl + C* because the `STOP` keyword is used for terminating each goroutine of the program.

Executing `concTCP.go` and connecting to it using various TCP clients, will generate the following output:

```
$ go run concTCP.go 1234
-> Hi!
-> Hello!
-> STOP
...
```

Remote procedure call (RPC)

Remote Procedure Call (RPC) is a client-server mechanism for interprocess communication. Note that the RPC client and the RPC server communicate using TCP/IP, which means that they can exist in different machines.

In order to develop the implementation of an RPC client or RPC server, you will need to follow some steps and call some functions in a given way. Neither of the two implementations is difficult; you just have to follow certain steps.

Also, visit the documentation page of the `net/rpc` Go standard package that can be found at `https://golang.org/pkg/net/rpc/`.

Note that the presented RPC example will use TCP for client-server interaction. However, you can also use HTTP for client-server communication.

An RPC server

This subsection will present an RPC server named `RPCserver.go`. As you will see in the preamble of the `RPCserver.go` program, the RPC server imports a package named `sharedRPC`, which is implemented in the `sharedRPC.go` file—the name of the package is arbitrary. Its contents are the following:

```
package sharedRPC

type MyInts struct {
    A1, A2 uint
    S1, S2 bool
}


type MyInterface interface {

    Add(arguments *MyInts, reply *int) error
    Subtract(arguments *MyInts, reply *int) error
}
```

So, here you define a new structure that holds the signs and the values of two unsigned integers and a new interface named `MyInterface`.

Then, you should install `sharedRPC.go`, which means that you should execute the following commands before you try to use the `sharedRPC` package in your programs:

```
$ mkdir ~/go
$ mkdir ~/go/src
$ mkdir ~/go/src/sharedRPC
$ export GOPATH=~/go
$ vi ~/go/src/sharedRPC/sharedRPC.go
$ go install sharedRPC
```

If you are on a macOS machine (`darwin_amd64`) and you want to make sure that everything is OK, you can execute the following two commands:

```
$ cd ~/go/pkg/darwin_amd64/
$ ls -l sharedRPC.a
-rw-r--r--  1 mtsouk  staff  4698 Jul 27 11:49 sharedRPC.a
```

What you really must keep in mind is that, at the end of the day, what is being exchanged between an RPC server and an RPC client are function names and their arguments. Only the functions defined in the interface of `sharedRPC.go` can be used in an RPC interaction—the RPC server will need to implement the functions of the `MyInterface` interface. The Go code of `RPCserver.go` will be presented in five parts; the first part of the RPC server has the expected preamble, which also includes the `sharedRPC` package we made:

```go
package main

import (
    "fmt"
    "net"
    "net/rpc"
    "os"
    "sharedRPC"
)
```

The second part of `RPCserver.go` is the following:

```go
type MyInterface int

func (t *MyInterface) Add(arguments *sharedRPC.MyInts, reply *int) error {
    s1 := 1
    s2 := 1

    if arguments.S1 == true {
        s1 = -1
    }

    if arguments.S2 == true {
        s2 = -1
    }

    *reply = s1*int(arguments.A1) + s2*int(arguments.A2)
    return nil
}
```

Here is the implementation of the first function that will be offered to the RPC clients—you can have as many functions as you want, provided that they are included in the interface.

The third part of RPCserver.go has the following Go code:

```
func (t *MyInterface) Subtract(arguments *sharedRPC.MyInts, reply *int)
error {
    s1 := 1
    s2 := 1

    if arguments.S1 == true {
        s1 = -1
    }

    if arguments.S2 == true {
        s2 = -1
    }

    *reply = s1*int(arguments.A1) - s2*int(arguments.A2)
    return nil
}
```

This is the second function that is offered to the RPC clients by this RPC server.

The fourth part of RPCserver.go contains the following Go code:

```
func main() {
    PORT := ":1234"

    myInterface := new(MyInterface)
    rpc.Register(myInterface)

    t, err := net.ResolveTCPAddr("tcp", PORT)
    if err != nil {
        fmt.Println(err)
        os.Exit(100)
    }
    l, err := net.ListenTCP("tcp", t)
    if err != nil {
        fmt.Println(err)
        os.Exit(100)
    }
```

As our RPC server uses TCP, you need to make calls to net.ResolveTCPAddr() and net.ListenTCP(). However, you will first need to call rpc.Register() in order to be able to serve the desired interface.

The last part of the program is the following:

```
for {
        c, err := l.Accept()
        if err != nil {
                continue
        }
        rpc.ServeConn(c)
    }
}
```

Here, you accept a new TCP connection using `Accept()` as usual, but you serve it using `rpc.ServeConn()`.

You will have to wait for the next section and the development of the RPC client in order to test the operation of `RPCserver.go`.

An RPC client

In this section, we will develop an RPC client named `RPCclient.go`. The Go code of `RPCclient.go` will be presented in five parts; the first part is the following:

```
package main

import (
    "fmt"
    "net/rpc"
    "os"
    "sharedRPC"
)
```

Note the use of the `sharedRPC` package in the RPC client.

The second part of `RPCclient.go` is the following:

```
func main() {
    arguments := os.Args
    if len(arguments) == 1 {
            fmt.Println("Please provide a host:port string!")
            os.Exit(100)
    }

    CONNECT := arguments[1]
```

The third part of the program has the following Go code:

```
c, err := rpc.Dial("tcp", CONNECT)
if err != nil {
        fmt.Println(err)
        os.Exit(100)
}

args := sharedRPC.MyInts{17, 18, true, false}
var reply int
```

As the `MyInts` structure is defined in `sharedRPC.go`, you need to use it as `sharedRPC.MyInts` in the RPC client. Moreover, you call `rpc.Dial()` to connect to the RPC server instead of `net.Dial()`.

The fourth part of the RPC client contains the following Go code:

```
err = c.Call("MyInterface.Add", args, &reply)
if err != nil {
        fmt.Println(err)
        os.Exit(100)
}
fmt.Printf("Reply (Add): %d\n", reply)
```

Here, you use the `Call()` function to execute the desired function in the RPC server. The result of the `MyInterface.Add()` function is stored in the `reply` variable, which was previously declared.

The last part of `RPCclient.go` is the following:

```
err = c.Call("MyInterface.Subtract", args, &reply)
if err != nil {
        fmt.Println(err)
        os.Exit(100)
}
fmt.Printf("Reply (Subtract): %d\n", reply)
}
```

Here, you do the same thing as before for executing the `MyInterface.Subtract()` function.

As you can guess, you cannot test the RPC client without having an RCP server and vice versa—`netcat(1)` cannot be used for RPC.

First, you will need to start the `RPCserver.go` process:

```
$ go run RPCserver.go
```

Then, you will execute the `RPCclient.go` program:

```
$ go run RPCclient.go localhost:1234
Reply (Add): 1
Reply (Subtrack): -35
```

If the `RPCserver.go` process is not running and you try to execute `RPCclient.go`, you will get the following error message:

```
$ go run RPCclient.go localhost:1234
dial tcp [::1]:1234: getsockopt: connection refused
exit status 100
```

Of course, RPC is not for adding integers or natural numbers, but for doing much more complex operations that you want to control from a central point.

Exercises

1. Read the documentation of the net package in order to find out about its list of available functions at `https://golang.org/pkg/net/`.
2. Wireshark is a great tool for analyzing network traffic of any kind—try to use it more.
3. Change the code of `socketClient.go` in order to read the input from the user.
4. Change the code of `socketServer.go` in order to return a random number to the client.
5. Change the code of `TCPserver.go` in order to stop when it receives a given Unix signal from the user.
6. Change the Go code of `concTCP.go` in order to keep track of the number of clients it has served and print that number before exiting.
7. Add a `quit()` function to `RPCserver.go` that does what its name implies.
8. Develop your own RPC example.

Summary

In this chapter, we introduced you to TCP/IP, and we talked about developing TCP and UDP servers and clients in Go and about creating RPC clients and servers.

At this point, there is no next chapter because this is the last chapter of this book! Congratulations for reading the whole book! You are now ready to start developing useful Unix command-line utilities in Go; so, go ahead and start programming your own tools immediately!

Index

Made in the USA
Coppell, TX
02 May 2022